P9-CRD-783

PRAISE FOR *BABY, DON'T HURT ME*

"No one appreciates a scar more than me. I always loved Chris Kattan, but this book made me love him even more."

—Amy Sedaris

"Chris Kattan is one of the greatest physical comedians I have ever seen. He would play a small animal and believe he was 20 pounds. He would play a male stripper and believe that he was an amazing dancer. He would play an old lounge act and you would think he really had been trapped in a smoky Vegas room for 50 years. I've always admired his commitment to his characters but also his thirst for learning about comedy. He is a real student of the craft, and he was always great to me and gave me good advice on top of 'laugh until we are in tears' moments on *SNL*. This takes me back."

—Jimmy Fallon

"I highly recommend this book to anyone who wants to succeed in comedy as a performer or a writer. Chris Kattan gives a rare, detailed look behind the scenes of *SNL*. His stories are laugh-out-loud funny (driving Mrs. Koogle!) and very touching. He bares his heart in this riveting memoir."

—Molly Shannon

BABY, DON'T HURT ME

BABY, DON'T HURT ME

Stories and Scars from *Saturday Night Live*

CHRIS KATTAN

with Travis Thrasher

BenBella Books, Inc.

BenBella

BenBella Books, Inc.
10440 N. Central Expressway, Suite 800
Dallas, TX 75231
www.benbellabooks.com
Send feedback to feedback@benbellabooks.com

Printed in the United States of America
10 9 8 7 6 5 4 3 2 1

Library of Congress Cataloging-in-Publication Data is available upon request.
9781944648497 (trade cloth)
9781944648763 (electronic)

Cover photography: Emma Dunlavey
Lighting/Digital Technician: Damon Corso
Grooming: Annie Ing
Wardrobe Stylist: Bailee Edgington
Animal trainer: Rick Nyberg, Performing
   Animal Troupe
Retouching and compositing: Ramon Rivas
Cover design: Sarah Avinger

Editing by Alexa Stevenson and Laurel
   Leigh
Copyediting by Scott Calamar
Proofreading by Greg Teague and Cape Cod
   Compositors, Inc.
Text design by Katie Hollister
Text composition by Aaron Edmiston
Printed by Lake Book Manufacturing

Distributed to the trade by Two Rivers Distribution, an Ingram brand
www.tworiversdistribution.com

Special discounts for bulk sales (minimum of 25 copies) are available.
Please contact bulkorders@benbellabooks.com.

This book is dedicated to you. Yes, you, the reader, for without you, this whole thing wouldn't be a thing.

To the kindred spirits who dream of succeeding in comedy, or at least want to make a livable wage at it!

To the trusting, the gullible, and the pure of spirit. Keep that, and try not to get jaded.

To my father, my mother, Marc, Andrew, and my Billy, Jennifer.

To the people who put me back together: my surgeon, Carl, and my physical therapist, Karen.

"Silence is of the gods, only monkeys chatter."
—**Buster Keaton**

"Been hiding my scars in broad daylight bars /
Behind laugh tracks on TV."
—**Arcade Fire**

CONTENTS

FOREWORD BY SETH MEYERS

I will never forget the first time I saw Kattan as Mr. Peepers eat an apple. It wasn't the speed at which he did it, it was the precision; the ability to rip it apart like a lawnmower through grass while also managing to spit it directly at his scene partners. With no exaggeration I believe it to be the most impressive live act ever performed on *SNL*. I also believe it to be a perfect distillation of what I love about Chris Kattan. A kinetic, yet controlled tour de force.

Kattan (I have never called him "Chris" in my life and I'm not going to start now) was a workhorse in the *SNL* cast that brought the show back from the brink in the mid-90s. And I'm not kidding when I say the "work" part. No one sacrificed himself more physically for a laugh (and as you'll find out in this book the sacrifice was real). *SNL* needed a reinvention, and Kattan was exactly what the doctor ordered. Enthusiastic character-driven comedy in bold colors. Red! (Peepers) Blue! (Roxbury Guys) Pink! (Mango).

Kattan was fun. Genuinely fun in the way the best *SNL* cast members are. He was fun to be around during the week and he was fun to watch on Saturday. Hosts liked to be in scenes with Kattan because whatever fears they had about doing the show were erased by his contagious, joyous energy.

And, more importantly to me, he was kind. He looked out for me when I started in 2001, giving me small parts in his sketches and saving me from weeks in which I had no lines at all. But while that was nice, my biggest debt to Kattan will never be repaid. In the summer of '08, he invited me to his wedding and I met Alexi Ashe, who is now my wife and the mother of our two amazing boys. When people ask Alexi and I what we have in common, the one thing I know most to be true is, "We both love Kattan."

Lastly, my first season at *SNL* was 2001. My first show was two weeks after 9/11. Everyone was wondering when you could laugh again, and I'm not sure I did at all during that first show. But in the *second* show, during "Weekend Update," Jimmy read a story about a German historian who asserted that Hitler was a homosexual. Kattan entered as Gay Hitler and, with a perfect delivery of his only line, "Sprechen Sie Dick?" made me laugh exactly how I needed to.

INTRODUCTION

First off, I'd like to formally thank you for buying my book. Clearly, you have good taste. I'm not saying you had poor taste on any level prior to picking up this book, but now . . . congratulations. It's official.

Some of comedy's most memorable characters were born in studio 8H, on the eighth floor of 30 Rockefeller Plaza in New York City. That studio, home to *Saturday Night Live*, was also home to characters like Wayne and Garth. Stefon. Matt Foley. Debbie Downer. Ed Grimley. Stuart Smalley. The Samurai. Mr. Robinson. Mary Katherine Gallagher. King Tut. Master Thespian. Opera Man. They were created by legends like Bill Murray, Chevy Chase, Gilda Radner, Eddie Murphy, Mike Myers, Phil Hartman, and an overwhelming list of others—artists who have gone on to make us laugh for decades and will forever be known as some of comedy's greatest.

In my almost eight seasons on *SNL*, I was fortunate enough to create a few memorable characters myself. I'm probably remembered from my years on the show as the physical and energetic short guy who brought to life such deeply bizarre individuals as the androgynous stripper Mango, goth teen (and Cinnabon employee!) Azrael Abyss, or the apple-eating, face-humping Mr. Peepers.

It's a little strange to know you're mostly remembered as other, fictional people. When I'm dead, lying in a casket located at what I can only hope will be one of the more prestigious mortuaries in Southern California, I'm sure someone will walk up to my coffin and say: "Oh, God. Such a terrible loss. And such a good-looking guy, too." Then, grabbing a fistful of my Silver Fox hair, they will surreptitiously bop my head back and forth like one of the club-hopping Roxbury guys.

In 1995, twenty years after its historic debut, *Saturday Night Live* was in serious jeopardy of being cancelled. The so-called frat pack of Adam Sandler, Chris Farley, Chris Rock, and Rob Schneider had all left or been fired due to pressure from network executives, and mainstay Mike Meyers had departed for Hollywood. Producer Lorne Michaels was faced with the unenviable task of finding a whole new cast of proven sketch performers who would click with viewers, please the network, and prevent him from losing the show he'd created.

He found the majority of that cast—including me—at the Groundlings Theatre & School in Los Angeles. Since its founding in 1974, the Groundlings Theatre has become the foremost comedy training ground in Hollywood, counting among its alums such notables as Paul Reubens, Phil Hartman, Kristen Wiig, and Melissa McCarthy—not to mention the great Kip King, who was one of the original Groundlings cast members and, more importantly, my dad.

When I made my *SNL* debut late in the 1995–96 season, I knew I had only had the season's six remaining shows to create an impression that would get me invited back. Thankfully, my six years as a Groundling had prepared me well, and I arrived in New York with a trunk full of characters developed on the same LA stage where, as a kid, I'd watched my father perform.

What followed were some of the most intense and enjoyable years of my life. I always felt that the *SNL* of the second half of the 1990s was more of a performer-driven show than a writer's show. Obviously, you need both kinds of talent to make the show work, but the strength of the cast in those years leaned heavily toward the ability to bring a full-bodied character to life on stage rather than a knack for writing clever sketches. From 1996 to 2003, my cast included Will Ferrell, Amy Poehler, Tina Fey, Jimmy Fallon, Tracy Morgan, Seth Meyers, Fred Armisen, Molly Shannon, Will Forte, and Maya Rudolph, among others. Looking back, I feel we were one of the sharpest and most gifted *SNL* casts in its forty-plus years of history—in part, because we were allowed to stay together and grow. I've always thought Lorne knew our particular group was exceptional, and he wanted to preserve it. We worked together for years as part of an ensemble, creating and collaborating and churning out characters and ideas.

Saturday Night Live and pop culture media in general were a lot different then. We had no YouTube, no Funny or Die, no podcasts, Twitter, Instagram, or Snapchat. There was no means for a sketch to go "viral" moments after it aired. Today a cast member can appear on just a few episodes and wind up in a Judd Apatow film. Back then, it was rare to see a cast member working on a film while doing the show. As long as you were on the show, you were still a "not ready for prime time" player. You weren't focused on the "next big thing" because the chances of moving on and becoming a Bill Murray or an Eddie Murphy were slim. We all felt lucky to be "Live from New York" every Saturday, and there was a certain etiquette about extending yourself too much in film and other media: It wasn't cool to do commercials or bunches of TV guest spots. Today, it's not only acceptable, it's almost expected, as if *SNL* is just a step toward something else rather than the ultimate destination.

For years, people have been telling me to write a book about my time at *SNL*. Whether because of my improv training, or the way I grew up, I was always very observant of the details of my surroundings and experiences, almost as if I were outside of myself watching events unfold. Sometimes, during my years on the show, I felt like I was a journalist disguised as a cast member. There have been some really great books written by former *SNL* cast members. For my part, I want to tell what every cast member knows or has experienced but, for whatever reason, fails to mention when given the opportunity to write about it. Rather than just stories and anecdotes told for the purpose of being funny, I feel the need to tell a deeper truth, choosing "raw" over "fluff." This is not a comedy book; it's a book about a comedian. My story is one about a guy with dreams who makes it, but it's not exactly typical.

I grew up shuttling between a world of monks and a world of movies, and my career trajectory hasn't been what you'd call linear. I'm hoping that reading about my exhilarating years on *SNL*, how I got there in the first place, and what life's been like since, will be entertaining, sure, but also that it will encourage some of you with similar aspirations. Allow me to save you years of anxiety, and many hours of expensive therapy, by sharing what I have learned about patience, achieving success, and surviving it.

For a long time after I left *Saturday Night Live*, I was in a bad place. Beaten down by pain, major surgeries, and personal tragedy, I had trouble even seeing the point of living. I felt as if I wasn't needed anymore, and almost as if I were already dead. Perhaps that was it for me, I thought: I was just someone who did something really well years ago and now was forgotten. Maybe all people would ever think of me was: *Whatever happened to Chris Kattan? Who knows? What a waste.* This refrain played in my head for a long time, and things like being left out of *SNL* anniversary shows or not being asked to be in certain movies only further convinced me that not only was my career dead, its gravestone read: *Chris Kattan—was briefly amazing.*

Eventually, something shifted inside of me. I was sick of misery and self-pity. I grew tired of being embarrassed about the injury I sustained on the show and lying about the impact of the pain and surgeries that followed. I began to surround myself with supportive people who believed in me. And with their belief in me, I started to believe in myself again. That's when I got back out into the world and reconnected with my fans and my love of comedy through stand-up. I've spent the last few years touring the country and making people laugh face-to-face again, remembering what it feels like—it feels like there is nothing you can't do. This outlook opens you up to the fruition of new ideas from your imagination.

Bill Murray once said that after four years on *Saturday Night Live*, you can do anything. And he's right. The pressure you endure and the technical skills and lessons you learn can't be found anywhere else. You walk out of there shell-shocked, relieved, grateful, and hopefully fulfilled. You learn to be a survivor.

I've had this beautiful life, and I've felt and experienced so many amazing things. Every day now I'm able to wake up and see that. I'm a much stronger person than I used to be. I don't bullshit anymore; I don't spend all my time looking back over my shoulder. I don't have expectations, so I'm rarely disappointed. I feel grateful. I feel blessed.

Thank you for reading my story.

—**Chris Kattan**

Chapter 1

NO, PEEPERS! NO!

S
o there I was, hanging upside down by my bare feet, which were wrapped around the neck of a seven-foot-tall gentleman by the name of Roy Jenkins.

Holy shit, I thought to myself, *I'm hanging upside down with my feet around someone's neck. When did I learn to do this?*

It was a Monday night in 1993. Monday night's class was the one you never wanted to miss because not only was it the one time you got to do improv exercises, it was the only night to pitch sketches that might get you in the lineup for the upcoming Groundlings Sunday show.

The Sunday show director was Melanie Graham, who'd started as a member of the Groundlings main company and would years later become a writer for *SNL* for a few seasons while I was on the show. Melanie bore a strong resemblance to Edna Mode from Disney's *The Incredibles* (as well as to legendary Hollywood costume designer Edith Head, who I believe the

Incredibles character was based on). Melanie was intimidatingly smart, but encouragement was not her forte. She was critical, with high expectations, and it was easy to feel like she was being too hard on you. But ultimately, Melanie's expectations made us all better performers and better writers. At the time, I didn't realize that writing was such an important backbone of comedy. Looking back now, I can honestly say Melanie was one of the greatest teachers I've ever had.

Anyway: Monday night, 1993. We were just finishing warm-ups, and Melanie instructed Roy and me to go onstage and do a scene as poorly as we possibly could, breaking every improv rule. This was one of my all-time favorite exercises. I mean, to do a scene where you got to make the worst possible choices without any justification? Oh my God, I loved it!

For the top of the scene, Roy was alone onstage while I waited offstage for my cue. Roy began by doing terrible "space work." He held an invisible glass and pretended to make himself a drink, then walked over a couple feet and—forgetting he was supposed to be holding a glass—grabbed a sword out of nowhere with two hands before returning to make his imaginary drink. His imagined props just kept disappearing and reappearing without any visual justification. It was really funny. Then I heard Melanie's scratchy, dehydrated voice belt out, "And Kattan enters!"

Without having a single thought to back me up—no character in mind like you're supposed to when entering a scene in an improv—I threw open the weightless stage door and galloped, gazelle-like, over to Roy and leapt up with my arms opened wide enough to wrap around his chest. Then, some mysterious impulse combined with an enormous surge of strength took control. Like an Olympic athlete executing a pole vault, my feet swung up toward the theater lights, my arms let go of Roy's chest, and my calves wrapped around his neck as my bare toes locked together. Roy, now on the phone, still holding a drink, continued, as if totally oblivious to the fact that all 138 pounds of me was swinging from his neck like a human pendulum. More like a monkey, actually.

The talented Roy Jenkins was one of the most prolific cast members in the Groundlings' Sunday show, which featured Will Ferrell, Cheri Oteri, me, and a few others. Roy and I were both good friends with Will, but Roy and Will had been a team months before I came into the picture. In fact, the first time I ever saw Will was in a sketch with Roy where they played a barbershop-type a cappella duo singing to passersby in the Main Street section of Disneyland.

Roy and I both recognized my vault onto his neck for the golden nugget of possibility it was, and knowing how rare the birth of an original idea can be, we immediately rushed to find each other during the break to talk about it. Now we just needed to structure some kind of story around . . . whatever we'd just come up with.

At the time, I did not know one person who wasn't a fan of Johnny Carson. He was so engaging, so funny, you would need to have the worst comedic taste not to like him. He was there for us five days a week for thirty years, so you could take him for granted, forgetting that someday he might not be on the air anymore. When Jay Leno took over *The Tonight Show*, everyone missed Johnny. And Doc Severinsen and His Orchestra. And Ed McMahon. I especially missed Johnny doing Carnac the Magnificent or acting as the host of the "Tea Time Movie" (who, by the way, Horatio Sanz does a dead-on impression of). I even missed the prescription sunglasses that Ed McMahon wore when he was drunk. But what I missed most of all was when zookeeper Jack Hanna was a guest, bringing along some supposedly well-trained animal. Inevitably, the creature would misbehave and do fun animal things, like jumping on Johnny's desk and trying to cuddle up behind him. The cameras would zoom in on Johnny laughing while some koala or something played peekaboo from behind his earlobe. Adorable. Then for the big closer before they cut to commercial, the animal would pee in his eye. If they were really lucky, meaning the encounter would eventually make it on to some volume of *The Best of Carson,* the creature would take a classic *Tonight Show* dump on Johnny's desk, right next to his coffee mug.

So, you'll never guess what Roy and I decided our sketch should be about. Yep, you got it on the first try. Roy would be the Jack Hanna type of guy and we'd get Will to be the talk show host, but we didn't just want to write a straight parody of *The Tonight Show*, and, well, I didn't want to pee on anybody. So for the "blackout" of the sketch—the Groundlings' term for the bit at the end of the sketch that gets the big laugh to turn the stage lights out on—I'd do something even more innovative. Namely, I'd hump Roy's face while I "suck-slapped" Will's.*

The only difficult part was choosing what kind of animal I was supposed to be. It obviously had to be some sort of monkey, but an impression of an actual monkey species wasn't seminal or funny enough, and besides that had been done. What really made the scene work wasn't my character but what I was physically able to get my body to do with (or on) Roy. That hyperphysical interaction carried the scene. Finally Roy came up with the idea of this animal being the "missing link" between man and monkey. And, since he was a captive creature, he obviously had to have a moronic pet name that a child would remember at the zoo.

---

*suck-slap \ sək-slap \ probably a verb: **1a** to draw recipient's face toward mouth through suction force produced by movements of the lips and tongue, meanwhile or/ and then striking same or second subject sharply with or as if with the open hand; **1b** as unpleasant for recipient(s) as it sounds.

I stood up straight, put down my notepad and pen, and asked him what part of my body looked bigger or more obvious than that of most people.

"I guess your eyes," Roy told me.

"Like, my 'peepers'?"

"Mr. Peepers would be a funny name to yell at an animal when they're misbehaving, don't you think?"

I tried it out, and yelled: "No, Peepers! No!"

And . . . it just worked. I have no idea why.

Then I asked Roy if there was some trick I could do. Like a trained seal at the circus spinning a ball on its nose or playing a horn.

(Why they make seals play horns at the circus, I have no idea. Why just seals? Why not a squirrel? Anyway . . .)

"Is there something you can throw to me to catch?" I asked.

"A banana?"

"Too cliché."

"What about an apple?"

"Yes!"

There was something hypersexualized about Mr. Peepers. I imagined him like somebody's overexcited puppy who goes around humping everyone's leg. Except, instead of your leg, Mr. Peepers might go straight for your face. The apple became a part of that same ravenous quality, and when Peepers finally got his hands on the forbidden fruit, he didn't just bite into it. He *devoured* it.

As a boy, I used to watch this old Mickey Mouse cartoon from the '30s called "Mickey's Trailer" on one of those old, portable projection screens on a tripod that my dad kept in his garage. In it, there's a scene where Goofy eats an ear of corn on the cob in like five seconds: holding it at both ends, he gnaws swiftly from one end to the other, a row at a time, rotating the cob like an old manual typewriter carriage as he goes. This was my inspiration. But since Goofy was animated and this wasn't something I'd seen a human do before, I had to practice, figuring out how to eat the apple in as many bites as possible in a matter of seconds, without biting my lip off. I eventually worked out how to get through an entire apple in one ravenous attack, but there was no way I could swallow fast enough to keep the pace while chomping the entire thing.

"Spit it out!" Roy suggested.

When we finally put it all together in front of the audience that Sunday, it was an unpredicted smash.

The following week Melanie scheduled the sketch as the first-act closer for Sunday's show, which was traditionally the slot given to the biggest crowd-pleaser of the night, and it remained there in the lineup for another year and a half.

There were no lines for me to memorize because Mr. Peepers didn't speak; he just barked out an unthreatening "Baa! Baa!" whenever he was hungry or confused.

But while there was some comfort in not having to deliver any lines in order to get laughs, I had to work twice as hard physically. In order to continue performing Mr. Peepers for a year and a half at the same high-energy level the character demanded, I had to stay constantly in shape. By the time I ran backstage to the dressing room, I was usually totally out of breath with my heart racing. A lot of nights I'd make it through the entire apple (it had to be a Red Delicious because they were the softest) and afterward discover that my mouth was full of blood because I'd gnawed open the insides of my cheeks without noticing it.

As grueling as it was, playing Mr. Peepers gave me one of the best experiences I ever had performing at the Groundlings. After milking and trying out every new physical possibility with the character, I finally ended up leaping off the stage and into the audience—Peepers gave me the perfect excuse to "break the fourth wall." I climbed over people's shoulders, did pirouettes on top of their seats, and crawled from one audience member's head to another until at last I stopped to arbitrarily grab some stranger's face and dry hump it. I know it may not sound all that sophisticated or funny, but the energy of the sketch became its own animal. You had a nonvolunteer audience member nearly being physically abused, and they were hysterically laughing the whole time. There was something amazing about seeing how lucky they felt to be the chosen victim. "Hump my face! Hump my face! Quick! Someone take a picture!"

After my debut in the last six episodes of *SNL*'s 1995–96 season, I came back for my first full season no longer just a "featured player" but a full-fledged regular cast member. And my seventh show, the first show of the 1996–97 season, was the busiest one I'd had yet. First off, Will Ferrell and I did a Roxbury Guys sketch—another sketch first performed at the Groundlings, introduced on my second appearance on *SNL* the prior season. This time, we head bopped with the week's guest host, Tom Hanks. Lorne came up with the idea of filming a pre-tape of the three of us bopping our heads in the middle of Times Square. I remember Tom Hanks being such a sport when we filmed this. He didn't break character, even when some unknown asshole yelled out, "Hey, Forrest! You're fat!"

Knowing I needed to have more than just a Roxbury guy as a recurring character, I decided to pitch Mr. Peepers to Tom Hanks. That season, I shared a seventeenth-floor office with Colin Quinn. Colin was just a writer at the time and the perfect office mate. Despite being incredibly funny and sharp, he didn't have that comedian thing of being always "on."

He was quiet, wise, and maybe because he was older than me, very open and unguarded. He also had probably the most attractive, well-lit office there—I think it was the only one with a plant that was actually alive. When I first moved in, he admitted that he suffered from vertigo, which did raise the question of why someone on the show had placed him at a desk right in front of a seventeenth-floor window—the only window in the office—not to mention why he'd decided to stay there. I offered to switch sides, but Colin said, "Nah, don't worry about it. It's good for me."

Anyway. Tom Hanks made the rounds of the offices to hear pitches for sketches featuring him for that week's show. When he arrived at our office, Colin was at his desk, and I was on a couch under a poster for Adam Sandler's *The Wedding Singer* that then *SNL* head writer Tim Herlihy—who wrote the movie with "Sandman," as his friends lovingly called him—had put in Colin's office as a joke when the movie became a success.

Tom took a seat in my desk chair, and I began telling him about Mr. Peepers. I explained that Peepers was the missing link, described how he ate apples, and told him that it was really funny, which is never helpful to say. The more I talked, the worse it sounded. This was one of my biggest problems during my run at *SNL*. Getting a physical character or idea across in a pitch without any type of demonstration, or by reading it in script form during a table read, is almost impossible.

But guess what, bitches: I came prepared. I had video of the sketch being performed at the Groundlings. So I stopped trying to explain and popped in the VHS tape of me, Will, and Roy.*

---

* You can watch the 1993 Mr. Peepers Groundlings sketch on my YouTube channel: https://www.youtube.com/watch?v=7dsFjN4niDE

Tom Hanks laughed from the very beginning to the absolute end. I'm not talking a polite little chuckle here or there. No: he laughed so hard he *literally fell off the rolling chair onto the floor*. He laughed until he started coughing. What a crazy surreal moment this was for me. Tom frickin' Hanks was on the floor in hysterics, curled up like a fetus.

At first, it was incredibly flattering, but when he kept going, it actually became a little scary.

Jesus, is he okay? I thought. *Do I wait until he's done? Should I go tell someone this is happening? Tom fuckin' Hanks is on the floor having a conniption fit. Would it be wrong of me to take a picture? What the fuck do I do?*

I looked at Colin, who was staring at me accusingly. I mean, come on, what was this? What if we actually hurt Tom Hanks and it was all my fault? Finally, the seizure lessened. Tom got to his knees and said, "What do *you* got, Colin?" And Colin said, "How the *fuck* am I supposed to follow *that*?"

The next day, about an hour before the table read—where the cast gathered to read through all the sketches before the final lineup was selected for air—I saw Tom exiting the executive producer's office, carrying the stack of sketches in his arms. As he spotted me, he stopped and put one of the manuscripts right under his nose, pretended to smell it, and said, "Nope, not funny." He smelled another one. "Nope, not funny." Then he pulled out one last sketch, held it toward me so that I could see the title, "Mr. Peepers," inhaled a long, grateful sniff and said, "Now *that's* funny!"

Everyone packed into one room for the read through. There was never an empty chair, and people who didn't have seats in the room—research assistants, interns, and assorted others—would sit on the floor just outside in the hallway, reading from the same packet of sketches while we waited for Lorne, sometimes for hours.

Lorne was always the last one in. He wasn't late, just the last one. It was part of the clockwork routine that kept the show's pre-production process working perfectly and predictably for decades.

When he entered the room, Lorne would squeeze between the backs of the cast members seated around the table and the fronts of the network censors and script department people seated in chairs against the walls. Then, on his way to his spot next to the guest host at the far end of the table, he'd reach over between the shoulders of writer/producer Steve Higgins and director Beth McCarthy, grab a handful of green, seedless grapes, and pop a few in his mouth. The assortment of fruit and cold cuts the interns provided for the read-through table was the same every week, and so sad looking and visibly unfresh that no one touched it—except Lorne. No kidding, I think he popped these grapes in exactly the same manner every single week I was there. Like I said: clockwork.

Like any read through, the norm was to stay seated while reading aloud a piece you were cast in. It didn't matter if it was a musical parody or the sketch included a dance number, or if it was one of those "Update" features where Fallon or Sandler played the guitar. There was an unwritten understanding that no matter how much the sketch relied on visuals, to get up and perform would be awkward and uncomfortable for everyone else (and would probably work against you in terms of having your sketch selected for the show). But with Mr. Peepers, I felt like I really didn't have a choice.

So as soon as the sketch started, I took off my shoes and socks and jumped onto the table. I remember keeping my eyes low so I wouldn't be discouraged by the sight of everyone in the room looking at me, wondering why I felt the need to not only get out of my seat but put my bare feet onto the fucking read-through table. I dashed across, cautiously avoiding the fruit plate—yes, the same fruit plate that provided Lorne's precious seedless grapes—and scurried into Tom Hanks's arms just inches away from Lorne, who, by the way, was the only one not watching me. He just kept reading the sketch. Never looked up once. Not knowing where to go next, I jumped up onto the windowsill behind Lorne and, while trying to balance on one foot, I rested against the glass, seventeen stories up, and ate manically through an apple.

Staff writer Matt Piedmont, who was a friend and wrote the "How Do You Say? Ah Yes, Show with Antonio Banderas" sketches with me, and later *Casa de Mi Padre* with Will, yelled—and I mean *yelled*—"Jesus, Kattan!" The rest of his thought was unspoken, but clear: *We get the joke, dumbass—now would you get the hell away from the window?*

My commitment to staying in character had landed me somewhere that was probably neither safe nor smart. If I'd jumped a little harder or the window had been a little flimsier, I would have died. But at least I'd have died in character. Well—a character that never would have made it on air. That would have been the real tragedy. Honestly, even if I'd fallen out, I think Lorne would still have been obliviously reading the scene direction when they were scraping me off 44th Street in front of the 30 Rock entrance.

About two hours later, during the read-through break, Tim Herlihy told me that if the sketch didn't make it in, it was probably because Lorne didn't like the character. This was the second time I'd been told he wasn't a Peepers fan. But the Peepers sketch *did* make it in, and not only that, it became the first sketch of the Tom Hanks/Tom Petty show, right after the monologue.

Hanks plays a character named John Bumbry from the San Diego Wild Animal Park, a guest on *The Tonight Show,* with Darrell Hammond as Jay Leno. When the sketch begins, I am in front of them, perched on a bar stool and hidden underneath a blanket.

"That's a big bulge underneath that blanket," Hammond/Leno jokes. "What do you got—Dennis Rodman under there?" (Yes, it was written to be a bad joke. Nothing against Jay, but sometimes his one-liners weren't exactly home runs.)

As Hanks finally unveils Mr. Peepers to the world, I pretend to be waking up, sitting, and then standing and stomping my feet and letting out loud "Baa" sounds. My outfit consists only of red shorts, held up with suspenders. After clapping like a trained simian and nimbly raising one of my legs, I jump onto Hanks and began clambering all over him as he tries to keep talking, half out of breath.

"Believe me," he says as I lick his cheek extravagantly and then try to gobble his ear while my left hand explores his head, "if there were more of these little fellas, I'd be a busy bee!"

I hang upside down from his waist. After Hanks manages to disentangle himself, he puts me back on the stool, announcing that I have a vocabulary of over five thousand words.

"Peepers, say 'Jay Leno.'"

"Baa!"

"Jay Leno!"

"Baa!"

"Jay Leno!"

"Baa!"

I am rewarded with an apple, which I begin furiously masticating, tearing through the flesh of the fruit and spitting it out—then I demand another before finally jumping off the stool, attacking Jay, and then humping the other guest, Andie MacDowell as played by Ana Gasteyer.

I thought Mr. Peepers's first television appearance might be his last, because for some reason, the sketch didn't go over as well as I'd hoped. The character's weird energy just didn't feel as wild and immediate as it had on the smaller Groundlings stage. And I couldn't exactly break the fourth wall, because everybody behind that imagined wall was sitting at home watching through a television. *Oh, man,* I thought, after it was over, *Are all the characters that I wrote back home even going to work?*

Lorne didn't care about making sure everyone's particular talents and pet characters were showcased, he cared about one thing: what was best for the show. I was going to have to tailor my repertoire specifically for the *SNL* format or I wasn't going to last. And finding the perfect balance between looking out for myself and working for the best interests of the show as a whole? That was going to be tricky.

Another problem with bringing Mr. Peepers back a second time on live TV was finding a guest host who saw the humor in getting face humped. Tom Hanks's enthusiasm is the reason I got to do Mr. Peepers on the show in the first place. But not everybody is as cool as Tom Hanks. (To answer the question that everyone always asks: Yes. Tom Hanks is by far one of the greatest guests I ever worked with on *SNL*.)

I got another shot at making Mr. Peepers into a recurring character that January, with guest host Kevin Spacey in the first episode of 1997. This time, the setting was a monkey lab. Will Ferrell played Spacey's lab assistant. I cast him not just because he'd done Peepers before and was reliably funny in any sketch, but because he was really the only cast member capable of holding me. Will was tall enough for me to wrap my legs around and swing upside down from—which I did—while Spacey riffed off his domineering, abusive *Swimming with Sharks* character and yelled at me. At one point, I stood on my stool face-to-face with Spacey while we shouted "Baa!" back and forth at one another. I devoured an apple with the usual gusto, and then Will chased me around the lab and got his face violently sucked when Peepers went into "attack mode."

Not only did the sketch land better with the live audience this time, it was also appreciated more by the audience at home. In fact, this time Peepers worked well enough that the show would bring back the apple-spitting, dry-humping, half man, half monkey a dozen more times.

One day in 1997, Adam McKay, one of the best writers on the show, called out my name as I passed his office. He told me he had an idea for Mr. Peepers and wanted to write it up.

Adam didn't tell me what the idea was, but I was so dumbstruck that he actually wanted to write a Peepers sketch that I didn't even ask. Of course, McKay would go on to co-write and direct various movies with Will, including the *Anchorman* series, *Talladega Nights,* and *Step Brothers,* and then to write the critically acclaimed dramas *The Big Short* and *Vice.* With *The Big Short*, Adam became the only writer to come out of *SNL,* write a dramatic screenplay, and win an Oscar for it. In fact, he was the first *SNL* alumni to ever win an Academy Award at all. *SNL* cast members had been nominated, but they'd never won. It's really quite impressive to succeed in writing both comedy and drama, and even back when I was on the show, everyone knew how gifted Adam was.

In the past, whenever I'd gone to Adam's office to pitch him an idea, he'd offered to take a look when I was done but never seemed interested in working together. But he did write this sketch for Mr. Peepers. And during the read through, the sketch got more laughs than Peepers ever had before. I performed in the room like I always did now, but the laughs this time had nothing to do with my antic agility. It was all the script.

Well, almost all—there was one person seated at the table who was laughing at my antics, and that was the guest host, Claire Danes.

In the sketch, Will is once again Peepers's handler, and Claire plays Will's assistant. The two of them stand behind a jeep in the heart of the jungle, having brought Mr. Peepers back home to where he was found and saying a last goodbye to him. Unlike the written jokes that got the best reactions in the read through, the biggest laughs when the sketch aired were once again my circus-level humor and dry humping. This time I am humping the back of the jeep, and Claire Danes keeps breaking character and laughing.

The joke of the sketch is that every time Claire completes a heart-wrenching goodbye, Peepers runs off into the jungle . . . and then immediately comes running right back and jumps into Will's arms.

In the scene, there are four of these very emotional goodbyes where Will and Claire think Peepers is finally off to find his real family, but no. The cute, spastic, slaphappy little simian has no interest in leaving his captors at all. Will, by goodbye number four, is completely fed up, so eventually he grabs a prop gun from the back of the jeep and starts yelling, "Get the hell out of here! Now! Go!" At last, Peepers gets the hint. He waves his fifth and final goodbye to his *Homo sapiens* friends and leaps over to the set's foliage, twirling and "baa"-ing as he exits. Suddenly, a Peepers family of three—Ana, Jim Breuer, and Cheri—appear among the leaves to welcome Mr. Peepers home.

It didn't come to me until a few days later: *They were trying to keep Peepers from appearing on the show ever again!* Even though the audience liked Peepers, it had become pretty obvious that almost everyone else on the show was tired of him. Will might not have been performing when he yelled at Mr. Peepers to get the hell out and just go.

But you can't keep a good monkey/man down, and in November 2000, the high-strung primate ne'er-do-well finally found love. And I experienced something I will never forget: working with a female guest host who was unabashedly fearless, a woman who wasn't afraid to "unleash the beast" during a sketch. No surprise, this was Charlize Theron. She seemed to turn her performance into an extended dare, taking it as far as she could within the limits of not-ready-for-prime-time sketch comedy. I may have been responsible for creating the atmosphere with the scenario in the script, but what she did with it was 100 percent her own—we never discussed it prior to walking on set.

The sketch took place in the high-rise office of a conservative sex therapist. Molly Shannon played the therapist, and Charlize played a patient diagnosed as unable to experience any level of arousal. Amazingly original plot, I know. Charlize is on a couch, and Molly, seated in an armchair, hands her a blindfold to cover her eyes. Then, instead of bringing out a compatible human match for Charlize's character, Molly calls for Mr. Peepers to come out and perch next to Charlize on the couch.

We practiced all this at dress rehearsal.

"Now, Mr. Peepers is going to eat some fruit," Molly says, and as expected, a juicy fat delicious-looking apple is scarfed up and annihilated.

"Now, open your mouth. Peepers is going to try and arouse you," and I begin spitting chunks of what's left of that poor juicy apple into Charlize's mouth.

"How does that make you feel?" Molly asks, which Charlize can't answer because of the unpeeled banana that I'm stuffing in her mouth, followed by a bottle of milk. Most of the milk spills down her neck and all over her blouse. Charlize, drenched in this fruit massacre, is now yelling, borderline Meg Ryan in *When Harry Met Sally*, "Give it to me! Ohh, I want you so bad," as scripted.

Never had I seen a guest this committed to a scene, completely trusting. After all, she was blindfolded. Was it funny? Yes, but probably in an "I guess you had to be there" way. I was actually a little surprised the sketch made it into the lineup, not because it didn't work—it definitely worked—but because the network censors weren't exactly enjoying themselves watching us.

After dress rehearsal, Lorne had one note for the three of us in the sketch—and yes, I do mean the three of us because apparently Molly had been getting pretty riled up as well and I hadn't even noticed—and that was, "Could you pull back on the . . . not go so far with . . . you know." He didn't even know what to call it! He just couldn't come up with a word for whatever the fuck was happening.

I'm not sure what it says about me, or maybe human nature, that when an authority figure says something that could be considered controlling, my natural reaction is to rebel. But, well . . . ten seconds before the sketch went to air after the commercial break, while we stood by the set's door waiting for Jenna the assistant director to wave a two-finger silent cue to enter, Charlize looked at me and whispered, "Let's just fucking go for it!"

Without a beat, I answered, "Yeah! Let's just fucking go for it!" I mean, why would I say no to *anything* Charlize Theron asked me to do?

Halfway into the sketch, Molly says, "Now take off the blindfold." Charlize whips off her blindfold and chases after me while I spin and twirl around the office. When I perform, every now and then when I'm not nervous, I'll have a sort of out-of-body experience and watch myself in the sketch as if behind the cameras, from the audience. This is what happened. But my vision is not always accurate: I saw myself spinning around the room just like the Tasmanian Devil, when in reality, I twirled around maybe two times. Not even close.

Anyway, after knocking over everything in the room, as scripted, I jump over the couch and land on all fours on the coffee table, facing the camera. Charlize lands right up behind me, her legs cradling mine. Meanwhile, Molly's unleashed beast is cheering us on.

Then—*un*scripted—Charlize grabs hold of my wig while her other hand is latched onto my waist, and she starts pumping me from behind. I don't mean to get graphic, but she was doing some crotch slamming! I remember thinking: *What the fuck did I do? It's like I'm Dr. Frankenstein, and I've created a monster with barbarous hormones!*

And then—not only have I never experienced this, but I've never seen it happen again—after a few intense dry humps, the screen went to black and the sketch ended before it was technically over. Someone pulled the plug.

Afterward, Charlize and I walked offstage, out of breath, trying to process what had occurred on stage. Then she started laughing.

"I can't believe I tore your wig off!" she said. "What just happened?"

I tried to think of an answer, but I couldn't. But I knew one thing: whatever it was, around eleven million people had just watched it.

If Charlize Theron brought out the sexual side of Peepers, then Katie Holmes produced the romantic one.

When I first met her, a few minutes before the cast gathered outside Lorne's office for the pitch meeting, she was in an empty office down the hall with her publicist. She wore a fitted tan trench coat and sunglasses sitting on top of her head. I introduced myself, and she stood up and shook my hand. It was 2001. She was still on *Dawson's Creek,* so there was no Tom Cruise, there was no Scientology, and she seemed genuinely like that one girl you would always dream about in high school. She had the most delicate smoky eyes, and when she smiled, the right side of her lips turned crooked, and her bottom lip curled up when she laughed. I was so infatuated with her. She was the kind of girl you would write a song to and then stand outside her bedroom window and serenade. During every sketch we did together, and there were a few, it was almost impossible for me to communicate with her without flirting. And most of the time, she flirted back.

I remember rushing from the seventeenth floor down to studio 8H Friday afternoon to watch her rehearse the opening monologue. In it she takes her clothes off, revealing a sexy outfit, like something from the musical *Chicago*, and dances with all these buff guys in ties. It was a strange choice for the monologue to have her do a Broadway-themed song-and-dance routine, because she wasn't known as a singer or dancer. It was also not very funny. But I remember saying, "Oh, my God. The monologue is amazing. Did you guys see it?" and "Her voice is so beautiful, I didn't know she could sing so well!" and "Did you see her dancing? It's so good." I was so smitten that week I thought everything she did was unbelievable.

In the Peepers sketch, which had three sets and a pre-tape, the last set was her bedroom. The sketch was a parody of *Dawson's Creek*, and the story was that the school had a new exchange student named Mr. Peepers. In the last scene, Katie's depressed because she's gotten pregnant, so she takes a bunch of sleeping pills and passes out on the floor, as one usually does when depressed, according to teen dramas. Suddenly, Peepers appears, looking in through the back window. He backs up a few steps, spins around, and crashes in through the frame. He rushes over to Katie on the floor, realizes she's possibly near death, and then lies on top of her and humps her back to life. I should specify that when I humped her, my genitalia were not placed over her . . . area. I was humping a few inches down on her upper thigh.

When I'd gotten as many laughs as I could humping her leg, I moved my face up to hers—keep in mind that she's pretending to be dead, so her eyes are closed and she can't move until I give her the cue to come back to life by tapping the left side of her ribs. As rehearsed, I started sucking various parts of her face, then listened to her heartbeat, sucked her face again, and listened to her heartbeat. When I moved back up to her face a third time, she whispered—with her teeth clenched and her lips barely moving so the audience couldn't see—*"Don't you dare touch my mouth."*

I was slightly taken aback. It felt like that moment when you go out to dinner or a movie or something with someone, and then afterward you drive her home, or walk her home or whatever, and when you get to her front door, you move in for a kiss goodnight . . . and she pulls away and says, "Don't you dare touch my mouth."

So I didn't. I may have been spoiled by Charlize's fearless method performance and gotten carried away, who knows, but after that it seemed safe to assume that Katie probably didn't want to hang out any time in the near future, ever. At the after party, she arrived wearing a blue bob wig, the kind Scarlett Johansson wore when she sang karaoke in *Lost in Translation*. I have no idea why Katie was wearing the wig; maybe she thought wigs were a way of letting loose and celebrating, I don't know. But she looked great, regardless, and I did talk with her for a few minutes. We had the kind of brief conversation you have when the music is so loud that you need to lean in to each other, put one hand over one ear, and then yell directly into each other's ear canal.

Imagine my surprise me when she gave me her phone number. She wrote it in ink on a dinner napkin, but the strange thing is that she wrote it in what I guess you'd call a code. It was a poem about how she'd enjoyed working with me, but every line had a number hidden in it, looking just like one of the letters. It was really clever and almost brilliant in a kind of *Da Vinci Code* way, to be honest. Eventually, I figured out the number—by asking one of the *SNL* writers from Harvard to do it for me—but I wanted to play it cool, so I waited a couple of weeks to call her, and when I did she wasn't home, so I left her a message. These were the ancient days when people left messages for each other on actual machines they kept for this purpose at home.

A few days later, I got a message from her in return. This was the message:

"Baa! Baa! Baa!"

Despite his successful run on *SNL*, I never felt Mr. Peepers fully translated from stage to screen. I eventually concluded that part of the problem was framing. When an audience member is watching you perform on stage, they can, at least peripherally, see the entire stage and every activity that's happening on that stage. Regardless of where the main "action" is, they can choose to look at any part of that stage at any time they want. Sometimes the best part of a sketch is watching the reactions of the actors who aren't even meant to be the focus of the scene. Or the actions of background characters that another character is failing to notice.

Back when I was a young little tot watching an old comedy in my dad's garage, a lot of the scenes that I found the funniest were those that stayed on a wide shot. Especially those in silent films like Buster Keaton's *The General* or *College*, which are full of visual jokes. Or his short film *One Week*, which has that insane and unforgettable shot of the side of a house with an open window frame collapsing over Buster as he stands directly beneath it and just barely slips through, avoiding what could have been a tragic death. Or the famous mirror pantomime in the Marx Brothers' *Duck Soup,* where Groucho is in pajamas and Harpo is dressed as Groucho, also in pajamas, and pretends to be Groucho's reflection.

But on *SNL*, in order to sell the joke, it was pretty common for the director to have the studio camera shoot whoever had the line or was speaking at that moment, and seldom would they have the camera on someone's reaction unless by chance they decided to cut to it. In almost any modern film or TV setting, the camera does a lot of close-ups. For example, in almost every Norman Lear sitcom, including *All in the Family* and *The Jeffersons*, there was always a cult character with a famous catchphrase. And when it was said, the camera would almost always go to a close-up. When it was Archie Bunker whining "Aww, Edith," the camera would focus the audience's attention where the director thought it ought to be—on the joke. Sometimes that focus makes sense to a director mostly because it makes sense to the writer, who already knows where the jokes are. But for a performer, especially when you're doing something physical, it's not always your first choice. In pretty much every Peepers sketch on *SNL*, when we blocked it for the camera, I found myself constantly asking the director to stay on a wide shot so the sketch wouldn't suffer and fall into the standard close-up comedy trap. To me, Mr. Peepers worked best when the audience had a view of the whole scene. Maybe this was why Lorne wasn't initially a big fan of the sketch. Who knows? Maybe even though we never mentioned it to each other, we both felt that it would never work as well on television live from New York as it had onstage back in LA.

Now I often wonder if Peepers should have been left back home, at the Groundlings. Instead, Peepers made the leap from LA to New York like I did—which is to say after a long journey of multiple false starts, and an unfortunate incident with a poodle.

Chapter 2

I MAY HAVE KILLED THE POODLE

Months before we formally auditioned for *SNL* in 1995, Will Ferrell, Cheri Oteri, and I each met individually with Lorne Michaels and head writer and producer Steve Higgins up in Lorne's office on the seventeenth floor of 30 Rock. (Higgins no longer serves as head writer for the show, but he still does the voice-over and narrative for all the sketches today. And, of course, he's Fallon's "second banana" on *The Tonight Show*. Their *SNL* history is the reason they play off of each other so well. Because impressions were Jimmy's forte, he had a consistent spot as a contestant in the popular "Celebrity *Jeopardy*" sketches, and whenever Higgins was writing one, you'd always find Jimmy in his office adding jokes.) (By the way, Jimmy does an amazing Chris Rock.)

As I was saying, before you cut me off . . .

For this "sit-down with Lorne," not only did neither Will nor I know what was expected of us, we had no idea what Lorne was even like beyond whatever scraps of legend we'd heard over the years. The only thing we were told—by our agent—was that the meeting would probably last around ten minutes. Since my appointment was right before Will's, the two of us walked together up to 30 Rockefeller Plaza from the Paramount Hotel on 46th and Broadway, where we'd been put up for the night.

When I walked in to the meeting, Lorne was at his desk, with Higgins sitting off to the right. I sat directly across from Lorne, but even though Lorne and I were positioned for the conversation, Higgins did most of the talking. And by most of the talking, I mean Lorne may have said one word; I think he said "hmmm" when I came in. (Is "hmmm" a word?)

It didn't take long to realize things weren't going well. I couldn't tell if I was supposed to be funny or not. Was I supposed to talk about the creative talents I'd been honing since fifth grade or what? It was as if Lorne was bored with me before I'd even sat down. He just stared over my shoulder, holding a No. 2 pencil by both ends, twisting it back and forth, back and forth, and then back and forth again. I wanted to turn around so I could see what it was he might be looking at, but I knew I couldn't until the meeting was over. Which, judging by the level of Lorne's engagement, could have been any second. After seven minutes of this stimulating banter, Lorne contributed one last word to the conversation: "Goodbye."

I stood up, and as I turned around, I finally caught a glimpse of what Lorne had been staring at that was so fascinating —a poster of Steve Martin, Chevy Chase, and Martin Short dressed as 1930s mariachis in ¡Three Amigos! And so began my desperate quest for Lorne's approval, which would continue for roughly the next decade.

When I walked out of the office, Will asked how it went.

"I don't know," I said. "I'm not sure. Maybe someone could tell me."

As Will started toward Lorne's office, I noticed he was carrying a suitcase.

"What's with the suitcase?" I asked.

"I don't know," he said, with his eyebrows stretched up, looking wide-eyed and demonically playful. "I'm gonna try something. But I don't know."

"Do it. It'll be funny." Which was honestly all that mattered to us.

Dammit, why didn't I go in with something, like a gag? I couldn't stop obsessing. *Why did I just go in as myself? That was stupid.*

For the past few years, I had toiled as a chauffeur, waiter, and video store clerk so I could take classes, write sketches, and perform with the Groundlings. When it was finally my turn to be on that stage, I quickly discovered that it was harder than it looked. As a Groundling, you are habitually learning. (Now that I think of it, there is a little Buddhist overlap there, that idea of having "beginner's mind.") Your work is never done or good enough. The teachers and directors explicitly drill this into your head to prevent you from getting an ego, or getting lazy and complacent, creating a never-ending hunger to explore and create. Even if you are in almost every sketch and get the most laughs, you're still writing and proving yourself. If you don't produce and aren't funny, you're gone. On *SNL*, you might write two sketches and collaborate on a third, and if they don't go well, you won't be in the show that weekend. In the Groundlings, if a performance goes awry, you might not be part of the show until the next season when you can submit sketches again, unless someone drops out.

Yet despite the rigors of the craft, being a Groundling at that time was a thrilling experience. It was my first dream come true. Alternative comedy in LA was taking off, with new voices emerging everywhere, and the Groundlings were by far the most prestigious. If you were a Groundling, you obviously had what it took. The atmosphere of high pressure and high expectations created magic. I maintain to this day that I have never seen anything funnier than what I witnessed on the Groundlings stage, day after day, week after week. All of us were young, talented, completely without limits, and hungry for more.

I had made the cast of the Sunday show, a weekly live performance open to the paying public. All of the cast members would be voted on or off based on our performances, but the voting only happened twice a year. After eighteen months and three rounds of voting, you could either be voted out entirely or, if you were lucky, voted into the Groundlings main company, where you could perform two shows on Friday and two shows on Saturday. That is, assuming there was a spot for you. There were always thirty members, and sometimes even after a cast member had moved on to something bigger, they would hold on to their spot. If they were absent for a few years, the board would finally urge them to leave, since an empty spot was the only way a Sunday member who'd been voted up could ever make it to the main company stage.

I met Will on the first day of rehearsal for the 1993 Sunday show company. I'd been part of the cast for six months already, along with a group that included Cheri Oteri. Will and Roy Jenkins were two of the new additions, along with Chase Winton, Mary Jo Smith, David Jahn, and a few others.

Will and I became friends—and sketch partners—almost immediately.

We only had class once a week on Mondays, but I'd often get together with another cast member or two between classes to write something for the next week.

One of the first things I wrote with Will was a sketch where we played business partners who got together to "work" at home on a Saturday night while their wives went out. Once the wives were gone, our inner children were immediately unleashed. Turning the living room into our hideout, we began drawing stick-figure pictures and scotch-taping them on the wall, pretending a pen was a rocket, fighting over toys, and knocking over furniture. The first time we performed it in the show, the sketch went great—I knew it landed because Groundlings legend Mindy Sterling was in the audience, and I could hear her distinctive laughter from the stage. The second time it went even better, and I was sure it was going to continue to be a hit. I didn't take into account how crucial our timing was—it's a very physical sketch, and timing is especially important when you are doing physical comedy. The third time we performed the sketch in the Sunday show was our last. Our chemistry was great, but our timing was off, and for some reason it just wasn't funny.*

This first sketch would turn out to be the only one Will and I wrote that failed to make it into regular rotation at the Groundlings. Every other sketch we wrote was a success; Will and I knew early on that something special happened when we worked together. Our timing and comedic instincts were aligned, making it easy for us to play off each other. This wasn't something we ever really discussed, or even felt the need to mention. We just had this alignment when we performed together and always trusted it.

---

* The sound quality isn't great, but you can watch a Sunday show version of this 1993 sketch at: https://www.youtube.com/watch?v=3XJqXZsyJLY

Whenever we wrote at Will's apartment in West Hollywood, he'd usually cook dinner, which more often than not was spaghetti. He'd stand over the sink straining the pasta again and again before adding a jar of Newman's Own tomato sauce. Knowing what was on the menu, I usually ate beforehand. Will lived in a sparse duplex apartment just off of Beverly Boulevard. He always had the latest copy of the *LA Times* on top of a tall stack of unread copies of the *LA Times* from the past six months, and every time I went over there, a fresh Burger King "crown" sat on the kitchen table. I pictured him asking for a new crown every time he stopped at the drive-thru.

Will and I once worked a paying job together long before *SNL*. He played Santa and I played an elf, and we walked around Pasadena in costume in the middle of a sweltering December, handing out plastic-wrapped candy canes to children. We had to stay in character for six hours a day. On the third day, by about the fifth hour, a sort of delirium began to creep in.

"You know, Elf, you're looking pretty good," a suddenly pervy Will would say as he rested his arm over my shoulder.

"Oh Santa, you old shit. Your dementia is acting up again," I'd reply in a high-pitched and disturbing voice.

Meanwhile, all the kids around us looked deeply uneasy—for a while, until the novelty wore off. Then they'd just go back to pointing at and mocking us.

But back to what I was saying about me and Will. There was just something about our dynamic together that worked: our chemistry, banter, and—eventually—timing was almost effortless. That's what I miss the most about performing as a Groundling or on *SNL*—working with someone that good and playing off each other perfectly without even trying.

The closest you can get to this experience outside of sketch comedy is doing a play, or a movie, or a whole series opposite each other, which is rare for comedians, and even those things aren't quite the same. It's too bad, but today the comedy world, whether you're talking about improv schools or TV shows, doesn't seem to encourage the kind of partnerships that gave us so much classic duo comedy. Lorne is an exception—he especially likes talk show premises with two hosts, and he often gives duos a chance in general. I've come to enjoy doing stand-up, but it can feel lonely; it's always been much more gratifying and easier for me to collaborate with others. Of course, you need the right partnership. It would be hard for me to write anything with David Spade. He's his own machine; it's hard to take risks in those conditions, and risks are what make great comedy.

A few months after my nearly wordless meeting with Lorne and Higgins in the spring of '95, NBC flew me back to New York to officially audition for *SNL* along with Will, Cheri, and the very funny Jennifer Coolidge. By this time, we were all members of the Groundlings main company, but that didn't make it any less intimidating. Not only did our auditions take place in studio 8H, but we actually performed them on the iconic, original monologue/"good night" stage. To make things even more unnerving, there was no way to tell how many people were watching the audition, or who they were, because the studio was completely in the dark. The only thing visible was a tiny red light on top of one of the cameras, signaling that it was recording.

When I was done, I gathered my props and stuffed my character outfits into a sports bag, stepped off the stage, and walked through the studio doors past the page desk feeling as if I might be in a slight state of shock, and once again having no sense of what had just happened. Later I was told that it was Lorne Michaels, Steve Higgins, a few other head writers, and executive producer Marci Klein who were standing just a few feet from the camera in the dark, watching us.

For the audition, we'd each been asked to do three original characters and one impression, and with the training that we'd had in the Groundlings, we were more than prepared. The first original character I chose was Suel Forrester, a gibberish-spouting, slow-strutting substitute teacher who sounded like Tommy Lee Jones, only unintelligible. For my second character, I performed as my "unnamed slick guy dancing in his apartment while on a date." I chose this character to show that I was indeed capable of playing a masculine and normal person and didn't always rely on oddball original sketch characters. In the sketch, my character is sitting on the couch with a date, and just as I'm about to make a move, I stop short of her lips and instead walk over to the other side of the stage to the nonexistent, imaginary stereo to find the perfect song to dance to on the way back to the couch. (Major kudos to Marci Klein for volunteering to play the girl sitting on the couch during my audition.)

My third character was Mr. Peepers. I ate through an apple while balancing on one foot on top of a wooden stool, while a boom box that sat on the edge of the set played my voice narrating an introduction to the half-man, half-monkey creature. To commit like this without hearing one laugh or see even a smirk was excruciatingly hard. Then, for my impression, I played Christian Slater interviewing a vampire in a scene from *Interview with the Vampire*: "So, you're a vampire? The story you're telling me is amazing. It's incredible."

We boarded our flight back home to LA and tried not to obsess over our auditions. (FYI, the flight was on American Airlines—at the time,

NBC had some sort of a deal with them. This was also back when they served caviar in first class. I swear, the '90s were the best.) There was no point thinking about what we should and shouldn't have done; it was over, and now we had to wait. Coincidently, a few months earlier, Will, Cheri, and I had all also auditioned in LA for Fox's new sketch-comedy show, *MADtv*. All three of us were turned down. Being that it would be competing with *SNL* by airing at the exact same time on another network, I remember the three of us sharing the same reaction: "Who gives a shit."

We tried to suppress our expectations of actually making it on to *SNL* because it had been understood for a few years that Marci and Lorne were done hiring from the Groundlings. They felt the Groundlings were "hack." The last person they'd hired from the group was Julia Sweeney, and when she chose to do an *It's Pat* movie without Lorne as a producer (even though he turned down the producer offer in the first place) and without his consent, he was not pleased.

I knew the truth even back then: When someone is fixated on a label they choose for you, there's not much you can do about it. This is true in entertainment in general, in high school, and it was definitely true at *SNL*. (Even—especially—after you leave.)

Jennifer Coolidge was a tall, messy, sexy, tough, charmingly crass Boston-native bombshell who was considered unattainable by all. But this didn't stop me from crushing on her. While often recognized as Stifler's mom in the *American Pie* movies, the beautiful masseuse from the classic *Seinfeld* "Masseuse" episode, or her roles in various Christopher Guest comedies, her best work—as is the case with many super-talented performers—was back when she was onstage at the Groundlings. I'm by no means saying the amazing Jennifer Coolidge and other Groundlings

alums were never as good later in their careers. But in your first years on
that stage, there is a freedom you're encouraged to use, and it allows you
to discover a kind of brilliance you never knew you had that unexpectedly appears in your performance. Eventually, you learn to recognize what
you're gifted with. What makes you different than anybody else. What
can make you not just funny and or even hilarious but *fuckin'* hilarious.
When you recognize and then learn how to control it, hopefully you'll
be able to use it like a tool whenever you need it. And when you discover
how to be confident and playful with it, your gift can become many things,
including a new comedic persona that might eventually make you a star.
It was while in the Groundlings that Melissa McCarthy discovered a gift
like Coolidge's—a wild and grounded, brash and vulnerable persona that,
along with her go-for-broke physical comedy, has made her one of the
funniest women today. The process is truly magical when it happens. But
it's not easy to hold on to this gift for the rest of your career.

The first time I saw Coolidge perform, she was doing a show in the
Groundlings' main company. I had been in the Sunday show for a year
and had another six months until I'd either get voted up into the main
company or perhaps get kicked out entirely, which was always a possible result. When I first saw Coolidge doing an improv set, what really
struck me was the unique timing of her delivery. There was something
just slightly off about it. The only other person I can think of with a similar kind of timing is another Groundlings alum—Lisa Kudrow. When
Jennifer was in a sketch doing one of her recurring characters, she had a
tendency to drift off into a far darker place than most other performers.

I finally met her during an improv exercise one night in a Groundlings class. We were all on stage, lying on our stomachs, and I was right
next to her. Her sweater was covered with various lengths of numerous

colors of cat hair, including this little wad barely hanging on to her shoulder, so I said, "Hey, your cat just called and asked me to tell you he wants his sweater back." Something like that. Anyway, she liked it enough to ask me if I would walk her to her car after class. I was baffled. It felt like I was in an episode of *Happy Days* and Potsie had just been asked out by the worldly-wise Pinky Tuscadero.

The following week, when Jennifer and I were called up onstage in class to do an improv together, I knew exactly what was going on. Someone had probably seen us and had told Melanie, our director, that I'd walked Jennifer to her car. At the end of class, Melanie assigned the two of us to write a sketch sometime in the following week, and if she liked it, we could try it out in the Friday late show.

Two days later, I was at Jennifer's apartment. She probably wouldn't appreciate me saying this, but her place wasn't exactly tidy. Every time I walked into a different room, I would say, "Oh my God!" And immediately I would hear her running toward me, yelling, "Get out of there, you fucking asshole!" Then she'd push me out and close the door, saying, "I haven't had a chance to clean up."

Our first sketch literally took about fifteen minutes to create. It was a funny concept, so we wrote out three acts based on this one idea that could be stretched into a three-to-five-minute sketch. Just a beginning, a middle, and an end. Not only did this sketch make it on to the Friday late show, it became a staple of the show for at least four months. Coolidge and I really were a great comedy duo. Shortly after meeting Jennifer, I was invited to go on a trip to a lake house out in the desert with Will and Roy Jenkins and their girlfriends. During this rare weekend getaway, we rode jet skis, ate barbecue chicken and hot dogs, and drank Coronas. I was still single, so instead of a girlfriend of my own, I brought

an eight-by-ten black-and-white headshot of my new obsession, Jennifer
Coolidge. Surprisingly, the headshot did fill the void I otherwise would
have experienced. I placed the photo on the seat next to me at dinner; I
taped a pair of sunglasses to her face down by the lake; I even took her
jet skiing, which was exactly when the joke ran out of juice.

Since Jennifer and I appeared to be physically incompatible (she is
five foot eleven and I'm . . . not) and she was totally out of my league,
nobody could believe it when we actually started dating. Fellow Groundling Michael Hitchcock once joked that our sex life probably involved her
smoking a cigarette and tapping it into an ashtray that rested on my back
while I went down on her.

A few years ago, I asked her what sparked that "You know,
I think I might just like this guy" feeling inside of her. She answered me in
this really funny, slow, sarcastic, "Mommy's gonna tell you a little story
before you go night night" voice: "Wellll, on the first night you came
over, when it was time for you to go and you started to walk out the front
door, you turned around to face me and continued walking backwards.
Then you said, 'Hey, do you want to go to Disneyland next week?' And
when I said 'Okay,' you started to blush. And then, just when you were
about to say 'Great,' you fell backwards all the way down the stairs."

By the time we auditioned for *SNL*, I'd been dating Jennifer for a year
and a half. Not only had I gotten over my Napoleon complex, but I'd also
gotten over the feeling that I didn't deserve someone that beautiful and
talented. Like that first sketch we'd written, our relationship just worked,
with very little effort involved. She'd invited me to go to Boston to meet her
father, and we left on a Wednesday, knowing we would miss a weekend of
Groundlings shows. Generally you tried not to miss a show because there

was a whole sketch lineup that you were a part of that depended on you, but this felt like an important occasion.

That Friday, Cheri called me in Boston to ask a favor. She wanted to do a sketch that she and I had written together with another performer. This was standard—if someone was absent, you had to ask the other person if you could do their sketch without them.

"Melanie said we could put some of our best sketches in tonight because Lorne Michaels is coming," Cheri explained.

I felt nauseated. No one had told me Lorne was coming. It was the only show I'd missed in my whole Groundling career. And it just had to be *this* particular show.

I stood holding the phone, feeling like I'd just gotten sucked out of an airplane window at thirty thousand feet above the ground. I could hear Cheri on the other end of the line shouting my name, still waiting for an answer.

"Why is Lorne coming?" I asked.

"I don't know—I guess to take a second look."

I was not only stunned, I was pissed off. Everyone knew I'd been trying to get *SNL* to come see us perform. The show had always been my dream, and now Lorne had decided to check us out on our home turf months after our New York auditions—on the very weekend I'd be gone. The selfish neurotic inside my head began shouting: *Why is this happening? I've worked just as hard as anybody else in the Groundlings. Maybe even a little harder to step out of Dad's shadow. Just to prove I'm worthy of being here. All that work and now this?? It's not fair!*

I tried like hell to get back to LA, but it was impossible. There were simply no flights available. It killed me to know Lorne and Marci were visiting the Groundlings, and I wasn't there.

Things with Jennifer, however, started to take a turn the moment I got on *SNL*. She had auditioned and been turned down, creating a delicate situation because it was so difficult for me to share my exciting news without feeling badly about it. She suggested a separation, but I was adamant we could work it out. I didn't want to lose the connection we had, which never was as much of a romantic relationship as it was a mutual attraction for each other's comedic gifts. I just didn't want to lose her. (Hold this thought for a few chapters.)

Then Will and Cheri received calls telling them that they'd gotten spots on the show. They were going to New York. I began to panic. I hadn't heard anything yet. The last thing I wanted to think about was the possibility that I wasn't going with them. I simply refused to contemplate this, instead continuing to believe that I was going, too—even as weeks passed with no word about my audition.

I was with my dad at his house in Sherman Oaks when the phone rang. I lifted the receiver to my ear while Dad and I stared at each other in silence.

"Chris, um . . . I'm sorry," I heard my agent say.

That was all I heard. Every part of my body felt like throwing up. It was confirmed. I wasn't going anywhere. And then it came, my first official nervous breakdown. At least, that's what I'd call it. It's possible that it was just an old-fashioned panic attack, but I like to think it was a dramatic, life-affecting breakdown. My body felt heavy, as if it was sinking. I grabbed on to the bedside table next to me, yet still managed to collapse to the floor. I felt oddly seasick, as if someone had duct taped my feet to a sinking submarine. As I looked at my dad, still wearing his baby-blue buttoned-up pajamas, I began to hyperventilate.

I think it took ten minutes until I was able to get my breathing back under control. When I did, I found myself crying uncontrollably, curled up like a fetus on Dad's disgusting, never-washed carpet. He held my hand and looked down at me helplessly.

Shortly after that dark day, I found myself parked in my black Honda CR-X, listening to "You Oughta Know" by Alanis Morissette and waiting to see whether I could bring myself to actually open the door and climb out. We were having a farewell barbecue for Will. He and Cheri had performed in a couple more Groundlings shows before wrapping up their lives in LA to leave for New York. The twenty-first *SNL* season would be starting in September.

I wasn't angry with Will and Cheri, obviously. I was just bitterly disappointed for myself. And, honestly, I didn't want to be at this party. I didn't want to see all our friends crowding around Will, congratulating him and giving him their best wishes. For twenty minutes, I sat with my seat belt on, sulking like a toddler. Eventually I cut the engine, climbed out of the car, and went to celebrate with my friend. I really was happy for him. He deserved this. In all my time knowing Will, there had never been any doubt that this would be happening one day. I told myself to just breathe and soldier up and get used to the facts.

My frustration over not making *Saturday Night Live* surfaced in my performances. Three- or four-minute sketches began to double in length. I'd really take my time milking the audience, making the characters not give a shit, improvising more and more because, well, why not? I simply didn't care. Ironically, in the long run this worked in my characters' favor. They became more real because I wasn't hunting for the quick joke.

I couldn't stop wondering how things would go with Will and Cheri. I'll be honest—I was hoping the show wouldn't be a hit. The night of the *SNL* season premiere, the Groundling cast members who weren't on stage were watching the episode in our green room, and I hung around waiting to see how Will and Cheri did.

Will happened to be in the cold opener, playing a newscaster in a sketch called "O. J. Today." When he flubbed a line, I knew he must be nervous. Actually, I don't think he ever flubbed a line in all his seasons after that one. The reality of the situation hit me again as I watched my close friend and former partner. We'd performed together so long. Now he was "Live from New York" while I was just "Living in LA"—with my dad.

Will and Cheri didn't get a lot of laughs at first. I actually felt a bit vindicated, but then again, I knew they weren't really being utilized. One sketch on the second episode with guest host Chevy Chase featured Will as a pilot flying an airplane and Cheri as a little kid visiting the cockpit. It had been funny when they did it at the Groundlings, but on *SNL* it just didn't work as well. That fall, I tried to convince myself that I was glad I didn't make the show. I would tell myself, *Oh, my god, this show is terrible*, and then try to believe that somehow I'd dodged a bullet. Maybe the show was going to end. Maybe it was over.

Then, on the fifth show of the season, Will and Cheri introduced the Spartan Cheerleaders. The sketch ended up carrying that episode and showed the rest of the world the Groundlings energy we were all known for. Will and Cheri weren't only incredibly gifted, they were also well trained. We were taught in the Groundlings that it wasn't enough to be *funny*, you needed to be better. Like me, Will and Cheri worked like machines and put incredible pressure on themselves to deliver.

The sketches were improving, and my friends were doing better each week, getting more and more laughs.

Meanwhile, I found myself Driving Mrs. Koogle. I worked as her chauffeur, driving her and her obnoxiously huge poodle, Rex, in a maroon STS Cadillac Escalade to openings at the Norton Simon Museum in Pasadena, Mozart festivals at the Hollywood Bowl, and patio lunches with friends at The Ivy on Robertson. I was paid $300 a week under the table so I could collect unemployment, and she let me wear sweatpants to work. As the ninety-year-old recent widow of a wealthy owner of a few diamond mines near Udaipur, India, Mrs. Koogle had begun to distrust family members—who were suddenly showing her a lot more attention, especially as she grew weaker with age. She would often confide in me which relatives she felt most deserved to inherit her fortune after she passed away.

I hadn't given up on my dreams entirely, but driving Mrs. Koogle and her massive poodle around sure didn't help my self-esteem. I wasn't the biggest fan of Rex. He was just so dumb and large. Rex would bark at anything, and he never had a clue who or what he was barking at. Rex even barked at nonmoving vehicles.

One day while driving Mrs. Koogle to her weekly hair salon appointment—which I never could understand the need for since she always wore a wig—Rex was in the back seat and started barking near the intersection of Beverly Glen and Sunset Boulevard. I turned to see that he was barking at yet another inanimate object, this time a tractor being hauled by a truck. The next moment, Rex had squeezed out of the slightly opened window in pursuit of the tractor. I slammed on the brakes, then tore out of the SUV and raced over to grapple him back into the car, despite the fact that Rex felt roughly as big as me.

I was the hero. I'd saved this idiot dog's life. Miss Koogle decided to increase my pay and began bragging about my heroic efforts to her ninety-year-old lady friends. Naturally, I felt pretty good about my bravery.

A few days later, I stopped by to pick up Rex to take him to a nearby park called TreePeople, a popular spot in Coldwater Canyon where you could hike, mountain bike, or in my case stand next to a dog while it barked at the ground—or, if the weather was right, a tire—for ten minutes. I walked through the garage into the kitchen (the way I always entered, as was proper etiquette for housemaids, cooks, and drivers) and found Miss Koogle sitting at the kitchen table reading the *LA Times* as she did ritually every morning. Yet this morning she looked more melancholy than usual.

"Good morning, Miss Koogle. Hey, your hair looks great!"

Actually, her hair just looked more purple than usual, but there had obviously been recent effort so a compliment seemed appropriate.

"Where's Rex?" I asked.

"Rex is dead."

"Rex is dead?! What are you talking about?"

Not only was I shocked to hear this, but I was shocked to find that my response was 100 percent sincere dismay.

Apparently, after I'd cleaned the glass sliding doors with Windex on my last visit, Rex had gone outside and licked the Windex off. Then he got sick and died.

"Oh my God! He licked the glass and *died*?"

"He licked all the Windex off that glass door. *All* of it."

I had no idea that a dog could die from licking Windex off a plate-glass window, but that's what happened. That's what she told me anyway; I'm not a veterinarian. Had I known Windex could kill an eighty-pound poodle, I would have said, "Mrs. Koogle, I would love to clean your sliding glass doors with Windex, as requested, but be aware that if for some reason Rex decides to lick the Windex off, Rex will die. Just FYI."

But it was too late for that. A few days later, Mrs. Koogle asked me to sit down with her in the living room. This was the first time I had seen the living room, and the only reason I mention it is because the house once belonged to Boris Karloff.

"Chris. . . I have to let you go."

"Why?"

Of course, I knew why. She thought I'd killed her poodle, which technically I guess I might have. But that wasn't the reason at all.

"I'm letting you go because you're too short, and I don't feel safe," she said.

I thought: *Wow. How racist.* Wait, that wasn't right. The word I was looking for was "biased," but I couldn't think of it at the time.

"Do you think you might get attacked?" I asked her.

"You never know, in this day and age," she said.

What day and age she thought it was, I'll never know.

So, in early 1996, I was twenty-five years old, unemployed, and still living at home with my dad. Then I received a phone call from Will.

We hadn't talked too much since he moved to New York, so it was really good to hear his voice. I missed the guy. Life at the Groundlings was different without him. I no longer had a regular scene partner to inspire me and play off of. I asked him how the show was going, and he was as honest and candid as ever. It was like nothing had changed, which was comforting.

"So, um, Lorne wanted me to call you," Will said eventually.

"Lorne asked you, instead of calling me himself?"

"Yeah, I know, right? So, Lorne asked me to ask you if you wanted to be on the show."

Excuse me?

"You mean join the cast? Next season?"

"No, now," Will said.

"But there's only six shows left!"

"I know."

"Holy shit!"

I felt a combination of shock and confusion. I hadn't gotten the show. I'd been rejected. My dream hadn't come true, and as much as I'd like to say I had moved on, I clearly had not. I was still hurt and angry, but I knew that if I was truly headed to the show, all those feelings of negativity would have to end. The only reason I could think of that Will might be calling was because we had created some great stuff together at the Groundlings and those ideas were just curled up in a trunk ready to go. They needed me, and I was getting a second chance. My shock, confusion, and anger gave way to pure relief. In fact, I've never felt so relieved in my life. What I had been waiting for my whole life was about to happen. And I didn't even have enough time to say "I can't fuckin' wait."

Chapter 3

STUDIO 8H

I remember seeing the Elmer Fudd–style hunting cap sitting on top of Will's coarse and convoluted head of hair and wondering why he was wearing it when it was hot as fuck outside. This was the sort of choice Will often made. I'm sure he found the cap comfortable enough, but he was probably wearing it mostly to throw people off.

I had just arrived in New York on the 8:30 AM red-eye from LAX to JFK, the best flight you could take to feel as if you hadn't missed a day on either coast. NBC put me up in a single at the Paramount Hotel on West 46th Street in the heart of Times Square, the same hotel we'd stayed at when we auditioned. It's not nearly as chic as the "Quatre Saisons" (that's French for Four Seasons), where the show's guest host always stayed, but it was temporary. Mike Shoemaker, *SNL*'s producer, had said that the show would accommodate me for three months, at which point I would have to rent an apartment of my own. This was the norm for cast members starting off, and it was perfect for me since all I wanted was a place of seclusion to focus on the show, and the last thing I wanted to do was to spend every morning looking for a decent one bedroom, something I'd never done in my life, especially in a city I'd visited exactly once before. They also gave me a fat per diem check, which I ended up spending in about five weeks. Chris Rock once told me, "The most money you'll ever make in your life is that first big check 'they' give you." This was that check.

(Okay, fine. It's shoddy, but I'll tell you. It was ten grand. Keep in mind this was back in 1996, before the recession. What that means I don't actually know, but let's go with it for now.)

It was great to see Will again. It felt like I was reuniting with the older brother I'd never had or ever wanted until now. When I walked out to meet him and saw him waiting just outside the hotel, not only was I happy because he was the closest friend I had on the show or in NYC, but because it said to me that he really wanted me there and on the show, and he didn't care if anyone else at *SNL* thought or even knew that he felt this way.

Riffing and giggling like two little schoolgirls, we skipped down Broadway. New York! What a city! Every time you'd inhale, the pungent stench of urine would sting the innards of your nostrils, but the sky was clear, which somehow balanced it out. Like any friend looking out for his buddy, Will gave me the rundown of his *SNL* experiences so far, both creatively and politically. As we walked over to Rockefeller Center, he told me things I would never have thought of asking about, educating me on subjects from what Lorne was like to what time it's okay to go home Tuesday nights. He told me about the best writers from Second City and the smartest ones from Harvard. Which writers came from stand-up and which ones were just starting out.

I was so busy taking everything in that it wasn't until we stepped through those big, gold-plated 30 Rock elevator doors inside that I finally noticed the brown Dickies one-piece he was wearing his hunting cap with. An outfit someone would choose for their shift at a Jiffy Lube. Little did I know Will would wear the same zip-up coveralls to almost every pitch meeting for the next seven years.

I could tell David Spade was less than enthusiastic about sharing an office space with me. The second I walked into what Shoemaker introduced as my new office, on the seventeenth floor, Spade gave off this vibe that made me feel as if we had known each other since junior high, and he was still pissed off at me for throwing his backpack over the fence. Spade was the last member of the "Frat Pack" to stick around *SNL*. He wasn't doing sketches anymore. He didn't even go to the pitch meetings. He was just there because he was still obligated to do his popular "Hollywood Minute" segment on "Weekend Update."

At the time, Spade was the big man on campus. I'd been a huge fan of his work since I first saw his "Buh-Bye" flight attendant sketch and his "Tom Petty Mad Hatter" "Weekend Update" feature (which by the wayside is still truly hilarious). Like Don Rickles, but much less obvious, Spade introduced me to a style of cynicism that was subtler in its humor. This cynical voice, in turn, ended up making me more critical of myself than I already was, as well as more critical of others. And yes, it was a long and difficult habit for me to break out of.

What I admired the most about Spade was his ongoing partnership with Chris Farley. I always had such respect for duos, who in my opinion were responsible for some of the best comedy ever. If you think about it, what makes a comedy duo work is mostly the chemistry that occurs when they're paired together. This chemistry is a mix of trust, admiration, and playfulness, and this magic doesn't click when they're paired with anyone else. Abbott and Costello. Laurel and Hardy. Nichols and May. Martin and Lewis. Cook and Moore. (That's Dudley Moore and Peter Cook for those who don't know. Ever see the original movie *Bedazzled*?) Cheech and Chong. The Smothers Brothers. Sonny and Cher (I guess they're a comedy team, I could be wrong). Burns and Allen. Hope and Crosby. And, of course, the always hysterical Frost and Nixon.

Even though Spade was slightly smaller than me (like an inch smaller—I like to say someone is "slightly smaller than me" any chance I get), he carried himself with such confidence it made him intimidating. I remember on that first day we met, he asked if I wanted to go down to the lobby with him and grab something to eat. Of course, I said yes. I was too nervous to say anything else. I mean, I just made a new friend—and it was David Spade! And now I was going to have lunch with him! Maybe even split a sandwich, who knew? I couldn't wait to tell my dad.

From my desk, where I was lost in reverie, I heard Spade's ever-so-salty voice yell out:

"Hey, Kattan! You coming or what?"

"Yeah, man. I'm coming!"

I remember thinking, *I hope that was okay—to say "man."* Quickly, I grabbed my wallet from my desk next to my keyboard and skedaddled toward him while he rolled his eyes and held the elevator door open for me. When I got into the elevator, I saw that a bunch of very cute temps and clerical staff from Lorne's office were joining us as well. Okay fine, they were joining Spade. When we got off the elevator, I felt like I was back in high school as I trailed behind the attractive clique of beautifully groomed blondes surrounding my new office mate.

Squeezing through this circle of cutie-patootie giggling groupies, I caught a glimpse of Spade doing something quite brilliant. He had a Calvin and Hobbes tattoo on his upper arm, which was actually done freehand by Sean Penn. (By the way, if you're gonna get a tattoo, don't just have any celebrity ink it, like Stephen Dorff or Fabio. Make sure it's somebody cool—get DiCaprio or Viggo Mortensen or Rihanna to do your tattoo. But not The Rock. For some reason I don't think his tattoos would come out very well.)

Anyway, Spade wore a white sleeveless T-shirt, and even though his arms were pretty skinny, he wasn't shy at all about exposing them. I could never get away with wearing a sleeveless T-shirt because I was self-conscious about my arms not having enough definition. But because he wasn't like I was, he flexed an arm for his female audience and said, "Check out these guns," making him instantly adored and the size of his muscles irrelevant. So if you've ever asked the question, "How does Spade get so much p***y?" . . . well, now you know.

A little later, Shoemaker suggested I "do a round of the offices" and introduce myself. It was disorienting being shown around the offices of *Saturday Night Live*—where I, Chris Kattan, now worked—and introduced to so many people I admired. I got to meet some fantastic writers Like Tim Herlihy (known for most of the Sandler movies including *Happy Gilmore, The Waterboy*, and *The Wedding Singer*), Robert Carlock (*30 Rock* and *Unbreakable Kimmy Schmidt*), Dennis McNicholas (*Land of the Lost, The Ladies Man*), Paula Pell (*Sisters*), Steve Koren (*Seinfeld, Superstar, Bruce Almighty*), Norm Hiscock (*The Kids in the Hall, Parks and Recreation*),

Dave Mandel (*Seinfeld, Curb Your Enthusiasm, Veep*), and Adam McKay (I already told you, weren't you paying attention?).

Molly Shannon's excitement when she saw me was a relief. I had met her in LA, back when she worked at the Mel & Rose restaurant next door to the Groundlings. At the time, she was also doing a one-woman show at the Promenade Playhouse in Santa Monica, where she first performed the Mary Katherine Gallagher character. I never saw that show, but word of mouth was that it was amazing, and everyone at the Groundlings would say, "You have to see this girl. She's unbelievable." Which turned out to be true.

I already knew Molly wasn't one to worry about boundaries while in character, and being that my style was similar, I was definitely excited to work with her. It was great to see Cheri again, too. Although I was a little thrown off when, probably twenty seconds after stepping into her office, she started listing the sketches we did together back at the Groundlings that we should submit for the show. I couldn't say whether this was my impression of her competitiveness or her drive or what. Whatever it was, it was my first glimpse of what a cast member needed to do in order to survive on the show.

A few hours later, I found myself in Lorne Michaels's office for the Monday pitch meeting—crammed in along with the entire cast, all the writers, and the essential crew. People were in chairs, on arms of chairs, on the couch, the arms of the couch, the floor, crouched next to Lorne's desk, behind his desk, on his bookcase, his windowsill, against his aquarium, and in the doorway of his personal bathroom, which by the way included the only shower on the entire seventeenth floor. The guest host always sat in one of the two leather saddle armchairs right in front of Lorne's desk. Since everyone had already claimed a spot when the season started, I found a nice pinewood armrest to perch on next to cast member Nancy Walls from Second City (where she'd met her future husband Steve Carell—who'd actually auditioned the same time as Nancy and I did, but didn't get on).

That week, John Goodman was hosting for the seventh time. The form of the pitch meeting never changed from that first week. Lorne would gesture to someone or murmur their first name, cueing that cast member or writer to pitch their idea. The unspoken rule, as I would learn, was that everyone would pitch one or two sketch ideas and who they'd be collaborating with. When you shared the idea, sometimes you'd get laughs, sometimes you wouldn't. Getting a response really wasn't that important, although sometimes people would pitch a fake idea just so they could get a room laugh, which would inevitably make Lorne laugh—which was always a good thing. For example, years later, after having done a few seasons, John Goodman was back again the day I pitched a fake idea called "Lunch Basket," which was a joke between me and writer Matt Piedmont based on an actual sandwich shop on West 24th Street in Chelsea. The fake pitch wasn't the funny part—what got laughs in the room was when Lorne called on Matt after I'd pitched the idea, and Matt said, "Hi, John [Goodman]. Welcome back. I'm just gonna focus on 'Lunch Basket' with Kattan."

Anyway, that first week, right before my first-ever pitch meeting, Shoemaker came to my office and said, "Lorne wants you to submit your 'Substitute Teacher' sketch." So that's what I pitched in that first meeting, feeling lucky that instead of being overwhelmingly green, I had the show's politics working in my favor, even if I didn't quite understand why.

They don't really give you a specific call time to come in on Tuesday, but typically everyone would roll in somewhere between two and four o'clock in the afternoon and continue writing until the next morning, sometimes all the way until 10 AM. That first week, I remember seeing Cheri and Molly being the first ones to go home, around 3 or 4 AM. I had it easy, because my sketch was already written. I didn't want to change it since it had gone so well at the Groundlings and I thought it would work fine on camera, so all I really needed to do was rewrite it into *SNL* script format.

Early Tuesday evening, as the guest host always did, John Goodman went around to everybody's office to hear what sketches cast members and writers had decided to actually write. When John came to my office, I pitched him my Suel Forrester idea and he chuckled. For me, a "chuckle" can be read two ways. As a laugh that's real but quiet, maybe because you're shy or don't want to be too loud, or as a gesture made just out of politeness. This was clearly the latter.

For the read through on Wednesday, the call time was usually 2 PM, but like I said before, the read through really started whenever Lorne showed up. On Wednesdays, a lot of us cast members and writers would wake up around midday on our office couches, having slept only a couple of hours after working through the night to finish writing. It was more convenient to sleep at the office than to take a train all the way back to homes in Brooklyn or wherever, just for a few hours.

Everyone in the cast was assigned their own seat at the read-through table. Right in front of your spot would be a stack of all the paper-clipped sketches that had been submitted, anywhere from forty to fifty of them, including "Update" features, cold openings, host monologues, and sometimes commercial parodies. On top of the stack were a few stapled pages like a table of contents, with columns listing the sketch, who wrote it, and who was cast in it as a performer or voice-over. The read through was the first time you got to see the finished sketches, punched up in a shoot-for-television script format that included stage direction, thanks to the Script Department, which came in at 10 AM.

Will was almost always the first one in the cast to arrive at the table. Which made sense since he had a lot more to look over in preparation for the read through than anyone else, because he was cast more than anybody else. Second to arrive was usually Darrell Hammond, because he had so many voice-overs. But Will was the staple of the show. "The Phil Hartman of his time," as Lorne once put it. That's how it had been at the Groundlings, too. Will was the glue of our cast, and he always delivered.

Once, a few seasons into my time on *SNL*, I was working on a "Crocodile Hunter" with the writer Hugh Fink—we also wrote several of the Mr. Peepers sketches together—and we were deciding who we should cast for one of the roles.

"Let's have Will play him," Hugh suggested.

"I love Will. He'd be great," I said. "But maybe we should cast someone who's light in the show this week."

"Yeah, but Lorne loves Will. If you want your sketch in the show, you gotta cast Will."

The first five to ten sketches we read were usually the ones almost certain to be in the show, like something featuring a popular recurring character, the monologue, the cold opening, and so on. If Herlihy wrote a Brian Fellows sketch for Tracy, or Rachel wrote a Debbie Downer with Tina, it was going to be one of the first sketches read because it was a shoo-in for the show.

I was never a huge fan of political humor. Don't get me wrong; I loved writer Jim Downey's sketches on politics, and of course it kept the show current and provocative, and the ratings steady. As important as it may have been at the time, though, and as funny as the sketches may have been about Dan Quayle, for example, I would always think: *Nobody's gonna care about a "potato-potatoe" joke ten years from now*. Sometimes late on a Tuesday night, after hearing Shoemaker give a rundown of what recurring character sketches were being written up for that week, Lorne would say, "Stallone's here. Let's do a Roxbury," or "Let's do a Cheerleaders. Duchovny's here." That's what I felt *SNL* was: a character-driven show. That's why I wanted to be on the show in the first place, and that's why I felt they'd hired me.

When we read the "Substitute Teacher" sketch, the room's response was awful. The sketch was exactly the same as I'd performed it at the Groundlings, where it had always played great, but it did not go over well at all at that first read through. Head writer Fred Wolf was smiling, and Lorne pensively rubbed one of his puckered lips while doing something like smiling, too, but other than an occasional snicker in the room, no one was laughing. It just didn't make sense to me. Actually, there was a moment when Cheri was genuinely laughing, but then she covered her mouth as if she was supposed to be quiet like everyone else. I couldn't understand the room's climate. Was it because I was new to the show, or did they honestly think the sketch wasn't funny? To have any chance of succeeding, I knew that I needed someone to have faith in me. Something I'd be asking for the rest of my life.

After reading sketches for nearly five hours, aside from an always on-time "ten-minute break," all the writers and everyone in the cast would go back to their offices to wait while Lorne, the guest host, and the head writers met in his office to discuss and decide on the sketch lineup for the dress show on Saturday. After anywhere from two to three hours, Lorne would finally swing his office door open, the cue for Beth McCarthy, Tom Broecker (head of the wardrobe department), Ken Aymong (producer), and

Leo Yoshimura (the head of the art department) to file in. They would make sure the preliminary lineup was feasible, looking at the time frame and budget, verifying whether the host and cast members had enough time for "quick changes" between one sketch and another, and working out the logistics for all the pre-tapes as well as the costumes, hair, prosthetics, wigs, makeup, and set changes. If your sketch was chosen, you and/or the co-writer would be the producer of that sketch, meaning you were responsible for making sure the costumes, the set, and the pre-tapes were all executed the way you envisioned them, working with the art director and the rest of the art department. I always thought the art department had the toughest job of all since they really only had two days to build everything after Beth was done mapping out the locations and camera blocking for each set in the studio.

After around thirty minutes, Lorne would swipe his jacket from the standing wooden coatrack just beside the office door, throw it on (at that time, he often wore a handsome black Prada coat), reach into his pocket, apply some ChapStick (whether it was cold outside or not), and depart. Leaving his door wide open (he never locked it), he'd stride down the hallway to the elevators, where he would hop in alone (always alone) and head downstairs to be driven home. After he left, everyone else trailed out of Lorne's office except the script supervisor, who stayed behind, copying down the preliminary lineup so that it could be typed and distributed to everybody's office. The cast, including me, would often happen to saunter by Lorne's open door at this point to sneak a peek at the big corkboard covered with index cards. The board was separated into three columns—identified by cards at the top that said 11:30, 12:00, and 12:30—each column representing a half hour of show time. Beneath each thirty-minute card were thumbtacked green index cards with the name of a chosen sketch written in black Sharpie.

That night, after my first read through, Lorne showed me some much-needed faith. "Trust me," he said to Goodman and the head writers in his office. "It'll work." Suel Forrester was given the first spot of the night, right after the monologue.

When I saw that my sketch had been chosen, I knew that it had nothing to do with the sketch itself. It had to do with me. I wasn't being thrown into a lion's den expected to fight for airtime; I was getting help, thanks to Lorne or NBC. They had brought me on with six shows left in the season to test me. But instead of obsessing over negative thoughts like, *What if it bombs? Maybe that's why they put it in as the first sketch, to watch it fail and then it'll be over for me*, I somehow managed to let go of all my thoughts wrapped in bullshit and chose to have faith. I just knew that when I did the scene in front of a live audience, it would work.

Waiting backstage, seconds before I walked onto the set in Studio 8H, live in front of the world, there was a moment when I stopped going over my lines in my head and suddenly remembered something a trench-coated, dark-haired, goateed psychic I'd met the past fall while dining at a tourist-trap Italian restaurant on Melrose had said to me: "I see you wearing glasses . . . and a tie, like a teacher, and people are laughing . . . a lot."

The hipster psychic was right. The audience seemed to laugh at every joke.

In the sketch, I bewilder a classroom of students—played by Will, Cheri, and Molly Shannon, among others—with my bizarre, unintelligible gibberish, only to become perfectly clear when challenged, or when the principal (played by John Goodman) comes by to check on the class.

Scribbling unreadably on the blackboard, I say something like: "Seventeen orreeee. Peter the Graay . . . After his leadership at the time . . .

Rudaaa, wanted to expaan his empiyaaah, closer to the Baaltehh to give eet a maah. And—I can't stress this enough—a *windowandakneee*." A student played by Jim Breuer raises his hand.

"Uh, yeah. I can't understand what you're saying."

I cross to him, look directly in his eyes, and say—sarcastic, but suddenly clear as a bell—"Well, then maybe I should *ar-ti-cu-late* it for you."

Later, I give the students a pop quiz, after which a confused Will raises his hand and says, "Yes, I couldn't take the test because I don't know what it's on."

"Well, I got an A!" says the teacher's pet.

"I got an L," Will replies.

It was just like it had been at the Groundlings, and during the live taping, there was an energy coming from the audience that made me feel welcome. It was scary how effortless it was. It was as if I had already performed it on the show and it went great, so in a surreal way, this time when we did the sketch it wasn't really happening. Because it had already taken place. Am I blowing your mind? Is this too existential? Fine, I'll be quiet.

Oh, cripes! I forgot to say this earlier, but on Thursday night at the rewrite table on seventeen (there was another rewrite table on the ninth floor—the sketch rewrites were split up so the writers could get them all done in time for blocking), one of the writers added a joke to the Suel sketch. In dress rehearsal, it was the only joke that didn't get laughs, but we kept it in. Later, for the live show, it still didn't quite work. I remember telling myself never to forget to trust my instincts.

If you feel in your gut that something's going to work, trust that it will. When you come up with an idea and then turn that inspiration into a sketch, don't question whether it will work or not and don't overthink it.

Don't assume someone else's direction for the sketch is better than yours just because they're a better writer than you are. You're the one who came up with the idea; you're the one who envisioned it. Sometimes it's even harder to trust your instincts once you start getting somewhere, because there's more to lose, but remember that your instincts are what got you there in the first place. I've always felt that when I began to listen to other people too much, years later, I began to fail.

There was a tremendous amount of pressure surrounding me that night. After the show, Ken Aymong, an *SNL* producer for over thirty years and one of the nicest guys you could ever work with, told me I was the first featured player to get a sketch on in their first week, and the first featured player to land the first sketch of the night after the monologue. It took Farley, Sandler, even Mike Myers weeks or months until one of their sketches made it on and worked well.

But during the sketch, I was surprisingly relaxed. Partly it was because I had already performed the sketch so many times before. But, more than that, I think it was something else. After I auditioned for the show and didn't get it, I'd been angry and devastated for months and I moved on. By the time Will called and I was hired out of the blue, the starry-eyed optimism and expectations I might have had if my dream had come true as I'd originally hoped were tempered by those emotions, along with the nervousness I would have felt.

I guess you could say thank God I was fortunate enough to feel what it was like to not get what I'd dreamt of before I actually got it.

Chapter 4

LIFE ON MOUNT BALDY

When my parents divorced, I was three years old. I vividly remember the moment my mom took me out of my dad's arms, opened the sliding door of a 1972 Volkswagen van, and buckled me into the back seat. Car seats for babies and toddlers weren't a requirement back then, so with no struggle at all, I slipped out from under my seat belt and crawled over to the other side of the vehicle. As I got to my feet and looked out the window, I could see Dad standing at the front door in his two-piece button-down cotton pajamas. My dad was a big fan of pajamas. Sometimes, if he was staying home, without any shame he would wear them all day. But right now he was crying. Crying more than I was—and that was a lot, since at that point I was somewhere between bawling and screaming.

When he raised his arms and reached out to me, like a scene from *Kramer vs. Kramer,* I did the same, yelling "I want my daddy!" over and over.

Dad decided to make the situation even more traumatic, yelling back, "My son! Give me back my son!"

A tall, intimidating man sat behind the wheel of the Volkswagen next to my mom. He was my soon-to-be stepfather, and he sported the first beard I'd ever seen. Fascinated by the amount of hair that could accumulate on someone's jaw, I would spend the whole ride staring at him. And his hairy chin. He started the van and slowly began to drive us away, giving my dad and me a few more seconds to milk our dramatic goodbye dry. I cried for at least another twenty minutes, and nobody told me to be quiet.

My mother's full name is Hajnalka Elizabeth Joslyn, but everyone calls her Hajni, which when spoken sounds like "Hi-knee." (Yes, it does sound like the slang for "ass." No, it's actually *not* funny, and it never really was.)

My mom is beautiful. Like timeless, classic, but also "Dude, your mom is so hot" beautiful. She's full-blooded Hungarian, born in Budapest in 1943 during World War II, but it wasn't until the 1956 Hungarian Uprising that Mom witnessed the true horrors of death that accompany a war. Hungary's revolution was successful for only a few days until the Russians put a bloody end to it. Forced to leave her dying grandmother behind, my mom and her family escaped the country on foot, finally reaching their freedom in Austria. I know my mom has held on to the guilt of leaving her grandmother for most of her life. To this day, it's still a memory she avoids talking about.

Shortly after their escape, her whole family moved to London, where my mom spent her formative years. She had trained as a dancer in Hungary, and in England, she became a working model and actress, despite the fact that she's roughly five feet tall. She lived in London's Mod fashion scene, modeling alongside Twiggy and hanging out with cultural icons like Jim Morrison and Jimi Hendrix. She even posed for *Playboy* and, as I often brag, was one of the girls chasing after the Beatles in the famous opening of Richard Lester's *A Hard Day's Night.*

My mom could be a real flirt but with no intention behind it. She even has a story about Michael Caine and William Shatner fighting over her at a party once. (To me, that image is just too weird.) She was unobtainable, a big-time heartbreaker, always faithfully committed to whoever she was with. She was never single; I don't think for even a day. Everyone loved her.

My mom and dad first met as Zen students at the Cimarron Zen Center in downtown LA. In 1969, their teacher was a Japanese Rinzai-ji Zen *roshi* by the name of Kyozan Joshu Sasaki, and he apparently told my mom and dad that they "must have baby." If Yoda were a Japanese man, he would sound a lot like Sasaki, and I guess if you say that line in a deep, confident, Yoda-like voice, it is pretty convincing. A few months after that, the luckiest guy in the world married one of the most beautiful women in the world. They were married at the Zen center, and on October 19, 1970, I was born in a hospital in Culver City, California.

I have almost no memories from the time Mom and Dad were together. I remember being tossed up in the air in the living room and then feeling my dad's hands catch me on my way down, one hand on either side of my waist. I remember once accidentally killing a lot of saltwater fish when I dropped a handful of crayons in the aquarium because I felt the water could use more color. The other memory I have is of lying on my back in my crib and screaming in agony because my asshole felt like it was on fire and I needed someone to change my diapers. It's not a lot to go on.

It wasn't until my twenties that I learned what led to my parents' split, but here's a polite oversimplified summation: Once my dad found a partner and started a family, his interest in the Zen center waned; my mom, on the other hand, was experiencing deep changes while discovering herself through the work she was doing there. People always explain breakups by saying they "grew apart" even if the truth is that someone slept with a nanny, but in my parents' case, it was true. As we all know, a chip can become a fracture in an instant. That's why you never touch the dent a rock makes in your windshield; the oils from your skin can get in there on a molecular level and separate the glass, causing that one little nick to become a giant crack. Real life lesson right there.

Shortly after my parents divorced, mom married my stepfather, a fellow Zen student. (Yes, my mom met two husbands at the same Zen center. Who needs Tinder when you have the eightfold path?) Mom and my stepfather are a true example of soul mates, and they have been married for forty-three years.

At the time they met, my stepfather was working to establish a new Zen center on Mount Baldy, located in a desolate national forest in the San Gabriel Mountains. And so, in their infinite wisdom, he and my mother decided it would be a good idea to move to a cabin on the side of a mountain with a wide-eyed enthusiastic toddler.

One of the interesting things I discovered during my many years of therapy was that, though I didn't realize it at the time, as a child I was very angry with my mom for leaving my dad. I saw Dad as the victim, even though Mom and my stepfather always included him in family gatherings and holidays, and we had a lot of good times together, which in retrospect was pretty unusual. As much as I loved Mom, I seldom had fun with her like I did with my dad, though that wasn't really about her. My mom and stepfather had me for the weekdays; they took on the job of making sure I went to school, did homework, did chores—clearly, not the most exciting of times. Granted, another factor was my mom and stepfather choosing to live on Mount Baldy. The setting was ideal for people who wanted to retreat from the world, but it was torment for a kid.

And, like many children who have a new father figure appointed to them, I did not like my stepfather. Everything, even his name—Marc Joslyn—bored me. It wasn't until my twenties that I finally learned to appreciate him for the interesting, knowledgeable, and brilliant man he truly is. Today, when visiting him and Mom on Bainbridge Island in Washington State, I often get lost in fascinating discussions with him—for instance, about the theory that all wars are really between banks and the strength of the countries' currencies—because he can talk about pretty much any subject you can think of.

But come on, what little kid really wants to hear about how a specific movement in Mozart's Symphony no. 40 in G Minor is actually quite similar to the chess movement where queen takes pawn? Marc's idea of a joke would be an anecdote Sigmund Freud once told about Vasco da Gama while walking in the woods of Helsinki. Marc just didn't know how to be silly. My dad, on the other hand, didn't know how *not* to be silly—his idea of serious was watching Judy Garland sing "Born in a Trunk" in *A Star is Born*. We even had our own secret language based around the sound of "ling." For example, instead of saying "Do you want to go out tonight?" you would say, "Let's ling it down." Simple! And brilliant. At least when you're seven years old.

Another topic I couldn't comprehend at all was Buddhism. I couldn't figure out what all the fuss was about, sitting cross-legged in silence every day. It wasn't like I needed to find an answer to "who," "where," or "why" I was at that age. Did I really need to understand how to be "one" with everything already? What really sucked was that Marc, my mom, *and* my dad were all involved in it. In my teens, Marc was even ordained as a monk. There was just no avoiding Zen. Now if someone had taken the time to tell me that the Force in *Star Wars* was basically the same idea, there's a chance I might have gotten it. Like if they'd compared Zen Roshi Sasaki to Yoda, that would have helped me for sure.

On and off, the Mount Baldy Zen Center attracted extraordinarily influential people like musician and poet Leonard Cohen or the great Zen philosopher Alan Watts (whose sessions I highly recommend listening to, by the way). But when I was growing up, our neighbors were mostly an odd, shady sort of bunch. Not to be rude, but if you were living on Mount Baldy, you were probably either not doing so well financially or hiding from the government, possibly both. Take Carlos Castaneda, the Pulitzer Prize–winning writer and anthropologist, a cult figure who was also hated for his controversial books on shamanism. Castaneda had a huge following throughout the 1960s, when he wrote about his experiences and experiments with a medicine man named Don Juan, and also about developing his mind with psychedelics in order to get the most use out of it. He'd dropped out of society and was considered missing, but I knew right where he was—in a one-bedroom, three cabins away from us. There were probably only five other houses in our community, and we all lived off the same ragged fire road.

The fact that I'd had no idea who he was is probably what made Castaneda comfortable hanging out with me. For almost a year, we went on long walks together. Sometimes we'd walk four or five miles, staying out for the whole afternoon. Carlos was friendly, and talking to him was enlightening, even to a kid, though to be honest he had a somewhat insane look about him, with excessively sharp, bright eyes. I always thought he looked a lot like the Tasmanian Devil from Bugs Bunny cartoons. He had a Cheshire cat grin, and his hair was tangled up and wild.

Years later, talking to Lorne during an *SNL* guest host dinner, it somehow came up that I'd known Carlos Castaneda when I was younger. He was so impressed he started choking on his soup at Orso's. I honestly think it was the only time I impressed Lorne.

I know a lot of intelligent people regard Castaneda as a hero of literature. One time he gave me a quarter with a hole in it and then told me that he "flew through it." This really confused me. I asked him if he would fly through it again and he said, "Maybe later." Whatever, Carlos.

When I wasn't hanging out with my mom and stepfather or various renowned weirdos, I played with the few other kids growing up on the mountain. Since we were all raised with very little money and were living in an isolated forest twenty miles from the nearest market or gas station, there really wasn't any need or opportunity to keep up with the latest fashions. If you had a favorite shirt, you'd probably wear it for at least two years. In fact, most of us were fine wearing the same outfit for four days straight without bathing. Sometimes we didn't even wear shoes to school. We were a dirty tribe that rarely behaved because we had nothing to lose and nothing to do. At least Mowgli had a goal in *Jungle Book*. We didn't have shit.

As I spent the weekends with my father, I began to live two very different childhoods: one on the remote mountain during the week, and another in the city on Saturday and Sunday with my dad, watching him perform at the Groundlings and screening old movies while he educated me on the finer points of classic comedy. One weekend, I showed up with stains around my mouth from a Popsicle I'd eaten a few days earlier, and my dad began calling me Mountain Boy. When he'd burp, he'd say, "Eughghuh! I've been around the Mountain Boy too long."

Weekends spent watching my father perform or sitting in the dark while Buster Keaton flickered on a screen shaped my career to come, but oddly, so did the time spent on Mount Baldy. The silence that surrounded me was often lonely, but it also made me incredibly observant of my surroundings. Not just nature and the physical world but people—their personalities, habits, characteristics, and behaviors. And all of us "Mountain Boys" were thoughtless daredevils. We climbed trees and mountains, bodysurfed down rockslides, swung on ropes that were long enough to swing us into traffic, and played sports like "throw heavy stones at each other." I built up a tolerance for pain and physical endurance, and a willingness to try things that anyone having common sense and lacking a death wish would probably have dismissed as a bad idea. All this prepared me for a particular type of comedy, one I'd find myself especially suited to, and that SNL hadn't seen—at least, not in quite that way—before.

Chapter 5

ZIP ZING

"**G**ood evening. I'm Rabbi Abraham Stein, and believe me . . . the pleasure is mine."

It's late on a Friday night, and an audience of about fifty are seated in the cozy, darkly lit Groundlings Theatre. It doesn't matter what seat you're in; there is an intimacy inside the theater that makes you feel like you're part of whatever is happening onstage, even in the last row. But my favorite spot isn't a seat at all. I'm happiest standing up in the back behind the audience, next to the sound booth, because from there I can go down the stairs and run backstage and hang out in the green room watching the cast do their quick changes and transform into sketch characters in their dressing rooms whenever I want.

My dad, Kip King, is standing center stage wearing the most salacious early '70s lounge tuxedo you've ever seen, with his bow tie untied à la Jerry Lewis telethon, doing one of his more memorable characters: a rabbi/stand-up comedian whose act is mostly one-liners about God, the Torah, Judaism, and what he would call a synagogue in Las Vegas: the "Benai Dunes." One joke I can't remember the rest of got a big reaction with the line "Moses said to God, 'Before I part this sea, I want some people here!'"

Being that I'm only seven years old, I don't quite comprehend Jewish wit. I just know that whatever my dad is saying is making a lot of people laugh. And that it's *SNL* and Groundlings alum Jon Lovitz's favorite character he's ever seen at the Groundlings. At least, that's what he tells me every time I see him. (I'm serious—every time.)

I looked forward to the weekends not just because I'd get to visit my dad, but because I'd get to watch him and the rest of his cast perform at the Groundlings. I had never seen my dad behave like this before in my life. I'd seen him hold court with friends and family, but to watch him hold himself with such confidence onstage, commanding the attention of strangers of all ages, was so impressive. If only I could explain what exactly he was doing, I would have loved to brag about it in school. He was just so fetching and hilarious. This was the venue where he was most powerful in my eyes. I never felt so unconditionally proud to be his son.

My father's birth name was Jerome Kattan, but because of the rampant blacklisting going on during the McCarthy era in the early 1950s—supposedly they were rooting out communists, but funnily enough it was having a Jewish name that seemed most likely to make you a target—it was decided he needed a new one. His agent suggested that "Kip King" had a certain "zip" to it. (Could it be because Kip rhymed with Zip? Just a guess.) Anyway, that's the name my father will always be remembered by.

At age fifteen, while still living with his family in his hometown of Chicago, my dad already had a job as a hired magician and ventriloquist. With dreams of becoming an actor and performing in front of the camera, Jerome decided to leave his magic tricks and dummy behind. Do you know how hard it is to leave your dummy behind in the world of ventriloquism? Let's just say it's not easy. But within a year of moving to Hollywood, he had an agent and had landed a spot on *The Aldrich Family*, a television show based on the radio classic. So, at only sixteen, my father went under contract with CBS—but that "tweren't nothin'," as I seldom say. He also became an apprentice to Stan Laurel, of the legendary comedy duo Laurel and Hardy. If you want to be a comedian, or are at all interested in the history of comedy, and you've never seen their 1930s black-and-white short *The Music Box* or the film *Sons of the Desert*, you have my permission to take a break from reading this book to go watch them now. Comedy brilliance that to this day still holds up.

In fact—and I'm sorry about the tangent, but it's not the first and it won't be the last, so you should probably get used to it—if you really want to understand the history of comedy in film, you should start from the beginning. And by "the beginning" I mean a time much further back than *The Hangover* or *Meatballs*, both of which are funny but, despite what you may have heard, do not qualify as "old-school." Honestly, to get the complete picture, you need to go even further back than Abbott and Costello in *Buck Privates* or any of the Bob Hope and Bing Crosby *Road* pictures. If you have a dream of being a comedian, a great comedian, or a great writer of comedy, do yourself a favor and start with the silent era: Buster Keaton, Charlie Chaplin, and The Little Rascals. Anything that comedy motion picture pioneers Hal Roach or Mack Sennett did in the 1920s. Then, *eventually*, you can work up to Dave Chappelle, Amy Schumer, and

Kate McKinnon. You might be surprised how often a comedy bit from the past shows up in the work of a more modern comedian—who is then credited with it. Just watch The Marx Brothers' *Duck Soup*, from 1933. The mirror bit with Groucho and Harpo? You'll say, "Hey, I've seen that bit a few times already; once was in *Austin Powers*!"

Annnd we're back from the tangent!

My dad met Stan Laurel after attending a comedy workshop taught by Jerry Lewis, who was pretty much the biggest comedic star in the world at the time. Think Eddie Murphy in *Beverly Hills Cop* in 1984. ("I ain't fallin' for no banana in my tailpipe!" Anyone remember that line? So fuckin' funny. No? Okay . . . moving on.) Anyway, Jerry Lewis found Stan Laurel's phone number in a friend's phone book and suggested my father give him a call, and my dad did.

Apparently, what happened next was that Stan actually offered to teach my father what he knew about comedy; I mean, how cool is that! Eddie Griffin told me he spent a lot of time with Richard Pryor during his last years, which I find extremely admirable. Sadly, a lot of comics hang out with heroes only if they're currently famous. My dad, who was a tad obnoxious at the time, told Stan—Stan Laurel, of *Laurel and fucking Hardy*—that this "wasn't how you did comedy anymore." Can you imagine? (Dad? What were you thinking, ding dong?)

Despite the rocky beginning to their relationship, Stan Laurel took my dad under his wing, and grew to care a great deal for him. Before Stan passed away, he gave my dad the actual bow tie that he wore in all his short films from the 1930s. Dad once said that Stan Laurel was one of the only movie stars he knew to be emotionally fit. "Everybody else was so fucked up, to be honest with you," he told me.

Young Kip King soon landed a role on the dramatic series *Playhouse 90*, at the time one of the most watched shows on television. When he was first starting out, my dad went back and forth about whether he wanted to be more of a serious actor or a comedian, and at that time, his goal was the former. And why not, when he was being offered roles in episodes of classics of the early days of television like *Dragnet*, *The Rifleman*, *M Squad*, and *Mister Ed*. When you watch them now, his performances seem a bit on the hammy side, but, in his defense, that was the case for most of the casts of television dramas in the 1950s and early '60s.

My dad also found work in popular films such as *Peyton Place* (with Lana Turner), *Kid Galahad* (with Elvis Presley), and *Breakfast at Tiffany's* (with Audrey Hepburn). Yup, that's my dad delivering booze and squirming through Holly Golightly's apartment during that raucous party scene while her downstairs neighbor, played by Mickey Rooney—doing a crazy, over-the-top Chinese man with buck teeth and glasses—complained about the noise above. During his early Hollywood years, my dad dated Betty Hutton (star of *Annie Get Your Gun*, *The Greatest Show on Earth*, and Preston Sturges's *The Miracle of Morgan's Creek*) and even got actress Ann Robinson, star of the original *The War of the Worlds*, to be his date for his high school prom—and she was eight years older than him. I don't know how he wooed these ladies, but he did. I guess that magic potion called "funny" can be powerful stuff.

It was writer Tracy Newman who first turned my dad on to the Groundlings, in 1975. She and her twin sister, Laraine, had founded the improv troupe, and Laraine had just left for New York to be in the cast of the brand new *Saturday Night Live*. As with most such theaters, there was no pay in performing on the Groundlings stage, so my dad's day job was selling ads over the phone for a Jewish newspaper. There he became friends with the very funny John Paragon, and convinced him to join the Groundlings as well. Paragon would go on to co-write *Pee-wee's Big Adventure* with Paul Reubens and Phil Hartman, as well as *Pee-wee's Playhouse*—where he also played Jambi the Genie. (Remember "Mekka-lekka-hi, mekka-hiney-ho?" No? Damn. I'm two for two.)

Sometimes when I watched my dad and his fellow performers at a Groundlings show, the lineup would include a new sketch featuring a character that had never been tried out on an audience outside of class . . . and the character would end up not working at all. Maybe there were two chuckles within the five-minute sketch. The obvious call was to say good-bye to that character and move on, and sometimes that's what people did. Not every idea is a good one, and getting comfortable with making mistakes and moving on from failure is a necessary part of being successful in comedy—and in life in general, I guess, really. (Deep, I know.)

But watching the process of creating a character at the Groundlings, I also learned that failure doesn't necessarily mean the character is dead. A lot of the time, because of the performer's passion and committed belief in an idea, what started as "a failure" would eventually become one of the most successful characters that performer ever created.

There are so many details that go into a person, and getting those details right can be what makes the character suddenly become real. As a kid, I saw what a tough time Paul Reubens had trying to figure out what his new character Pee-wee Herman would wear. It wasn't until Groundlings director Gary Austin suggested a gray plaid suit and red bow tie that he had hanging back home in his closet that it clicked. This might seem like a simplistic example—obviously there is more to developing a character than a costume—but it was something that I could actually understand as a kid. I was introduced to plenty of creative tools by watching my dad and his friends, but lots of them I didn't grasp until years later, when I actually had reason to apply them myself.

It wasn't so much that my dad's characters themselves were original and groundbreaking, like his fellow Groundling Paul Reuben's Pee-wee Herman, but as a performer he was just as strong as anyone else in the group, maybe because of the way his characters felt. Later, whenever I was developing a new character, my dad would remind me how important it was for the character to be likable, and that one of the best ways to achieve that was to show their qualities of humanity. Take, for example, another character of my dad's, Cry Baby Billy. The name pretty much sums it up: a grown man who would sob about various things and eventually cry for his mommy. Like most great characters in comedy, my dad's were sometimes uncanny, but they were also definitely human.

When it came to improvisation, my father's technique didn't always quite make sense. Phil Hartman once described it by saying, "Trying to control Kip is like trying to put wind in a box." My father loved this line so much he would quote it to others, usually when being told to do something he didn't feel like doing. A smart way to avoid taking responsibility, I say.

One of the greatest things my dad ever did was a series of prank phone calls he recorded. He would answer actual newspaper ads, while doing an offbeat but convincing-enough character. Mostly, he would call in response to for sale or wanted ads, but a few times he ventured into the morbid territory of the obituaries section.

My favorite recording by far—I think it was everybody's favorite—was a response to an ad selling a "Ski Outfit," complete with goggles, boots, poles, hat, and so on. In a rather dismal, depressed tone of voice, my dad began by asking a series of innocuous, general questions:

DAD AS FAKE CALLER: Could you tell me what color the ski suit is?

SELLER: I believe it's a bright orange.

DAD: Bright orange, okay. And what size is it?

SELLER: It's a medium.

DAD: Medium. Is it for a female?

SELLER: Yes it is.

DAD: Could you tell me the make of the goggles? Do they even call them goggles?

SELLER: Goggles, yes.

DAD: Or glasses? Or a mask? What do they usually call it?

SELLER: Goggles is fine.

DAD: Goggles. Okay. Bear with me I'm just writing this down. Is there a ski cap included? Or ski hat?

SELLER: There is a hat included. Yes.

DAD: Is it like a sock or a stocking and does it stay on when you ski?

SELLER: Yes, it fits.

DAD: Does the ski suit include a jacket? Like a ski jacket? Or is it one ski suit that has pants and a jacket in one ski suit?

SELLER: It's one piece.

DAD: Now the ski suit. You say it's orange. Are there any patterns on the orange ski suit?

SELLER: There is a rainbow pattern on the front of the suit in the chest area.

DAD: So is it a pattern of rainbow colors or the whole shape of a rainbow that's on the front of the ski suit?

SELLER: Both.

DAD: Both. Okay. Good.

After about fifteen minutes of this, the conversation took a dark turn.

DAD AS FAKE CALLER: Well, it sounds like the outfit is exactly what I'm looking for. You see, my wife died recently in a skiing accident, and we wanted to have an open-casket funeral, and because she loved to ski, we wanted to have her wearing the goggles, the scarf, the whole ski outfit. Also, her favorite color was rainbow. But instead of lying down, we were gonna have her propped up, holding the poles and positioned like she's skiing down a runway. With the scarf flailing behind her so it looks like she's actually skiing. She would have wanted it this way.

There were dozens of these calls. Unfortunately, the recordings never went on to become anything more than a bootleg tape passed around the comedy underground. Johnny Carson was known to have played it for guests during poker games at his home.

Years later, in 1989, like so many things in the entertainment industry, my dad's simple idea of recording prank calls resurfaced, when a comedy duo out of Queens known as The Jerky Boys did something very similar. Even though their routine became popular and was far more commercially successful, it felt flat to me compared to my dad's routine. Their characters were over the top and went right for the "in your face" moment, and as a result, the conversations The Jerky Boys had never lasted more than a couple minutes, making the whole routine one quick, outrageous joke. Rarely did the joke have a build. What I loved about what my dad did was that he convinced the person on the other end of the line that his character was a real caller, so much so that they became sympathetic; sometimes, the conversations lasted as long as forty-five minutes.

When I was fifteen, my dad's comedy career finally took me somewhere I could brag about to my friends. Other kids my age may not have heard of the Groundlings, but they sure as shit knew *The Smurfs*, and I got to sit in on the table reads, because Dad voiced one of the main characters, Tailor Smurf.

("I was the Jewish Smurf, I made the clothes," my dad would often point out, while in character.)

We'd drive to the old Hanna-Barbera recording studios (which are no longer there) on Ventura Blvd in Universal City (back when it still was called that), where I'd sit in the far back row and watch Dad read with voice legends like Lucille Bliss, who voiced Smurfette, and June Foray, who'd done the mice in Disney's *Cinderella* and Rocky and Natasha of *Rocky and Bullwinkle*. Everyone there had incredible resumes; they were the voices of *Scooby-Doo*, *The Jetsons*, *The Flintstones*. In later seasons, the awe-inspiring king of improvisation, Jonathan Winters—who Robin Williams considered the "Master of Comedy"—was there to voice Grandpa Smurf.

(Dear reader, if you want to be comically inspired, go to YouTube and do a search for "Jonathan Winters and Robin Williams" and then watch them do anything together. Everything else you've ever considered funny will go down at least two notches.)

By this time, having clocked hours watching him, whether sitting at a table read or standing by the sound booth behind a laughing Groundlings audience, I'd begun to understand how important this world was to my dad, and why. How fulfilling it was to work with a talented group of people to create something incredible out of nothing. The world that my dad inhabited was so full of life, I couldn't stop thinking about it. I wanted to be around it as much as I could. Unfortunately, at least for the time being, I was doomed to spend weekdays on Mount Baldy, sucking on rocks for fun. So I developed a goal. Something I could dream about, work toward, prepare for. Almost like a soldier honored to serve in the military, I was deadened to everything else around me, just waiting until the next time I could visit my dad and take in everything that he loved. I knew that someday, like him, I would be a performer.

On my weekend visits, I would stock up on what I later called "The Chris and Dad Tapes." As much like potential tabloid fodder as that sounds, the reality was much less exciting—at least to everyone but me. The recordings had no production value—we made them on one of those old-school tape recorders, the ones where you had to press the far left Record button and the middle Play button at the same time to record, that ran on three huge C batteries—and very little was even thought out. The only recordings that had any actual structure were the few where we performed sketches or played characters, unscripted and improvised, of course. That, and the ones where we would dub the voices of a movie of our choosing (and this was before *Mystery Science Theater 3000*). Otherwise, they were just recordings of the two of us performing every mundane task you could think of: driving, eating, talking on the phone, waiting for a call from someone before talking on the phone, talking to the plumber while he's over to fix something, you name it.

Mostly, they were recordings of my dad, made whether he was doing anything or not. Sometimes I'd record a whole hour straight because I knew that somewhere within that hour, ten minutes of brilliance would slip out of his mouth. I recorded him taking his vitamins. I even recorded from outside the bathroom door while he was sitting on the toilet reading *The New Yorker*.

A few times, I recorded my dad while he was in the car with a date, me sitting in the back seat with my tape recorder. Does that seem inappropriate? Completely, but he did ask his dates first. Sometimes, when my dad was just waking up, I would place the tape recorder on his pillow next to his face—and not discreetly, since the recorder was the size of a shoebox—press Record, and then quickly run to the living room. Sometimes his eyes would open and I'd hear him say, "Oh, God. Not the tape recorder again." Yes, it did irritate him sometimes, but so what? My dad, being the least-threatening person—man, woman, or child—I've ever known, was really funny when he got mad. And most of the time, he loved it. What comedian doesn't love an audience, even if it's just one person?

My father's sense of humor made me feel alive and blazed a path for my own creative instincts to follow. I'd listen to my stash of tapes over and over and over again, from recordings of old Groundlings shows and improv classes to those of us ordering takeout at Jack in the Box. I eventually had a box of probably one hundred cassettes. Those tapes were my number-one source of entertainment on weeknights before I fell asleep on Mount Baldy. Soon enough, I'd remind myself, Friday would come and Mom would pick me up after school to drive me and my little suitcase back to my dad's for another fun-filled weekend.

As much fun as I had with my dad, as a kid there was a lot I didn't realize about the influence my time with him had on me. He never quite understood the role of being a parent, so he became my best friend and my hero instead. In many ways, things remained like that for years, even after I came to understand that this wasn't exactly the role of a father.

In some ways, I took care of him as much as he took care of me. My father and I joked that our relationship was similar to the one between E.T. the Extra-Terrestrial and Elliott. When E.T. got sick, Elliott got sick as well. (Didn't the potted sunflower die, too? Lots of terrestrial codependency in that movie!) But actually, I don't think this was an accurate comparison; it was only my dad who seemed to have the problem. Dad had an oversympathetic hypochondriac tendency that would trigger whatever ailment someone around him was experiencing at any given moment.

"Oh, I have the worst pain in my left hip," someone might say.

"You're kidding. So do I!" And Dad somehow would magically develop a similar pain, one that remained with him for months. I remember once my cousin on my dad's side thought it would be funny to make up a nonexistent sickness just to see if my dad believed he might have it. And in only a few days, guess what? He did.

It wasn't until much later, well into my twenties, that I began to see a darker side to our uncannily close relationship. Whenever I looked to my dad for advice about a girl, he was unfailingly helpful and supportive. But when that girl and I fell in love, and (as often happened) started living together, I would spend less time with my dad. I'd find myself in the middle as she and my dad competed for my attention. Then, so subtly I rarely saw it at the time, Dad would undermine my romance, dissecting everything about our relationship and the reasons we fell in love in the first place. I'm not sure he knew what he was doing, consciously. After the inevitable breakup, I would turn back to my dad for support and consolation, and he'd blame my disastrous relationships on what he called "The Kattan Curse."

Whenever something bad happened to me, he'd say, ruefully, "It's because you're a Kattan." On the other hand, when I got good news, he would claim that I was "breaking the Kattan Curse," as if I was, finally, the chosen one from a long line of neurotic, ultimately unsuccessful ancestors. For years I tried to break free of this curse that supposedly loomed over us, but in the end, it became clear to me that The Kattan Curse was just a manifestation of his unconscious need to maintain our symbiotic connection. But, hey, come on. No one's father is perfect, right? Am I right? I mean, I am, right? Hello?

My weekends with my dad may have given me plenty to talk about in therapy, but they also gave me a master class in comedy's roots. An obsessive fan, he knew everything about practically every movie ever made that was considered a classic, up to and including the run time. "Impressive" wasn't a big enough word for the level of knowledge he had about film. And it wasn't just movies. He also knew old-time radio shows, television, and theater. Dad knew everything—as long as it was before the mid-1950s, which he considered the end of the Golden Age. But he was also intensely critical. He would get restless if he got stuck watching a movie that hadn't merited four stars according to critic Leonard Maltin, whose *Leonard Maltin's Movie Guide* was essentially my father's bible. My dad had plenty of opinions of his own, and he was happy to rank any group of titles from best to worst, with absolute authority.

Take the Hope/Crosby *Road* pictures. My dad would tell you that *Road to Rio* was the best of the series even though it was the fifth one made. The third, *Road to Morocco*, would be ranked second, followed by *Road to Utopia, Road to Zanzibar*, and then *Road to Singapore*. The only film in color, *Road to Bali*, was tied with *Road to Zanzibar. Road to Hong Kong* wasn't even mentioned because it was released in 1962, ten years after *Bali*, and considered forced and "terrible." In general, though there were exceptions like *Rio*, time wasn't kind to movie franchises, and the earlier entries were the better ones. The Abbot and Costello movies that Universal distributed (*Hold That Ghost*, *Buck Privates*, *The Time of Their Lives*, and *Abbot and Costello Meet Frankenstein*) were all excellent. After that, they got into doing "Abbot and Costello meet some monster," like the invisible man or a mummy, and the magic faded. Sure, there were a few funny moments in their later films, moments that were lifted from their radio show or vaudeville acts and rehashed, but the best one was probably in *Abbott and Costello in the Foreign Legion* and was actually taken from one of their vaudeville bits titled "Slowly I turn, step by step." *Abbott and Costello Go to Mars?* Don't even bother.

The Marx Brothers films were all good. Some were stronger than others, of course, the weakest being their third adventure with MGM, the 1939 release *At the Circus*. The films they did with Paramount before going to MGM were their best work, the greatest of these being *Duck Soup*, and then *Horse Feathers*, *Monkey Business*, *Animal Crackers* and, lastly, their first film ever, *The Cocoanuts*. Those first five had four of the Marx Bros., including Zeppo, who was the ladies' man and least funny. The MGM films after that just featured what became the famous three: Groucho, Chico, and my favorite, Harpo. God, I loved Harpo.

But even though their Paramount stuff was the strongest in general, their best movie of all, and probably their most popular, was the first one they did for MGM—*A Night at the Opera*, produced by Irving Thalberg in 1935. *A Night at the Opera* is on the American Film Institute's top one hundred films of all time. (And no, *Girl's Trip* isn't.) It includes the brilliant "crowded cabin scene," in which the brothers, who are stowaways on a steamship, keep ordering more food . . . along with the plumber, the mop lady, three women to change the linens, the engineer to turn off the heat, a very heavyset engineer's assistant, and a manicurist. Pretty soon a crowd of people is squeezed into their tiny cabin. At one point, the manicurist asks Groucho "Did you want your nails long or short?" to which he replies, "You better make 'em short. It's getting kind of crowded in here."

Just before everyone who squished in is about to spill out, a young girl knocks on the door and Groucho opens it:

"Is my Aunt Minnie in here?"

"Well, you can come in and prowl around if you wanna," Groucho says, with his pupils darting to the side and his eyebrows bouncing up toward his forehead. "If she isn't here, you can probably find somebody just as good."

Dad's magical nostalgic cerebellum could also recall every detail of all the best classic animated shorts (more popularly known as cartoons). Warner Bros.' Bugs Bunny and Daffy Duck meant introducing me to the works of Chuck Jones, Friz Freleng, and Leon Schlesinger; Walt Disney's Mickey Mouse, Donald Duck, and the *Silly Symphonies* series taught me the names of artists Ollie Johnston, Frank Thomas, Ward Kimball, Don Bluth, and Ub Iwerks. Tom and Jerry, Betty Boop, and Popeye were perfect for a lesson on MGM's William Hanna and Joseph Barbera, Tex Avery, Fred Quimby, and Max Fleischer.

I remember once watching a Mickey Mouse cartoon called "Mickey's Polo Team," which my dad loved because it featured dozens of animated versions of real Hollywood stars like Chaplin, Laurel and Hardy, Douglas Fairbanks, and Mary Pickford. My dad nudged me on the couch.

"Notice everyone playing polo is white?" he asked. "That's because Walt Disney was racist! Swear to God. If you don't believe me, I'll show you a cartoon called 'Coal Black and de Sebben Dwarfs.'"

Sure enough, when I finally saw the 1943 short, only one word came to mind. Yep . . . racist!

Other than the *Bugs Bunny/Road Runner* show on CBS every Saturday morning, Dad wasn't a fan of contemporary cartoons, defined as pretty much anything made after Truman was president. If I "accidentally" had the TV playing *Scooby-Doo* or *The Flintstones*, Dad would say, "Would you please turn that off or put on something worth watching? I'd appreciate it. Thanks."

With the exception of foreign films, documentaries, PBS specials, and his hidden porn (stashed in a very obvious top drawer in his bedroom dresser next to his rolled-up socks and a little bag of shake weed), if my dad watched it, I watched it. (By the way, even his porn was stuff like *Emmanuelle*, *The Devil in Miss Jones*, and *Debbie Does Dallas*—not the second through the ninth; just the first one. Only the classics!)

Long before Blu-ray, DVD, VHS, or Betamax, a videotape format known as three-quarter inch was really the only way to record something through a video source and play it back. These machines were not intended for home entertainment and were mostly used at news stations and for airing prerecorded television shows. Yet somehow my dad had one of these, along with a huge collection of classic movies taped on the giant five-by-twelve-inch, one-hour-long tapes it played, a collection that entertained me for years of Saturday and Sunday mornings.

But if the Golden Age of film ended in the 1950s, the Golden Age of my time with my dad began the day he taught me how to thread 16 mm film into his old World War II–era projector. The projector used to play newsreels for the troops on a Navy boat but was now in my dad's garage, sitting on a wooden stool playing films on a portable movie screen.

The garage was by far my favorite place at my dad's. It was just outside the living room, which had big French doors looking out to his garden and the rest of his half acre of land. My mom used to tell me that when they were married and she was still living there, she'd planted and maintained the most exquisite and liveliest garden in Sherman Oaks. Orange trees, plum trees, walnut trees, roses, tulips, lilies, even a handmade functioning koi pond. Unfortunately, when she left, the entire garden went to shit. My dad couldn't even keep an indoor ivy plant alive. Actually, not *all* of it died, at least not right away. There was an orange tree that struggled along valiantly, but eventually that died, too, thanks to the chlorine splashed on it every time someone jumped into the pool.

Instead of the garage being filled with tools and shovels, which would have been pointless since my dad barely knew how to hammer a nail, it was full of antiques, memorabilia, and film reels. There was a bottle of Coca-Cola from 1903 with its top still on that supposedly included the cocaine of the original recipe. A December 7, 1941, "A day that will live in infamy" Pearl Harbor thermometer. Every part of the cultural spectrum was there, from lurid, almost-ultraviolet trays and old Mickey Mouse watches to a beautiful set of Blue Willow plates. (By the way, if at any time you don't know what I'm talking about, your friend Google is always standing by—and probably helpfully recording your search history.) The décor featured movie posters from the 1920s to the 1940s, mechanics' garage calendars from the prime pinup years featuring long-legged, busty girls dressed in bathing suits, and a poster of a cowgirl sitting on a flying firecracker by the great and I'm sure horny Alberto Vargas. The antique bubblegum machines still had gum inside, and it always cracked me up when a guest came over and removed the loosened lid to scoop a handful of the round bubblegum, only to have my dad scream out, "Don't eat that! That's original bubblegum from the 1930s and 1940s!"

Unfortunately, much like my mother's garden, Dad didn't know how to take care of these collectable rarities he had accumulated. Even his precious 16 mm films were unevenly stacked one on top of another right against the moldy wooden walls. Fortunately, years before most of these films were either destroyed by the mold, eaten by mice, or disintegrated into nitrate, I got an education in classic comedy by threading them into the projector and watching them. It was the 1970s, remember, and back then you couldn't just order whatever classic movie you wanted to see off Amazon or stream it from a smart flat-screen or iPhone—unless it happened to be showing on regular television, you were out of luck until home video took off at the end of the decade, and even then, lots of classics weren't on video, or were so poorly transferred they were barely watchable. But somehow my dad had 16 mm reels of everything, even films that were difficult to find good copies of, like *A Night at the Opera* and *Road to Rio*. He had Charlie Chaplin in *The Gold Rush*—the one where Chaplin is starving in a cabin during a snowstorm and makes soup by basting his shoes in a pot of boiling water. He had W.C. Fields in *It's a Gift*, and Buster Keaton shorts like *One Week*. (Bucket list those two comedies, would you please?)

Watching these films in my dad's garage was like my own *Cinema Paradiso*. I couldn't get enough. I'd watch them over and over again, and I became obsessed with these performers and their comic timing. Their movements were so purposeful, so well orchestrated; it was almost like music.

When it came to physical comedy, Buster Keaton was by far the master. Of all the stars my dad introduced me to, he was the one I studied the most closely; besides watching him on the screen, I read everything my dad had about him. Keaton took incredible chances with his body in order to fulfill his vision and make the camera see what he wanted it to see, and he realized the only way to do that was to never think about it, to simply *do it*. Back on Mount Baldy, my daredevil tendencies evolved into more than just a way to play, and I began trying out some physical stunts. I became a bit of a Raggedy Ann doll, throwing myself down the steps outside my house. I soon found out that though I often got hurt, I rarely felt pain. I didn't know my limit, so I became fearless. That's right, fearless.

Even as a kid, something Buster Keaton once said resonated with me:

The secret is in landing limp and breaking the fall with a foot or a hand. It's a knack. I started so young that landing right is second nature with me. Several times I'd have been killed if I hadn't been able to land like a cat. Imitators of our act don't last long, because they can't stand the treatment.

Chapter 6

WHAT IS LOVE?

One night after a Groundlings class, Will and I went to grab a beer at a local place that had a meager dance floor. We noticed a middle-aged gentleman standing up against the bar, wearing a matchless blazer, a skintight T-shirt, and a glossy gold chain. The guy was moving his head and upper body to the beat of the music, while using his fingers to pantomime *Do you want to dance? You do? You don't? You don't? You do?* to any woman who ventured into his vicinity. Alas, no matter how hard he tried, not one interested glance came his way. The man got nothing.

Dismally dejected, he turned back around to face the bar and ordered another drink. Then, as Will and I watched, he once again turned to face the dance floor, and with a fresh cocktail in hand—and, apparently, excited by a new lease on life—he started in again, moving to the music, his fingers rhythmically miming yet another round of *You? Me?* dance invitations without a single response. He repeated this ritual over and over throughout the evening, seemingly expecting a different result each time—which, by the way, I believe is the definition of insanity. But the guy's tenacity was endearing. He had an underdog quality that made us root for him. And that quality was what inspired Will and me to write a sketch about him for the Groundlings.

At the time, I was a real sucker for cheesy, bubblegum techno/euro-dance music. (It was a short-lived phase. It was like Chinese food. I just ate it and pooped it out.) There was a catchy song on the radio a lot back then called "More and More," by a legendary and unforgettable—yes, I'm being sarcastic—1990s German outfit known as the Captain Hollywood Project. It went like this: *"More and more and more. I don't know where we're going to."*

I'm sure you remember it. But, lyrical accomplishment aside, honestly, "More and More" really made you want to dance—and that's why I chose it the first time we did the sketch onstage at the Groundlings.

Will and I pitched the sketch my second week at *SNL*, and it made the lineup. Phil Hartman was the guest host that week, but he didn't appear in the sketch. It was rare to get a new sketch in the lineup that didn't feature the host, but as a result, Will and I didn't have to worry about altering our sketch to include or showcase another performer; we were free to do it just as we had at the Groundlings. We basically replicated the original for the *SNL* audience, with a pair of hapless, dateless, but ever-hopeful guys shimmying in suits and slick chains as they try and fail to entice women through the power of gesture from their spot at the bar. That sketch from Episode 16 of Season 21 was the first TV iteration of head-bopping brothers Steve and Doug Butabi, a.k.a. the Roxbury Guys.

Being a featured player, especially a new one, especially a new one hired just six weeks prior to the finale, was a real test for me. If it hadn't been for Lorne or Fred Wolf—the co-head writer at the time—choosing my sketches for inclusion week after week, I probably would have failed. Fred was also debuting as a featured player. He was a close friend of Spade's, and an extremely nice guy who had my back from day one; along with Lorne and possibly NBC, Fred was the reason I received so much airplay in the beginning. But I delivered, week after week, reminding myself that if I could maintain this momentum, I just might be able to remain on the show. It helped that, for maybe the first time in my life, I didn't feel like I was beating my head against the wall just to get to the same level as everyone else. Not only did I have a trunk full of tried-and-true Groundlings material, I was reunited with Will, the partner I'd developed many of the sketches with in the first place.

Since the sketches I first submitted had already worked well at the Groundlings, I wanted what appeared on the show to re-create what was seen onstage back in LA, which meant as many wide camera shots as possible. The dialogue I wrote was rarely the element that made my sketches work—the words weren't usually the funny part. I was adamant about the visual presentation of each sketch, the camera coverage, and the music, and I learned to lay everything out for the art department, director, and music department all at once early on. That way, I wouldn't be viewed as some demanding little asshole constantly asking for changes, like "Can we please use this song instead?" or "Is there any way the camera can stay on me until after I say my line, and then cut to Gwyneth?" (Sorry, name-drop!)

When it came to music, many sketch writers and cast members were more flexible than I was; sometimes they didn't consider adding a song at all until after the sketch was chosen. For me, music was essential. While lots of sketch ideas originate in an observation, a moment, or a memory that you want to explore or make fun of or push further, plenty of times my original motivation for a sketch came from a song: one I'd just heard or one I remembered from the past that moved me or suggested a specific mood or scenario.

When you watch *SNL* in reruns, especially on another network, like Comedy Central or VH1, many of the songs that were in the sketches originally have been replaced, usually with ones I've never even heard of. This is almost always because the cost of paying to use the original is beyond the budget of the network in question—the permission to use the song doesn't transfer when the show goes into syndication. Sometimes this isn't such a big deal, but other times replacing it with something that works as well is almost impossible. Worst of all was when the show would arbitrarily choose a "royalty free" track without asking the sketch writer first.

An example of this is a series of sketches I wrote with Matt Piedmont, versions of the "Mood Music" sketch I used for my *SNL* audition, where I play a successful bachelor trying to choose the appropriate song to get my groove on with my date. On the version I did for the show, my date would be played by the guest host—on my fourth show, this was Teri Hatcher, and I put on Sade's "No Ordinary Love," Bryan Ferry's "Your Painted Smile," and then Paul Simon's "Diamonds on the Soles of Her Shoes." But the best of these "dating" sketches was the one I did with Renée Zellweger.

The sketch begins with Renée and me walking into the living room of an apartment where a stereo unit stands to the left, by the entrance (basically the same set design as the sketch with Teri).

"Wasn't dinner great?" I say to her.

"Yeah," Renée says. "I've never had Antarctic food before."

Just as we're about to sit on the couch, I ask if she'd like to hear some music. Then I strut over to the stereo, press Play . . . and the theme song to the TV show *Alice* comes grooving out of the speakers. (By the way, that song was sung by the star of the series, Linda Lavin. I know—Fascinating!) I dance back to the couch, but pop back over again to switch things up with the always-sexy theme songs from *Diff'rent Strokes*, followed by the sketch's third punch line, *The Price Is Right*. All the while, thanks to the props department, I've got a plastic bag filled with pureed oatmeal in my left pocket, connected to a tube running up the side of my button-down shirt and through my left sleeve, ending at my wrist. Toward the end of the sketch, a frustrated Renée goes to the stereo and puts on a more suitable song before returning to the couch and pulling me in for a kiss. At which point, I deploy my disgusting prop and throw up on her. Her response is one of my favorite lines from the show:

"You just threw up penguin all over me!"

Two years after I left the show, Lyle, one of Lorne's very cute blonde assistants (yes, I definitely had a crush on her at one point while on the show), called me at home in LA to tell me that Broadway Video wanted to release an *SNL Best of Chris Kattan*.* Which was very cool of Lorne—and the lovely people of Broadway Video, of course—to do. So, as requested, I put together a list of my favorite sketches and read it to her. I wanted to use the Jim Carrey Roxbury Guys sketch but couldn't, because that was already going to be on Will's *Best of*, so I chose our first Roxbury performance, from the show Phil Hartman hosted, along with selections of my other best-known characters and bits, including the Teri Hatcher date sketch and the Peepers sketch with Katie Holmes. When Lyle called me

---

* *Saturday Night Live: The Best of Chris Kattan* is available on Amazon.com. In case you're interested.

back, she had bad news. Thanks to the songs used, the "Mood Music" date sketches with Teri and Renée were out. Because the music basically *was* the sketch, there was really no point in replacing the songs, either. Today these sketches are nowhere and I mean *nowhere* to be found. Not in a rerun, not on YouTube, not even on the *SNL* app. (And they're both funny! Damn you, copyright protections!) Worse, the Peepers sketch I did with Katie Holmes was out, too. In it, I'd used five different songs, including Coldplay's "Yellow" and David Gray's "Babylon," and while I was told I could include the sketch as long as we replaced the songs with more affordable titles, I opted to choose a different Peepers sketch instead, one with no music at all. For me, it would have been like replacing Wagner's "Ride of the Valkyries" in *Apocalypse Now* with "It's Raining Men" by the Weather Girls. And that's honestly the best analogy I can come up with.

Right around the time I was taking my first classes at the Groundlings, another aspiring comedian struggling in LA took one of his regular drives up to Mulholland Drive to look out onto the city below and dream about his future. On this particular evening in 1990, as the legend has it, that twenty-eight-year-old hopeful wrote himself a ten-million-dollar check for "acting services rendered," dating it five years in the future: Thanksgiving Day, 1995. He stuck the check in his wallet, where it slowly began to disintegrate as the years passed.

By the time I met Jim Carrey the week he hosted *SNL* in May of 1996, he had already made more than enough to cash his check, having starred in the box office hits *Ace Ventura: Pet Detective*, *The Mask*, and *Dumb and Dumber*. He had just made news by becoming the first actor to be paid twenty million dollars—for his starring role in an upcoming dark comedy directed by Ben Stiller and produced by a young Judd Apatow. The two of them wrote quite a few scripts together back then but for some reason, as talented as they were, they never got anywhere. Anyway, that film—*The Cable Guy*—was slated to be released a month after his appearance on *SNL*.

Jim Carrey's twenty-million-dollar grin was front and center in Lorne's office for our pitch meeting at the start of that week. I remember feeling good about a sketch idea I'd pitched, which had actually gotten some laughs. After the meeting, as everyone dispersed back to their offices, I ran into Fred Wolf, fidgeting as usual with a cigarette he'd never smoke. He was just coming out of Norm Macdonald's office, by "Weekend Update," and he waved me down and suggested that Will and I bring back "those dancing guys" we'd introduced a few weeks before, when Phil Hartman was on, but this time add Jim as a third dancing guy. At that point Fred had no idea what he had just given birth to. I sprinted past the elevators and the reception desk over to Will's office, which he shared with Adam McKay, to tell him about Fred's brilliant idea. Will was into it, but he couldn't work on it with me then—he had already promised to write a Cheerleaders sketch with Cheri and writer Paula Pell. After that, he said, he would try to find time. One thing about Will: He was the opposite of "all talk." If he said he would try, he would try, and if there was any way to make it happen, he would always come through.

I muffled my excitement, and went back to the office I shared with Spade and began to write the sketch I had pitched at the meeting earlier. Honestly, I can't even remember what it was about, but it doesn't matter, since it didn't get in.

That night, back at the Paramount Hotel, I couldn't stop obsessing over the Roxbury sketch, as if it were a calculus equation I needed to figure out (which wasn't exactly easy since I didn't know jack shit about calculus). I had music playing while I brainstormed ideas in my tiny room, and at some point, I put on some garish MTV dance party CD, and one of the tracks was "What Is Love" by Haddaway. The song has no build; obviously it has a chorus, but I don't think it has a bridge or even a verse. In fact, it's really only that chorus looped over and over again, perfectly befitting use in a sketch, which is almost always about the length of a pop-ular radio-mixed dance song. Any part of the song would work for a scene in the sketch. It was super-catchy and relentlessly upbeat, teetering on the edge of annoying. To be honest, I always felt there was a fine line between annoying and addictive. And anyway, borderline-annoying manic opti-mism was a pretty good description of the quality Will and I had been drawn to in the guy who originally inspired the sketch in the first place, so it fit. I listened to other songs, but that one stuck. I knew Will would love it, too. Maybe not the song itself, but I knew he'd love it for the sketch, because he trusted me.

My excitement was dampened a bit when my dad called late that night, "wondering" if his good friend Kathleen, who went by the name Bunny and had the distinction of having once been on *American Band-stand*, could get work as an extra on the show that week while she just happened to be in town visiting New York. Oh, lucky me. I was slightly distressed by the whole idea, especially as I was only a feature player, but it was my dad, so I told him I'd ask.

The next afternoon, Tuesday, I showed up at 30 Rock dressed in my usual comfy Fred Segal FreeCity sweatpants, a Helmut Lang peacoat, and an LA Dodgers baseball cap—recently purchased, like all my hats, since I seemed to lose them all the fucking time. It was an outfit that Jimmy would christen as ". . . so cool." I checked around different offices to see who had already come in as usual, said my hellos, and so on, until

Will was free, and then the two of us went over to Steve Koren's office to talk about the sketch. Steve was known as a writer who was great at adapting preexisting characters—like he did with Molly's Mary Katherine Gallagher—for the *SNL* format. Not only was he incredibly talented at translating the unique chemistry of an improvised character into the television format, but whenever I had an idea while writing a sketch with him, he would stop writing, look right at me, and listen. He wrote down every word I said, every idea. And instead of judging an idea or editing while we wrote, we would wait until we'd finished the sketch and then we'd go back and "cut the fat" that didn't work. He totally understood our process and helped me trust my instincts as a writer. His style was a perfect match for a character-driven performer who would sometimes write stream-of-consciousness-style, like me or Molly.

Steve really liked the idea of having Jim Carrey as a third Roxbury guy, but he was writing a "Joe Pesci Show" sketch with Jim Breuer and wouldn't be done for a few more hours. Breuer's was already one of the more popular recurring sketches, so it was a high priority. While we waited for Steve, I went back to my office to finish the sketch I'd pitched the day before (yes, that's right, the one that didn't make it in), while Will went back to Paula's office to work on his Cheerleaders sketch with Cheri. At 8 PM, I opened the door to Paula's office to find Will sitting on a large, somewhat deflated medicine ball, throwing out various squad chants while Cheri jumped on the couch and Paula sat writing at her desk. I could tell Cheri wasn't too pleased about Will taking off to write another sketch, especially when "Cheerleaders" wasn't finished and they were still trying to nail down the "perfect cheer," but Paula said she could work around him, so off we went to Steve's office.

As Will settled into the shit-colored, dorm-conditioned couch, I put on "What Is Love." Right away, we all agreed that this could work. The song had the drive that we needed to carry the sketch from scene to scene—the guys, now a trio, would unceasingly bop their heads to the unvarying rhythm as they continued to try their luck at one place after another, the song sounding as relentless as they were. The first location would be the usual nightclub, from which the guys are quickly ejected, and then to build on the joke, they'd desperately go on to other parties or events already in progress: hitting a high school prom, then crashing a wedding. Now we just had to figure out how to solve the problem we'd heedlessly created for ourselves with those multiple locations, which meant multiple stage sets in the sketch. We came up with some funny bits that could be filmed as "pre-tapes"—of us back in the car each time en route to the next hot spot. The director could cut to these while we ran from one stage set to another, before cutting back to us live at the next location.

For the end point of the sketch, and our characters' desperation, Will suggested a nursing home as the third and final location, which we'd follow with one last pre-tape of Jim, Will, and me in the car again, this time accompanied by the only women we'd managed to convince to come home with us: three octogenarians.

Those were the beats of the sketch, we had them down, and we knew how many pre-tapes and how many sets we were going to need. Now we just had to, you know, actually write the scenes we had worked out.

Aside from being a movie star, Jim Carrey came with years of sketch comedy experience on *In Living Color*, so everyone knew our material for Wednesday's read through had to be exceptional. That day, when Jim stepped out of the elevator on floor seventeen, he was met by one of the talent producers, Ryan Shiraki, who led him back to Marci Klein's office, where our guest host had thirty minutes to settle in and enjoy a Diet Coke, his drink of choice.

"I'm addicted to these," he said to me.

Knowing there was limited time for Jim to skim through the nearly fifty sketches that sat in front of him, and hoping for a quick dance rehearsal, Will and I knocked on the door of Jim's temporary office and walked through the beats of our sketch with him, showing him the head bop and playing the "What Is Love" music cue. We bopped, then he bopped, and then we all bopped.

And . . . that's all there was to it, really. Jim's neck was so flexible that while bopping his head, his chin would touch the far corner of his shoulder. It was simply, as one might say, nut balls to witness. When they got to our sketch, about half an hour into the read through, the three of us got up as planned and stood together, bopping our heads to the left while the music played and Lorne read the stage directions. There wasn't a lot of reaction, just some scattered laughs throughout the room, which by now I was used to. But with Fred Wolf having suggested the idea, and Lorne trusting Fred's instincts, I knew we stood a good chance of making it on.

That evening, when Lorne opened his office door, threw on his Prada rain jacket, kissed his lip balm, and left 30 Rock, I was all but lurking in the shadows, and I ran over to see the lineup the second he was out of sight. While the other sketch I'd pitched officially hadn't made it, the word "Roxbury" was Sharpied on a card and thumbtacked to the board. Will, Steve, and I walked straight to the art department to discuss how we envisioned the sets and costumes. While I was talking to Brian, the head of extras casting, I remembered I'd forgotten to ask about finding a spot for my dad's friend, Kathleen. With a scowl that asked, "What are you, stupid?" he said "of course" . . . and then cast her as an extra in the

Roxbury sketch. Not exactly the sketch I had in mind, I just hoped she'd made quite the splash on *American Bandstand*.

As a cast member, when you finally arrived home Wednesday night, there would be a phone message on your answering machine from Hillary Selesnick, the coordinating producer, giving you your call time for the following day. For a sketch's first-ever rehearsal, each cast member got an individual call time for a forty-minute camera blocking. I wasn't due in until late afternoon that Thursday, but I came in around twelve so I could see Soundgarden's sound check for the songs "Pretty Noose" and "Burden in My Hand." Coincidentally, the band's bassist, Ben Shepherd, had been a year ahead of me in high school back on Bainbridge Island, Washington, where Mom and Marc moved us during my freshman year. Nearly every day after school, while I was on Bainbridge getting involved in theater, Ben took the ferry over to Seattle to hang out at the center of the growing grunge music scene. Seeing Ben on the *SNL* set was my first experience running into someone from my hometown who had found a similar type of success after graduating. After sharing a cathartic "Fuck, yeah, we made it!" I headed to my dressing room and waited for the phone to ring, requesting me to report to the writers' room on nine for rewrites on "Roxbury."

On Friday, I had a 2 PM call time to film the pre-tapes, two floors down in Studio 6H, the stage where *Late Night with Conan O'Brien* was located. In just two hours, that audience would be filing in. But first I had to go to Tom Broecker in wardrobe, then over to the hair and makeup department to gel my hair back and put on sideburns with "sticky gum." When I got to 6H, there on the *Conan* set sat an engineless car, positioned in front of a green screen facing two cameras, along with Will and Jim, lighting, the B-camera director, and the rest of the crew, including the infamous "Wally" on cue cards. (Yes, that is the same Wally you see holding cue cards on *Late Night with Seth Meyers*.) We hadn't decided where we'd be sitting; Jim went for the back seat so he could be center frame. Will, unselfish as usual, muttered, "I guess I'll be the driver," leaving the passenger seat to me, which meant I'd get to do the "something's wrong with the CD" joke. Someone yelled "Play back!" signaling for the music to begin; the director shouted "Action!" and the three of us started bopping.

(The CD joke, by the way, went like this: We are bopping away, when the music suddenly stops. Jim hollers, "What the hell is going on?!" and I eject the CD and hand it to him to inspect. Jim yells, "Dust!" then blows on the CD. He hands it back, I put it back in the player, and then the music starts playing again and we resume head bopping. Trust me, it was a good joke. Will and I thought of the CD-stopping bit, but Jim came up with the dust part while on set.)

There were three pre-tapes to film, and we only had enough time to do a few takes for each one. The shots each had to be set up and lit, and interior lighting in a car is a pain. There were two short linear fluorescent lights above each of us, makeshiftedly (Is that word? It is for the moment.) duct taped to our window visors, and one more behind, on the floor by Jim's feet. We had to be adjusted so that Will's and my bopping wouldn't block Jim's bopping behind us.

The last pre-tape was the final joke of the sketch, and the hopeful payoff—it's our ride back for the night, Jim in the back seat with his conquest from the nursing home seated on his lap. In the script, it was written that Jim would make out with his conquest, but just before the second take, he asked Props if they could get him some dentures, and then proceeded to pretend that he and his elderly lady friend had been necking so fiercely that he'd sucked her choppers right out of her mouth. He held the dentures between us toward the camera, exhilarated and announcing, "Look! A souvenir!"

(After filming, in a yellow cab going home, I wondered if the joke might be too broad for *SNL*, more suited to *In Living Color*. Of course, Jim's instincts were right on. What I really should have been wondering was why I was questioning Jim fuckin' Carrey.)

On Saturday, we rehearsed a complete run-through of every sketch—with pre-tapes, voice-overs, props, wigs, and wardrobe—from noon to 5 PM. The cast was never expected to perform in this run-through at the level we'd need for dress rehearsal, which was where we would finally see what jokes did and didn't work for the studio audience—the week he'd guest hosted, Phil Hartman had taken me aside on Saturday and recommended I "save my energy" in the eight-o'clock dress rehearsal for the live show. Some sketches are cut after the dress rehearsal, and I remember thinking, "How can he be so sure that his sketch will make it in?" And "How can he be so sure *I* could be so sure that my sketch would make it in?" At 5 PM, we broke for "lunch" and then were free to prepare, relax, or nap until exactly 8 PM, when the approximately two-hour non-telecast dress rehearsal with an in-studio audience began.

At last, sometime between 10:40 and 11:10 PM, everybody would scurry over from their dressing rooms or the ninth-floor writers' room or wherever and squeeze into Lorne's main office. Similar to the Monday pitch meeting, everyone would sit wherever they could find a place—the couches, floor—but this time we were there to see the final rundown of the 11:30 live show and to hear Lorne's notes on each sketch that was now on the board, from the cold opening to "Goodnights." The show was an hour and a half, and each thirty-minute block would have to be cut down to about twenty-two minutes of sketch material to make room for commercial breaks. If your sketch didn't play well in the dress rehearsal, it would mostly likely be cut and wouldn't get a second chance. Ever. If your sketch played great, but for some reason it still got cut, you had to let it go without an argument or even a question. There was nothing you could do about it. It was about the show. Not you.

Five minutes before the show went live that week, my dad's friend Kathleen walked into my dressing room and plopped all her stuff down. She was out of breath, probably from running from the elevator to get there. Instead of being with the rest of the extras, she was decidedly set on sharing my spacious fifteen-square-foot dressing room for the rest of the night. *Thanks, Dad!*

During the show, I was being pulled from set to set so quickly by the assistant director that it was nearly impossible to gauge how the sketch was doing with the audience. But ten minutes after we'd finished, just after getting out of my costume, the stage intercom blared: "Jim, Will, Kattan! Please set yourselves for Soundgarden song intro immediately!" And so I hurriedly pulled the two-piece sharkskin suit back off its hanger, ripped the gold chain out of a ziplocked sandwich bag marked "Kattan" from Props, and somehow successfully threw everything back on. Then, being the little half-Jewish desert twister that I am, I darted like the wind to meet Will and Jim at the "Goodnights" stage. This was definitely new. The guest host always introduced the band alone. This was the first time they ever had the characters from a sketch join the host to introduce the musical guest—and these characters had only been introduced a few minutes before! This was the first hint that our sketch might be a success.

The show's after-party took place down on Rockefeller Center's ice rink—sans ice, since it was summer. This was the season finale, and it was by far the biggest *SNL* after-party I had seen, the biggest party I'd been to so far and, with the exception of the fortieth anniversary, it remains the biggest SNL party I have ever been to. I remember struggling to get through the crowd that night to congratulate Jim, but it was impossible to reach him. This was his prime, and the excitement around him was remarkable; everyone was vying for his attention—in fact, it had been hard to connect with him the whole week. He had this amazing energy and was a blast to be around, but it was almost as if his feet weren't on the ground.

That night, I never would have guessed how that four-minute sketch would end up changing my life. Today, more than twenty years later, it is popular enough that YouTube has a ten-hour-long loop of the three of us in that car, heads bopping to Haddaway, *with over twenty-two million views.*

Even though I'd found some immediate success with my sketches during that first half season on the show, I didn't feel stable enough to exhale. Like I said before, I wasn't nervous, but I wasn't necessarily optimistic, either. Lorne was obviously helping out when it came to airtime, but I still didn't feel like I'd made a decent connection with him. Every interaction I'd had with Lorne had been somewhere on the spectrum between a glance as he walked by me in the hallway and a single three-syllable sentence. I took some comfort in the fact that when I mentioned this to others, pretty much everyone reacted the same way: "That's just Lorne," they'd say, holding their forearms out and palms up in an elaborate shrug or rolling their eyes. It wasn't until twelve years later that head writer Steve Higgins told me something that explained almost every bizarre dynamic I experienced that first half season. Steve said the reason I was hired for the last six weeks of the season was to "light a fire under everybody." (Maybe that's why Norm Macdonald was always such a sweetheart to me . . .)

I left for LA the week after the season ended, even though I still had two weeks on my room at the Paramount. I suppose I could have used the time to look for an apartment, but I was leaving for a four-month summer break, and anyway, I wasn't sure whether I was going to be back. You didn't find out until a month before the new season, when your agent called to tell you if your contract had been picked up or not. Again, everyone told me not to worry, "Of course you'll be back!" they'd say, "Kattan, come on!" But really, you just never know. Maybe after my initial rejection, I was more aware of that than most.

When the time came, and I found out that not only was I going back to New York, but I was going as a full-fledged regular cast member, no longer a featured player, it was the most surreal, intoxicating feeling. On one of my first days back, I remember passing *SNL*'s then executive producer Mike Shoemaker, who is now the showrunner and producer of *Late Night with Seth Meyers*. He was having dinner with his wife at the Mustard Seed restaurant in the lobby of the Paramount Hotel, my (until I found an apartment) New York home, and he stood up to give me this incredible hug. A year before, I'd been renounced, depressed, and driving Mrs. Koogle; now I was beginning to feel fearless again.

Chapter 7

CHRIS ON A HOT
TAR ROOF

Even though I had a few playmates on Mount Baldy—my fellow Mountain Boys—only one kid my age lived within a mile. Most of the time, it felt like I had the entire mountain to myself. Whenever I complained about being lonely, my mom would stress how important it was to "learn how to entertain myself." I became a prodigy in this particular arena. With a teeming population of twelve within a fifteen-mile radius, I really didn't have a choice.

My stepfather tried to engage with me, but he did this by regaling me with Gestalt's hilarious anecdotes on behavioral assimilation or tales of Brahms's charming struggles to compose while growing up in Hamburg, when I would have preferred to play a simple game of throwing rocks at each other, one of the more popular activities available to children on the mountain. And as if actually living in near-total isolation wasn't enough, we barely ever left the forested confines of Mount Baldy for a visit to civilization. I knew civilization was out there, because when Friday came around, I'd be back in that small, dark theater on Melrose Avenue with my dad, watching Phil Hartman perform long-form improv as "Chick Hazard, Private Eye," but it was like my parents occupied two different dimensions. It was hard to believe they could possibly exist on the same planet, much less both within the Los Angeles metropolitan area.

Don't get me wrong, our home was beautiful—my mom would never have let us inhabit uninspiring surroundings, and she poured her creativity into our living space. But during the week, we barely ever left the goddamn house! No movies, no dinners out, no nothing. Every two years my mom took me to buy new clothes for the school year, but that was as close as we got to a family outing.

Even errands were rare—my mom drove to Vons every couple of weeks for groceries, and, of course, I begged to go with her every time. She was an amazing cook—and still is. Unfortunately, when it came to lunchtime, our tastes weren't exactly simpatico, and I opened my lunch pail at school every day with a mix of dread and resignation, like I was facing a firing squad. Other kids would get a peanut butter and jelly sandwich and a bag of Cheetos or a Ding Dong; I had two pieces of whole grain bread with the density of a neutron star, stuffed with cucumbers and a handful of watercress my mother had plucked from a nearby stream. And yes, of course it was all very healthy and today would probably cost around seventeen dollars at Whole Foods, but I just wanted some Pop Rocks! Of course I heard the story about the kid who drank a bunch of Coca-Cola, ate twelve bags of Pop Rocks, went on the Colossus at Six Flags Magic

Mountain, and then exploded. I still wanted them! I just wanted some-thing wrapped in plastic with a fucking cartoon image on it, like a Twinkie dressed up as a musketeer with a mustache or a cowboy with a lasso.

We rarely had visitors because we lived off an unpaved fire road, and driving on this road for a mile was hard on a sedan. If your vehicle didn't have four-wheel drive or the word "Baja" in its name, it was pretty much fucked. But my mom and Marc did have friends, and maintaining these relationships occasionally forced them from the mountain. A few days before Christmas of 1979, one of Marc's psychotherapist friends took us out to dinner. It's the only time I remember us going to dinner in a restau-rant, which may or may not be related to what happened afterward, when we were back at the psychotherapist's house and someone called asking to talk to Marc right away.

"Marc, what is it?" my mom asked when he'd hung up the phone.

"Our house is on fire."

Driving back up the mountain, I curled in the corner of the VW van, lis-tening to my mom and stepdad as they listed all the important items they may have lost.

"What about Winni?" I interrupted in terror. Winni was our per-fectly spotted Dalmatian. (Yes, we lived on a fire road with a Dalmatian, mascot of firehouses everywhere. We still didn't see this coming.)

When we pulled up to our house, three massive fire trucks blocked our driveway. The firefighters were attempting to save what was left of our cabin, pumping water at it from hoses attached to the trucks. They didn't have an unlimited supply, since one of the other conveniences Mount Baldy lacked was fire hydrants. I jumped out of the van and went looking for Winni. When I finally found her, she came running toward me in a panicked fury with her tail ablaze. (Actually, not true, but that's what I told people. I guess because it'd be a cool visual?)

Four hours later, when the fire was finally contained, there was nothing left of our home but a couple of soot-covered rooms. Most of it was just . . . gone. When I was able to get into my bedroom to survey the damage there, it looked like the abandoned snow-covered house in *Dr. Zhivago,* except completely black. I picked up a charred *Empire Strikes Back* action figure from my charcoaled bookshelf and noticed the perfectly clear footprints left underneath. With the exception of a few books and some silverware, every item we had bought or created was destroyed.

For the next few nights, we stayed at a friend's home about seven miles north in the village of Mount Baldy. On our second night there, the temperature plummeted. Like quite a few homes in Mount Baldy, this one didn't have heating; there was a potbellied stove, but it was in the living room, and the room where I was sleeping was frigid. My mom found a heating pad in the laundry room, and being the loving mother that she was, slipped it under my bedsheets. Hours later, after I fell asleep, I dreamt of being on a small boat with a tiger, very much like the setting in the film *Life of Pi.* In my dream, the boat caught on fire, and then the fire spread to my legs. Suddenly, I woke, elbowed myself up, and saw flames dancing right between my real, non-dream-life legs. I leapt off the mattress, ran to the kitchen for a glass of water, and threw it onto the flames. (The moral of this story, I suppose, is if you're going to use an electric heating pad manufactured in the 1970s, you might not want to turn that dial up to ten.)

For many people, the story might continue with their family picking up the pieces and attempting to return to normalcy as quickly as possible, the house rebuilt by a hired contractor and construction team or maybe even sold off. Instead, we pretty much rebuilt it ourselves, like

Swiss Family Robinson. Thanks to having fire insurance, we could afford a three-man construction crew to do some of the highly skilled labor, but my mom, Marc, and I worked on it in some manner almost every day for about four years. To this day, the palms of my hands are as rough as a blacksmith's. I truly believe it's from carrying stacks upon stacks of burnt wood beams along with all that nailing and hammering, sawing, stripping, painting, plastering, sanding, chiseling, and so on we did as a family of do-it-yourselfers. Along with calloused palms that remove the need for oven mitts, I also got the lovely nickname "E.T. hands" in high school.

Less than a week after the fire, we moved back into our house, such as it was. Our water tank, half a mile away, was finally functioning. One bathroom worked, and the three of us lived in oppressive togetherness in one of the more habitable rooms. Spending years living and working in the hollowed-out, skeleton-like remains of your former home is extremely depressing, especially when you're also seeing your parents weeping every other day and becoming increasingly downtrodden and overwhelmed by the work they had taken on. Whenever I come across faded Polaroids of Mom and Marc from between 1979 and 1984, they always seem to be scowling. In some photos, even the dog looks resentful.

I never asked much about it then, but I knew finances were a big part of the reason they were doing this to themselves. At the same time, I think it was also just the way they were—or should I say, the way we were. *Memories . . .*

As one half of my family was rebuilding our home on Mount Baldy, I watched my father get remarried, then re-divorced. Dad wasn't the best "how to" example when it came to relationships, and his second marriage was no exception. He met his second wife while attending a weekend

EST seminar. EST, short for Erhard Seminars Training, was very popular during the '70s. It was basically a cult that offered a two-weekend brainwashing in exchange for a lot of your money. Participants were preached a tangled combo of existentialism and feel-good narcissistic solipsism for four sixteen-hour sessions with two bathroom breaks and no food or water, with lots of role-playing so they could throw grown-up tantrums and call each other "asshole." My dad later created a character at the Groundlings based on someone who had gone through EST. His character just kept saying "Thank you for sharing" to everyone.

Dad, the hypochondriac, was all over this latest self-help craze and naturally assumed that I could benefit as well. He shared what he'd learned, but I abandoned it pretty quickly—the second I tried it out around my mom and she yelled, "Stop playing the victim like your father, for Christ's sake!" But if Dad was doing some self-help thing, he would always include me; it was his version of bonding. At one point, he brought me to a John Bradshaw inner-child seminar, after which he convinced me that I needed to establish a stronger relationship with my own inner child—my outer child, at the moment, being all of nine years old. Before I'd ever kissed a girl for the first time, Dad was already trying to educate me on why all women eventually would leave me. (Somehow, everything always came back to the problems he had with his mother.)

I'm not saying everything my dad taught me was negative—he had a lot of motivationally positive aspects as well. My mom always said that if a pool was freezing cold, Dad would be the first one to jump in, and I actually think that was a great way to approach a lot of choices in life. But it had a definite downside for my dad when it came to marriages, investments, important legal matters, and overall common sense. Maybe he should have seen the ominous writing on the wall the day he and my stepmom got married, when a huge-ass bumblebee stung my left eye while I, the ring bearer, carried the ring up the makeshift aisle on a pillow during the ceremony in his backyard. My new stepmother, as my dad would discover, was a welter of neuroses, and their relationship became unhealthy and abusive almost immediately.

One time while visiting my father, I went to the garage to watch a movie and opened the door to find my stepmom lying flat on her back on the floor. Her skirt was raised just enough to see her hand gripping one end of what looked a lot like a microphone held to her private area. Absolutely petrified, I did an immediate about-face and scurried back to my bedroom with my stepmom chasing after me.

"Do you know what I was doing?" she asked, after finally convincing me to *sit down and hear her out for just one minute.*

I wanted nothing to do with this conversation, but I knew the sooner I answered her, the sooner this unnecessary explanation would end.

"You were recording yourself, but you were doing it down here," I said, pointing to my crotch.

"No, Chris. What you saw is called a vibrator."

She then went on to explain that when a woman isn't being satisfied in her relationship, she often seeks other means of pleasure. Keep in mind, I was nine years old. She went on to explain orgasms—what they were and why they were important to a woman. She was so insistent on educating me on the topic of female self-pleasure that every time I raised my hands to cover my ears, she would pull my arms back down to make sure I heard every single detail.

A few months later, after what was only one of many unsuccessful attempts at hashing out their issues, my furious stepmother marched out of the house in the middle of a screaming match. My dad was close behind, and he became so angry that he pulled off one of his slippers and threw it at her. When my stepmom found out that his violent slipper beating might give her grounds to sue him, she kicked my dad out of his own house. The subsequent divorce process dragged on for almost four years. Finally, around the time our house on Mount Baldy was completed, my dad got his own home back. And my stepmom? Well, if you haven't guessed already, she eventually found happiness in a career writing children's books.

In school after the fire, I barely talked. I remember feeling dead inside, going through the motions with no interest in anything around me. I was so unable to focus that the teacher would have to wave at me to get my attention during class. My school eventually suggested that I be taken out of class for a few months.

During the time I was out of school, we worked on the roof of our house, putting on a fresh coat of hot tar before placing the asphalt shingles on top—every kid's favorite way to spend the day. But I discovered that as the hot tar dripped off the sides of the roof onto the ground, it would harden, drying into all different shapes and sizes and creating the perfect action figures to play with, at least now that all my real toys were gone. You could play army games by pretending that one bulky piece of tar was a US tank barreling down the cobblestone streets of Aachen, Germany, during WWII. Or games of fantasy, pretending that one piece of tar with sharp edges was a dark, evil dragon flying through the skies before attacking a village of innocent people. Not all my tar games were centered around anger. I also taped a blue jay feather to the "head" of one long piece of tar and pretended it was Superman.

I barely remember most of those few years after the fire, rebuilding the Mount Baldy house and watching Dad's marriage corrode at the seams. I pretty much checked out and surrendered to darkness. The one thing that I was able to find some solace in was this—creating something out of nothing.

When I returned to school, I brought my tar-made action figures to play with, and this kid Troy, who was an absolute asshole and a real bully, snatched my tar from my hands during recess and wouldn't give it back. That was what finally broke the near silence I'd retreated to. In the middle of class that afternoon, after I grew tired of him teasing me from across the classroom while we were taking a test, I marched over to where Troy was seated at his desk, leaned into his smug bucktoothed face, and yelled, "Give me back my tar!" This was of course years before Mel Gibson yelled "Give me back my son!" into his phone in the movie *Ransom*.

I wasn't exactly the most threatening kid in the schoolyard. In fact, I only got into one physical fight during my entire school career, and it was with the same snide dip turd, Troy. I was playing a rather intense round of four square, and you know how vicious that game can get. Troy kept throwing the ball *at* me instead of *to* me. Finally, I snapped. I mean, I just went big-time "cray" on him.

"Do you wanna fight?" I shouted. "Is that what you want? Huh?! Do you want some?! Huh!? Is that what you want?!"

Because I was too young to know how to properly hit someone in the face, I grabbed him by the throat—he was about two feet taller than me—and hissed, "Let's go fight in the office!" I still remember how intense my hissing was, because the air I exhaled through my clenched teeth was so unexpectedly cold that it hurt the insides of my teeth. I'm serious. (Could my teeth be my version of Achilles' heel? Who knows.)

Anyway, our eyes were locked as we made our way across the playground, using only our peripheral vision—under the swing sets across the chalk-graffitied asphalt and around the monkey bars, all while maintaining a grip on each other's necks. All the way to the principal's office, kids were holding the doors open for us, commanding, "Make room! Make room everybody! They're gonna fight in the office!" Finally, after at least a solid two minutes of testosterone-fueled absurdist theater, we found ourselves in the office, trying to strangle each other directly in front of the secretary at her desk and the school principal, who was seated at his desk on the other side of the office, trying to talk on the phone.

"What are you two doing? And why does it have to be in here?" asked the addled and slightly exasperated principal.

But I wasn't going to answer him. How could I? And what kind of a question was that anyway? I wanted to show everyone how much Troy deserved to be punched in the face, and yet part of me was thinking: *If I get my ass kicked, I want Troy to get in serious trouble for it.* Hence, let's go fight in the principal's office, I guess. Honestly, I don't know what the fuck I was doing. Nobody did. But you have to admit it was a valiant attempt; at what, I'm not quite sure. Anyway, Troy and I both got detention, but I made myself believe that I'd proved a point, and that was good enough for me.

My cozy depression morphed into insecurity as I reached my early teens. Minor concerns became major, like whether my new pair of slightly tight jeans made me look like I had camel toe. I always dreamt of having a real, authentic Members Only jacket or a black-and-white-checkered Vans skateboard hat, the kind with the weird foreign-legion flaps in the back.

But my mom was a strict nonbeliever in fashion labels. Instead, she made most of my clothes. My mom was insanely talented, but she couldn't understand how important name-brand labels were for newly fad-aware teens. The preppy fashion phase was just beginning, and when I pleaded for a short-sleeved Lacoste shirt, one I could wear with the collars straight up, Mom's response was, "Why should I waste money when I can make you the same shirt and sew a stupid alligator on it myself?" She did have a point.

I also dreamt of owning a mountain bike—like a bitchin' BMX or a radical Diamondback or a even a gnarly Mongoose like other kids had, some kind of ten-speed mountain bike that would actually serve a purpose for a dauntless energetic kid like me. Miraculously, this time my mom was more sympathetic to my pleading, and for my next birthday, I was given a bike. Yes, it was an actual bicycle! And the ugliest bicycle that you can possibly imagine. (Nope—even uglier.) It looked strong, strong enough to hold a very big person (which I was clearly not), but good Christ, was it ugly. It had springs the size of a Slinky on both sides of it for I don't know *what* the fuck. There was no insignia or name brand anywhere on the bike, just one sticker near the bottom of the frame that read "This bicycle has one speed." Because the bike was clearly used, Mom and Marc had tried their best to freshen it up by spray-painting it a vulgar baby blue. It was bulky, awkward, thirty pounds too heavy, and had a basket in front of the handlebars that didn't come off, which I know because I tried to remove it when my mom wasn't around—I didn't want her to feel bad, because I loved her for buying something that I'd asked for. Especially when I knew we were far from financially stable.

On the first day I could, I rode my garish bike for three miles along the fire road to school. During recess, this obnoxious kid pointed at it and asked if that was my new bike. I said "yes," and he grabbed it and threw it over the edge of a cliff, and that was the end of my bike.

I went to Mt. Baldy School for nine years, kindergarten through eighth grade, with about fifty other kids. Lots of mornings, I got a ride with my best friend's mother. Varan was my best friend mostly because he was the only kid who lived somewhat nearby. He's the only person named Varan I've ever met and probably the only one I ever will. Our moms traded off carpooling every other week, and one morning when I got to Varan's house at seven thirty, I was asked to sit on the living room couch next to their dogs and wait a few minutes while his mom finished getting ready. Varan was the youngest of three brothers who had been living on Mount Baldy since they were born, just them and their mom. Compared to other kids they were . . . let's just say, *different*. Of course, anyone who grows up in a secluded mountain setting might turn out a little different. (Ahem.) Anyway, their mother came out of the shower and was walking around without any clothes on. This was the first time I had ever seen a woman's completely naked body, and it made me feel incredibly awkward. So, I politely covered my eyes. Varan's older brother responded to this by threateningly putting the edge of a knife to my stomach. With a sick villainous look on his face, he asked, "You like seeing my mom naked?" His mom walked back across the living room, still dripping wet but now with a towel wrapped around her waist, leaving her voluptuous breasts totally exposed, and said—slightly annoyed but not at all shocked—"Ian! Come on. Knock it off."

(Apparently when Varan's brother grew up, he actually murdered someone. It was a surprise when I heard the news because I always thought he would go on to become a social worker or something.)

Anyway, when I ran a mile over to Varan's house in the morning instead of following the road, I took what wasn't even a trail; it was just a route I created and ran along every morning on the weeks I rode to school with Varan's mom. It was completely unsafe, but I had a ridiculous amount of energy and agility when I was a kid, and I loved running down this ragged mountain trail. I had to jump over streams and land on rocks camouflaged with moss, leap from one unstable rock to another with one foot here and another foot there, do a spin, and then grab an oak tree branch and swing to the next rock. I moved something like Mowgli and Gene Kelly combined. I tried out different moves, pushing my alertness and dexterity as far as it would go. I never fell down or slipped and injured myself. Because I ran the same path for years, I developed a technique, a dance so perfect and complex that it somehow became a necessary part of my daily life growing up.

With the exception of a few barking dogs, nobody ever saw me doing this. Not my mom, not Varan, nobody. It was my secret dance of extreme crafted lunacy, on some level my own expression of what I learned from hours of watching Buster Keaton and Chaplin do stunts. It was a part of my unconscious, athletic mentality, something self-discovered and self-trained and unique to me.

Despite my growing physical prowess, I didn't have much interest in playing sports like basketball or football—"Shirts against skins!"— or anything. I was always the last kid chosen to be on someone's team. "I guess we're stuck with Kattan," they would say. But it didn't matter, because somewhere along the way I had become interested in something a lot more fascinating: girls. I wouldn't describe it as a pheromonal sexual thing, or even a juvenile pursuit of the answer to the "Why am I getting a boner?" question. No, I would describe it as obsession. An intense teenage crush on a different girl every two or three months. Not surprisingly, my infatuations were usually chosen from among the eye candy, the cutest and most popular girls in my class, but getting the girl wasn't the point, the point was the obsessing itself.

I became a helpless romantic with a very big imagination. I would construct fantasies about different scenarios, usually with the same small cast: the girl I was currently obsessing over, the nemesis or bad guy—i.e., whoever it was I currently hated—and, of course, me. So what if the story line was predictable? My fantasies had a rather high production value, so the sets, location, and lighting were always compelling. Sometimes I would put myself in a harrowing action scene where I had only minutes to save my beloved from the perils of the villainous bad guy. And my well-staged fantasies always included music. Not the typical epic and sweeping soundtrack score, nothing classical. Instead it was usually a doo-wop song that had a certain heart-tugging sadness, like "Earth Angel" by the Penguins or Roy Orbison's "Crying."

At recess, everyone couldn't wait to get out from behind their desks to run outside and play. (I sure do miss using that word "play." *Let's go outside and play! Did you ask your mom if you can come over and play?*) During the twenty-or-so minutes of recess, while other kids were dangling from the jungle gym or "playing" on the grassy field, what I liked to do the most was to sit alone on the swing set over by the sandlot and, being that I had one of the greatest gifts technology had given us—that's right, I had a Sony Walkman!—I would swing back and forth wearing my giant orange foam earmuff headphones, listening to melodic music and dreaming about my latest obsession. After school, I would lie in my bed at home with my head next to the portable boom box speaker and do the same thing, working myself into such a state of melodramatic attachment over my latest infatuation that I would cry. I don't know if this was common for someone my age—or anyone, actually—but I enjoyed it. Maybe it was unhealthfully therapeutic.

Even later, in high school, I always had a crush on somebody, and realism was never required. At one point, I had a hopeless crush on Marilyn Monroe, and she had been dead for over twenty years. "Norma Jean!" I would correct people. "Her name is Norma Jean!" Offscreen she'd been so troubled, and somehow, I thought I could have saved her from depression, taken care of her, and made her happy. I remember weeping while watching a Betamax videotape of a collection of Marilyn Monroe newsreels, one of which featured her coming out of a clinic after a miscarriage and being absolutely mobbed by photographers. When nobody was home and I was watching, I would sometimes yell out, "Leave her alone!" while sobbing.

In general, when it came to shared interests, I sometimes wondered if I had been born in the wrong era—maybe a side effect of my dad's influence, though Marc's lectures on Buddhism and whatnot probably didn't help. I didn't think there was anything wrong with me for having totally different interests than anyone else in my school, and yet I was frustrated that I couldn't find anyone who liked the same things. Once on a school field trip, some parents volunteered to help out with driving since the one bus was full. I sat in the back seat of a car with two other kids, and the mom driving turned the radio to K-EARTH 101, a popular oldies station. "The Lion Sleeps Tonight" was playing, and because I knew and loved it, I began to sing along to the falsetto part. The mom turned to me wide-eyed and impressed and said, "I can't believe you know this song!" Of course I knew the song. I knew it word for word. In fact, every song from the '50s and '60s played on that trip, I knew. It was like a scene from *Rain Man*.

The other kids in the car naturally thought I was an absolute weirdo, but at least I had found a person with whom I shared some interests. In fact, there were a lot of them, but they all were twice my age and usually female. That was the story of my life as a kid: I got along with the parents of the kids I went to school with much better than with the kids themselves. I once read somewhere how important it is that kids learn the tools to socialize and communicate between the ages of seven and eleven—the years that I wasn't around many other kids. Without a doubt, this had an effect on me.

One of the few movie character obsessions I had in common with other kids my age was Indiana Jones. My stepbrother Leif, Marc's oldest son, knew this, and on one of his visits he brought me the perfect gift: an actual, no-bullshitting-you, fifteen-foot-long bullwhip. Leif loved taking his shirt off to do Tae Kwon Do at six-thirty in the morning by the nearest streambed, Swayze *Road House* style. Once, when I was ten years old, I told Leif I was allergic to pollen. "I hope you're not allergic to pussy," he replied. I know, hilarious.

Anyway, this bullwhip was the single greatest toy any overimaginative loner Mountain Boy could have asked for. It was the real deal. Leif got it from Mexico, probably in trade for some old-fashioned Costa Mesa peyote. Who knows. I loved it. Loved it! And as if getting me the whip wasn't enough, Leif even taught me how to crack it like Indiana Jones. Like a very loud snap. "It's all in the wrist," he said. (By the way, is it just me or does it seem like there are an awful lot of things that are supposedly "all in the wrist"?) Anyway, after a few months, I got so good that with a flick of my wrist, I could wrap the end of the whip around a thick tree branch and swing across a pretty good distance.

I decided to try out another cool visual from the movie—the way Indiana Jones sent the whip twisting around Marion Ravenwood's waist and used it to pull her toward him and into his arms. Two Mount Baldy girls around my age named Phoenix and Kelsey loved reenacting that scene with me! I brought the bullwhip with me to school and showed off some of my Indy tricks with my whip during recess. It was so impressive, girls actually lined up for a chance to have me wrap the whip around their waist and pull them into my arms. I was finally coming out of my shell.

Then one day, Phoenix's mother came to see my mom. "Well, I don't mind it," she said to my mother, "but Kelsey's mom feels differently. She's telling everybody that your son has been whipping our daughters with a bullwhip." Of course, when she put it like that, it didn't sound very good.

The other modern obsession that began to take hold—and that would get me in a lot less trouble than whipping girls after school—was *Saturday Night Live*. Eddie Murphy changed my life. This was when my desire to grow up and be a performer began to become less vague, and I started to feel the pieces—those weekends digesting comedy with my dad and my own specific talents—finally slipping into place. Before *48 Hours* and *Beverly Hills Cop*, what he did on *SNL* from 1980 to 1984 forced nearly every other comedian to back off from the limelight to watch in awe, waiting for him to stop raising the bar so that it would be safe for them to emerge in front of an audience again with a new and improved bit. Eddie exploded into stardom so fucking fast at such a young age, it was ridiculous. While on the show, I heard many times from other writers that Lorne wished he had some credit in making Eddie a star, even though he was already credited with "discovering" some of the greatest comedians of all time. But like Lady Gaga once said—or maybe she said it a few times after Madonna once said it. Or maybe Madonna said it a few times herself. Or maybe . . . you know what, never mind. Anyway, someone once (or multiple times) said, "There could be one hundred people in the room and ninety-nine of them believe in you. Except there's one person that doesn't believe in you. You're only going to remember that one person." Murphy was with the cast while Lorne was on a five-year hiatus. I always wondered whether, if Lorne had been there, he would have tried to control him by cutting down his sketches so as not to lose his rising star so quickly.

"Gumby," "James Brown Celebrity Hot Tub Party," "Mister Robinson's Neighborhood," "Mr. White," and "Buckwheat's Assassination" were probably Eddie's most memorable sketches, but the moment that I remember as life-changing came on December 15, 1984, when I saw him do a character called "Shabazz K. Morton." In that sketch, called "Black History Minute," as he was addressing the camera, something amazing happened. It started when Eddie flubbed his line.

"A black man named George Washington Carver developed a new method of soul . . . *soil* . . .improvement through crop rotation."

A few audience members laughed at the blooper, and Eddie, still in character, said aggressively to the camera: "So, I messed up—*shut up*! . . . Stop clapping before y'all make me smile!"

When Eddie said, "So, I messed up—shut up!" it felt like all my blood went racing to my brain. It's hard to explain why that moment affected me the way it did. I had never in my life seen a comedian so comfortable and confident about acknowledging a fuck up. That moment spoke right to me, and it said: *Look what you can do. Look at the power you can have on live television in front of millions of people.* As long as you remain confident and relaxed, you can change the rules permanently. You can make a mistake into a victory.

After Eddie Murphy's breakthrough, from then on, everyone was allowed to break the fourth wall. You can make comedy history when you're a cast member on *SNL*. It was an incredibly powerful opportunity, and one every cast member had, but at the time it seemed like Eddie was the only one using it, like he was on another level that no one else even attempted to reach. Not taking advantage of that opportunity seemed like something a person might regret for the rest of their life, but maybe Murphy was the only one who cared enough to look like he didn't care. He often made the rest of the cast seem like an unmemorable group of supporting players. I have no idea how he felt about his fellow cast members, but I'm almost positive he never compared himself to them, or worried about what they were doing or what they thought of him, because if he had, he never would have been secure enough to do what he did.

When Eddie Murphy yelled *"shut up!"* at the *SNL* audience, I was fourteen years old. I decided then that I knew exactly what I was going to do with my life. I wasn't just going to perform, I was going to perform *there*. I didn't how I was going to get on the show or what that path would even look like, but I knew that *Saturday Night Live* was where I belonged.

Chapter 8

"SO, WHAT DO YOU WANT? YOU WANT ME TO FU . . ."

orne Michaels said this about writing on *SNL*, not directly to me but in an interview: "If it works, it's yours. If it doesn't work, it's yours." Luckily, I'd started *SNL* on a creative roll, and that roll lasted into the beginning of the 1996–97 season, my first as a regular cast member.

The night of the second show of Season 22—my eighth show so far—as I was hopping two steps at a time down to the eighth floor, I passed Lorne on his way up to his office on nine. He stopped in the stairwell and,

I shit you not, pulled out his ChapStick and applied some before speaking to me for almost the first time ever.

"Nice work on 'Bellhops.'" Not only was it four whole words, it was four whole words of *praise*. A moment to brood over.

Lisa Kudrow had hosted that night. She was promoting this not-very-popular show—*Friends*, I think it was called. Or *Besties*? Something like that. Anyway, I'd first gotten to know Lisa back when I was in a summer improv class that she taught at the Groundlings. A lot of alumni taught classes to make some extra money. This was around the time she was going out with Conan O'Brien, and I remember how supportive and particular she was with me, even years before I made it into the Sunday show. On *SNL* that week, two sketches I wrote made it on. One was a Suel Forrester sketch that hadn't been done at the Groundlings and was the first Suel sketch specifically written for camera. In it, Lisa played a helpless stewardess trying to land an airplane while communicating with Suel, this time an air traffic controller, who once again spoke only gibberish.

"You're gonna *hadda lada plaay,* or else you're gonna die!'

The other sketch I got in the show was one I wrote with Will and Jim Breuer in which the three of us played bellhops working in the lobby of a five-star hotel. The idea was simple: whenever a hotel guest trustingly gave us their luggage, or a postman dropped off a FedEx package, we would say we'd "gladly take care of it," and then, as soon as they left . . . we immediately destroyed whatever they'd entrusted to our "outstanding" care by throwing it against the wall, tossing it behind us, or stomping on it.

We came up with the idea while hanging out by the elevators on seventeen next to a tall stack of large, empty watercooler bottles. While walking by, I accidentally knocked one over, and for some reason (what am I saying—of course the reason was to get a laugh), I reacted by grabbing it by the lid and throwing it against the wall. Breuer thought it was funny, grabbed another watercooler bottle and did the same thing, but broader. Jim and I kept throwing watercooler bottles all over the place. Then Will walked over from McKay's office and got in on it, and pretty much everything Will does physically is funny. But what made it worth writing up as a sketch, to me, was the sound the bottles made when they hit the walls. It was loud, it was obnoxious, and I loved it. At read through there wasn't room to demonstrate without giving some poor intern a concussion, so we ended up performing the sketch halfway in the hallway and halfway in the room. If the room couldn't quite get all the physical stuff, they could at least see that it was noisy and loud and it was going to be funny. Which it really was. On Saturday night, I honestly think the sketch turned out closer to a 1930s physical comedy than any other sketch I've done. Even though the sound of the loud water bottles was what had inspired the sketch, it worked even better on camera with the luggage joke. I even threw a perfect pitch where I chucked a suitcase over my shoulder without looking and took out a light on the wall. It is still one of my favorite sketches I've ever done on the show, and the unexpected compliment from Lorne later that night suggested that he felt the same way.

I'd introduced Mr. Peepers the week before in the first show of the season, when Tom Hanks hosted, but it was actually another sketch from that week that stood out the most. It was just on the heels of the Summer Olympics, and we'd somehow gotten the tiny gold medal winner and gymnast Kerri Strug to fly out and make a guest appearance on "Weekend Update," even though she was still walking around on crutches. In case you've blocked out the events of the 1996 Olympic gymnastics competition for personal reasons, let me refresh your memory: Kerri Strug became a legend when she stunned (and slightly horrified) the world after landing this incredible vault literally *right* after having severely sprained and torn the ligaments of her ankle on her first of two vaulting attempts. Her feat earned the US squad their first-ever gymnastics team gold, and she was famously carried to the medal podium in triumph by her coach, the great Béla Károlyi.

Robert Smigel, the writer behind *SNL*'s infamous cartoons "TV Funhouse" and "Ambiguously Gay Duo" (which was voiced by Steve Carell and Stephen Colbert), was really responsible for making the sketch work. Smigel is one of the best writers I've ever collaborated with (and I'm not just saying that because he wrote two voices for me in *Hotel Transylvania 2*), but my favorite talent of his has to be his work on *Conan* as the puppeteer-voice of "Triumph, the Insult Comic Dog." ("For me to poop on!")

Anyway, after I gave Smigel a taste of my Kerri Strug impersonation, he suggested I should play her fictitious twin brother, Kippy. So that Saturday afternoon, I dressed exactly like Kerri and sat next to her for a "Weekend Update" closing spot alongside anchor Norm Macdonald. It was one of those sketches that you could just tell was going to work the first time we did it at the run-through. The dialogue exchange between Kerri and me was only a page long, but when we performed, it took a full three minutes to get through because the audience was laughing so much.

And then it happened. The unthinkable. Norm Macdonald actually laughed on the show. At me! And believe me, I'm the last person in the world he wanted to be laughing at. It was a real laugh that made him stumble over his lines. Yep, he actually "broke character." It was a great start to the season. And probably the official beginning of the Norm and Kattan bickering that would continue until a few seasons later, when NBC unfairly fired him from the show.

Four days later, the sketch landed a full page in *People*—my first national magazine appearance. When I saw it, I remembered the time Dana Carvey was on *Letterman* and the audience went crazy just at the mention of his Church Lady character (another Smigel collaboration). "Wow!" Carvey responded, "the power of media." My brief turn as Kippy Strug ended up making it to CNN and is still used in basically every broadcast of the Olympic Games.

I began to receive all kinds of positive feedback from the world outside of the show. I think the appropriate word would be "buzz." In the third week of the season, *Access Hollywood* did a whole segment on me, and I didn't even have a publicist. Everything seemed to be going so well, yet I wasn't hustling to get anything or to be anywhere other than where I was. Lorne even got me a spot on *Late Night with Conan O'Brien* (where he was a producer at the time) as a second guest, on after Samuel L. Jackson. My first talk show. (Yes, I was nervous. Are you kidding me?)

But the incredible high of making it to *SNL*, getting sketches on every show week after week, and that feeling of becoming increasingly confident couldn't last forever, like an upward roller coaster that has to tilt down again eventually. Perhaps it all began to dissipate as early as the third show that fall. Bill Pullman was the guest host, and Will and I did another sketch that we'd originally done at the Groundlings. We titled it "AT&T," and in the sketch we played two Southern female telemarketing phone operators. So, naturally, we were in drag, finally. We were each wearing what I would say was probably a taffeta day dress, circa 1905. But there wasn't really any physical comedy in the sketch; instead, we sat at a switchboard that wasn't there, because we were facing camera, sometimes getting out of our seats to walk to the back and scream, "Where's my cheese Danish?! I want my cheese Danish!" in scratchy, high-pitched Southern accents. We were chosen to be the first sketch of the night, but it was the first sketch I did on the show that did not go over well with the audience. Not well at all. Even worse, it turned out that the man who had my back, who believed in me, who fought for my sketches to be in the show, was leaving. It was Fred Wolf's last night on *SNL*. Oh fuck.

The next episode was hosted by Dana Carvey, and I kept wondering how Fred's absence might affect the show for me. Was I being silly to think he was the only one in that room that really fought for me? Well—surprise, surprise—this was the first week of my entire run thus far that I didn't get a sketch in. Not even in Wednesday night's preliminary lineup. Not one. I know I shouldn't bitch about it, and I didn't (at least I don't *think* I did). Everyone had a light show now and then. But unfortunately, this was the beginning of a very rough back-to-back six-episode streak of me getting pretty much zero airtime without any explanation. To put this in perspective, the number of shows I'd appeared in was quickly in danger of being eclipsed by the number of shows I hadn't. Fred had been looking out for me, and with him gone, it suddenly seemed like no one was. I couldn't stop obsessing about who in Lorne's office during the lineup decisions didn't want to put my sketches in anymore. Who wasn't a fan? Could it be all of them? Was I just being paranoid? I sure did hope so.

There was actually one reason for my airtime drought that made sense to me at the time. Out of the six episodes I was absent from, five were hosted by former *SNL* cast members: Dana Carvey, Chris Rock, Robert Downey Jr., Phil Hartman, and Martin Short. I'd started to learn that when alumni hosted—or, I should say, alumni with popular recurring characters—they'd usually come into the pitch meeting already knowing what they wanted to do on the show. Almost like a "Best of," really.

Obviously, this didn't sound like quite as much fun to the writers and other cast members, but after hearing everybody's ideas, Dana was going to do Church Lady sketches and Mike Myers would do "Wayne's World." This is what the viewers expected to see again; any fan would. Otherwise they'd be saying "Well, why didn't he do the blah blah guy?" In practice, though, this meant the guest hosts created a lot of pressure on themselves, because it seemed so vital that their sketches and recurring characters worked just as well as they had back when they were in the cast. The point is: when alumni were hosting, part of the lineup was a given, especially for Lorne, who loved being nostalgic and knew how important it was for the audience and the show's place in history.

Once again, this proved to me the value in having recurring characters. By the time the second part of Season 22 came around, I was growing accustomed to my sketch ideas not getting chosen, at least not the ones with new characters. Occasionally, I'd be cast in a fun role in someone else's sketch, or I'd do a sketch I wrote with Will, like a "Shop at Home Network" parody where we would sell *Star Wars* memorabilia like Jawa ashtrays and a Chewbacca baseball card and Mark Hamill himself. Of course, we got to do some screaming. (Will screaming was always, always funny. Does anybody remember "Get off the shed?") But what finally broke my streak was bringing Mr. Peepers back for a second time, and most of the rest of the shows for me consisted of characters I had already introduced, like Peepers, Suel Forrester, or the Roxbury Guys. Don't get me wrong, who doesn't want to be Mr. Peepers and get the chance to hump Sting? You can just imagine how much fun Sting had being dry humped by a thirty-year-old guy. After all, when you think fun, you think Sting. But I still wanted to come up with new characters.

Finally, in the first part of 1997, a few more of my alter egos made their *SNL* debuts . . .

JOSH ZIMMERMAN, HORNY HUSBAND OF LAURA ZIMMERMAN
(PLAYED BY CHERI OTERI)

The Zimmermans, or "the sex couple" as they were often called, were this sexually charged married couple that Cheri and I did back when we were in the Sunday show at the Groundlings. They were basically a healthy, happy suburban couple who had a surprisingly amazing sex life and managed to turn every situation sexual—I guess you could call it a type of role-playing maybe?—resulting in the discomfort/envy of those around them. A lot of the laughs came from the suggestive wordplay between Cheri and me, as we'd manage to sound completely filthy without actually uttering anything censorable. We'd end up in some sexual, compromising position, with my face shoved up against hers, and as both our lips quivered, I would say in the most passionate tone I could: "So, what do you want? You want me to fu. . . Huh? You want me to fu . . . *find* the right words?"

I have to admit, even *almost* saying the sentence "You want me to fuck you" was pretty risky at the time. What I found most memorable about performing the Zimmermans wasn't just the physical comedy that Cheri and I pulled off, but the ease of our back-and-forth banter, which came from that Groundlings-rooted chemistry.

For the second appearance of the characters, Molly Shannon and guest host Matthew Broderick played neighbors invited over for dinner.

"So, Laura, how long have you and Josh been together?" Molly asks.

"Seven years this month," I say.

"Uh-oh. Seven year itch," jokes Broderick's nice guy character.

"Oh, don't you worry about that, he knows what to do when I get an itch," Cheri says. "As a matter of fact, honey, I have an itch right now. Oooh."

"What do you want me to do about it?" I ask. We lustily stare at each other.

"What do you *think* I want you to do about it?" Cheri says, starting to move out of her seat toward me.

"You want a little of this? A little of that?"

We get more and more hot and bothered as I scratch her hip with a finger.

"Daddy's gonna work."

"Go to work, Daddy!"

"Daddy's working hard."

"Punch your clock, Daddy!"

As soon as Oteri sounds like she's having an orgasm, all the while repeating a phrase that sounds an awful lot like "push that cock," she stops and says, "Oooh, you got it," and then sits back down abruptly, like nothing unusual has happened.

"You know how it is," we tell our gaping neighbors. Molly Shannon glares at Broderick with pure hatred. "Yeah," she says, "I know how it is."

I wasn't surprised to hear that the network censors weren't the biggest fans of the sketch. What did surprise me was when Steven "fucking" Spielberg and his lovely wife, Kate Capshaw, a.k.a. Willie Scott in *Indiana Jones and the Temple of Doom*, came up to me a few months later and not only said that they "both really enjoyed the 'sex couple' on the show," but then literally acted out the "What do you want? You want me to fu . . ." bit, by heart, nearly verbatim, right in front of me. (Believe it or not, Julia Roberts also acted out part of the "sex couple" sketch for

me while bowling at Jerry's Deli on Ventura Blvd at the wrap party for
Erin Brockovich.)

I remember reading an interview that David Spade did for *Rolling Stone* around that time, in which he was talking about the difference between his days on the show and the present, and how much more you could get away with in terms of the network censors, and he used our sketch as an example of something they'd never have been able to get away with in his day. We brought Josh and Laura back a third time when Ben Stiller hosted a Halloween episode. It was probably the best of the Zimmermans sketches, partly because Stiller was always so good as the innocent boyfriend caught in a situation that he didn't exactly sign up for, like in *Flirting with Disaster*. In that episode, I made bobbing for apples look like I was simulating wearing a bondage ball gag, and while Cheri tried to help me uncork a champagne bottle that I was holding, I kept saying, "Stop talking. Just touch it! Just touch it!" And then, "Here it comes! Here it comes! Here it comes!" But the part that NBC had the toughest time with was after a number of strokes, when the champagne cork finally popped and the fizz came spilling out everywhere, and Cheri rubbed it all over her chest and around her mouth.

Spade was right. But somehow, I guess in the name of laughs, and with Lorne's help, we got away with every suggestive physical joke and verbal euphemism. The energy behind our sex games in the sketch was often so convincing that Lorne was sure that Cheri and I had been "hooking up." (We never did. If we had, the sketch probably wouldn't have worked nearly as well.)

AZRAEL ABYSS, CO-HOST (WITH MOLLY SHANNON) OF "GOTH TALK"

Another recurring character I introduced in 1997 was Azrael Abyss, The Prince of Sorrow. The spark of the idea for Azrael came from a voice. It was high-pitched, a bit like Kerri Strug's brother, Kippy, but without the adolescent spunk.

At this point on the show I had learned it was easier to collaborate with a writer—or to at least have the character 60 to 70 percent done. Especially with Fred gone and having trouble getting a sketch in. A writer could help find a world for your character. If you had the voice and mannerisms, sometimes that might be enough. Or maybe you just nailed the voice and said a couple of sentences. For Azrael, that was it.

Dennis McNicholas, one of the Harvard graduates, was the writer I worked with for these sketches. He had joined *SNL* as a writer in '95, and he would go on to become head writer in 2001. He's probably best known for *The Ladies Man,* co-written with Tim Meadows. He left *SNL* in 2004 for a bit, but came back (something that's rarely done) to write for "Weekend Update" with Colin Jost.

Anyway, Dennis jumped in on my Azrael character idea since he had once been a goth guy himself, growing up in Florida during the 1980s.

"How about a talk show?" he asked me.

So the idea became two goth teens hosting a public-access talk show to goth up their very un-goth suburban lives, talking about such goth topics as the forlorn grind of their job at Cinnabon. Directors always liked talk show sketches. Beth McCarthy used to tell me "Goth Talk" was her favorite sketch because it never had any pre-tapes attached to it, and there was no need to build other sets.

McNicholas and I felt the best person to do "Goth Talk" with was Molly Shannon, and when we asked her, she was excited and fully committed, just like she was with everything she did. Molly and I had a lot of mutual respect for each other, so our chemistry was always strong.

It was nice to have one of the show's best writers scripting a sketch for you. McNicholas wrote all the "Goth Talk" sketches and never asked me to come up with any ideas other than creating the original characters and working out the format. Who knows, maybe it was a Harvard thing because Robert Carlock—also a Harvard graduate—had the same methods as a writer.

The first appearance of Azrael Abyss was with Rob Lowe, who by the way, loves smoking stogies with Lorne—who I never in my life saw smoke a cigar with anyone *but* Rob Lowe. Jeff Goldblum, Sarah Michelle Gellar, Steve Buscemi, and Lucy Lawless all appeared on "Goth Talk" over the next year. I think guest hosts liked to do those sketches because they could dress up and act ghoulish and stupid. For them, it felt like Halloween.

KYLE DEMARCO, INTERPRETIVE DANCER

If taking Mr. Peepers to the *SNL* stage came from a subconscious sexual desire to bring out the "best" in some of the more intimidating actresses in Hollywood, like Charlize Theron, Jennifer Aniston, and a very uncomfortable Katie Holmes, then I'm sure my character Kyle DeMarco came from a similarly insecure, if much less perverted, subconscious desire to interact with the some of the music industry's biggest stars, like Sting and Eminem.

Whenever I watched the show, years before I was a part of it, I was always impressed when a musical guest made an appearance in a sketch. There was something so exciting about it. Every time this life-altering event would occur, I would yell madly for whoever I was watching the show with, most likely my dad, should they happen to be out of the room. "Dad! Oh, my God! Aerosmith is on 'Wayne's World'!" or "Dad! Oh, my God! Madonna and Barbra Streisand are on 'Coffee Talk'!"

I was envious, too, when a cast member was doing one of their recurring characters in a sketch, and the musical guest would drop in and say a couple lines. It was as if that cast member was now the coolest member of the ensemble because they'd convinced the musical guest to step out of their comfort zone and walk into the live-TV comedy world.

It wasn't until I was on the show myself that I saw how often the musical guest had absolutely no interest in being in a sketch at all. Like when asked I asked Bono to do a phony NBC "The More You Know" educational promo at the end of the Mango sketch in which Val Kilmer portrayed a competitive stripper named the Dutch Boy. Whether that falls under the category of being racist against the Dutch, I don't know, but it was probably a smart call on Bono's part to say no. Plus, the idea was really just a lame excuse to have Bono in my sketch, and didn't really add anything. There, I said it!

By allowing them to avoid some of the apprehension of doing live television, it was really Andy Samberg who ended up having the perfect draw to get musical guests to do the show after his "Lazy Sunday" short with Chris Parnell debuted in 2005. Whether he was solo or paired up with his Lonely Island team of Akiva Schaffer and Jorma Taccone, his digital shorts changed the show's format forever. Samberg and Lonely Island were actually ordered to do a film short for every single show that aired. As fun as that may have seemed, I would think it might feel more like a time-consuming weekly assignment, regardless of the millions of Twitter followers it generates. By the way, I have 48.5K followers. Two months ago, I had 24.3K followers. After I reunited with Horatio, Tracy,

Jimmy, and surprise guest Ariana Grande to perform "I Wish It Was Christmas Today" on *The Tonight Show*—and posted a picture of Ariana and me puckering up to camera in Christmas sweaters, which led to her following me—I suddenly gained 24.2K followers. Isn't that interesting? (Well you know what? It means a lot to me, so there.)

That first full season I was on, I came up with a character and idea for a sketch format that usually succeeded by focusing on the musical guest. My character, Kyle DeMarco, was a terrible interpretive dancer driven to land the job of a backup dancer for the musical guest, who in the sketch was auditioning dancers for their upcoming tour. It was focused on the guest and their music but didn't ask much of them, since the punch line would be told by me in the language of dance. You never really worried about whether the musical guest could act or not, but we wrote their dialogue to be relatively easy, just in case.

The first Kyle DeMarco sketch I did was with Sting and his wife, Trudie Styler. That was the March 1997 show that Sting was hosting, and despite the major lack of enthusiasm Sting had while performing with me, surprisingly both my sketches got in. (The other sketch was the Peepers monologue.) Honestly, I don't think Sting really enjoyed doing either sketch, though. In fact, I don't recall having a single conversation with him that entire week—about anything. Not even small talk. He's the kind of guy who today would always be texting instead of engaging with you, except they didn't have iPhones back then, so while in rehearsal he'd stand next to me, but face away to avoid communication.

All that week I couldn't stop thinking about Sting and Trudie and the twelve-hour Tantric sex they had in their castle back home in merry ol' England. Trudie was very kind, and she seemed to really like me. Especially when I dry humped her husband. I think she kinda enjoyed it in the way someone might laugh when they see someone else trip and fall or spill something on themselves or be hit in the crotch with a baseball by a child. A few years later, I saw Sting backstage before a concert he was doing with the Police in Edmonton, Canada, of all places. I was doing a strangely cast Christmas movie with Carmen Electra, Tim Curry, and Patrick Swayze, who tragically discovered he'd been diagnosed with cancer while shooting. Not a fun thing to discover while shooting a Christmas movie in Canada. And that's all we really need to say about that movie. When I introduced myself, Sting had absolutely no idea who I was. It's like, *Hey Sting! It's me! I dry humped you. Remember? I mean, what the fuck, Sting?*

Anyway, my favorite part of the Sting/DeMarco sketch was my tank top that said, "STING ALL THE WAY!" But what worked the best was my "interpretive dancing." It began with Sting playing "Every Breath You Take" on a boom box on a table, where he and his wife sat. For the line "Every breath you take," I would heavily breathe on him; for "I'll be watching you," I would hide behind him and then pop my head out while looking through a pair of binoculars and whisper, "*I see you, Sting.*" When the music switched to "Roxanne," during the line, "You don't have to put on the red light," I pulled out a red light bulb from my gym bag and turned it on.

Months later, when I said in a Monday pitch meeting that I wanted to bring Kyle DeMarco back for a second time, Mike Shoemaker suggested that I include another cast member as a dance partner. We decided to add Chris Parnell, now making us the DeMarco Brothers. We went on to perform with Paul Simon, Britney Spears, Lenny Kravitz, and Eminem, but because of the price of using copyrighted music, those sketches are sadly also totally unavailable online and rarely show up in reruns. By far the most popular (since it's the only one available) of these is one we did with Bon Jovi members Jon Bon Jovi and Richie Sambora. Chris and I wore (very short) denim shorts and tank tops that read, "Shot Thru the Heart" and "And You're to Blame" on the front, and "These Took 3 Nights to Make" and "Yeah, and We Missed Felicity" on the back.

Lorne always placed the DeMarco sketches at home base, which is where the show's opening monologue took place. In order to hide the *SNL* band behind us, there was a set blocking them. If your sketch was at home base, you considered yourself lucky, since it was the best vantage point from which to be seen by the audience, making it also the easiest place to get laughs in the studio.

The Season 26, Episode 4 appearance of the DeMarco brothers, in November 2000, featured musical guest Paul Simon, with host Charlize Theron playing a generically written bitchy casting director. On Thursday of that week, the sketch had just finished going through rewrites at the writers' table run by Steve Higgins on the ninth floor (the rewrites up in the seventeenth-floor writers' room were run by Tina Fey). Marci Klein came in and said that Paul Simon wanted to go over a few things in the sketch before we blocked it, which was literally in about an hour, meaning any changes he might have would need to be incorporated along with the changes we had just made at the writers' table. So, immediately, Parnell, writer Scott Wainio, and I headed down to the eighth floor to Paul Simon's dressing room.

We sat with Paul and went over the songs that we planned on dancing to, which were "50 Ways to Leave Your Lover," "The Boxer," and "The Sound of Silence." Paul was fine with our choices and didn't have any changes, but it was very important to him that he share with us the meanings of his songs. It was obviously a pleasure to hear this coming from Paul Simon himself, but it never really affected the sketch on any level. I don't know. Musicians are weird.

It was pretty well known that Paul was one of Lorne's closest friends, and when talking to him I noticed that his speaking cadence was similar to Lorne's. They even peppered their speech with the same habitual phrases in the same pattern, like ". . . you know" and "it's like . . ." and Lorne's famous "No, no, no, I know." I never had a long enough conversation with him to see for myself, but apparently Steve Martin, another close friend of Lorne's and the best man on his wedding day, has the exact same delivery and uses the same repeated phrases as Lorne and Paul. One of the writers—she'll remain nameless—told me that one time, Lorne's five-year-old son Henry pointed up to the sky and said, "Daddy, look, a star!" And Lorne relied, "No, no, no, I know."

I was so happy to be introducing new characters again at the end of that second season. I was even playing human beings, who (unlike Peepers and Suel Forrester, for instance) spoke actual words and even sentences in the English language, though I did notice that what I was doing on the show seemed to be making a lot of people wonder about my sexuality. This was annoying not just because it might affect my ability to get dates, but because it was an era when actors and other public figures thought to be anything but heterosexual usually faced discrimination from networks and their audiences. The irony was that one of the main sources of pain and drama in my life since I was a teenager had been how girl crazy I was, always falling for the right girl at the wrong time, or the wrong girl at the right time, or the wrong girl at the wrong time (there was always a wrong in there somewhere).

As we end what I find has turned out to be one of the more boring chapters of this book for some reason, I feel like I should leave you on a high note. So here's one more special moment from that season: One time, when I stopped by Lorne's office to speak to him and he wasn't there, I asked one of his assistants, Cerie, where he was. "I don't know," Cerie replied. "He should be back soon. Right now he's out shopping for socks with Paul Simon."

Which makes perfect sense. I mean, what else would you do with Paul Simon?

Chapter 9

GIRLS LOVE
FUNNY GUYS

After over three years of construction, we finished rebuilding our house on Mount Baldy, and it was more beautiful than ever. I was attending my first semester of high school at Upland High, about twelve miles downhill from home. Every morning I would wake up at 5 AM and walk two miles on the fire road until it ended at an actual concrete road, where I got on the school bus. Upland was a big change for me. About two thousand kids went to my new school, meaning I was introduced to more new people than I'd probably met in a lifetime on Mount Baldy. High school in Upland also introduced me to street gangs. My horizons were finally expanding!

Halfway through my first semester, just as I was about to introduce myself to a couple of Crips, my mom and Marc decided that instead of settling back into the home we'd just spent years building almost from scratch, we were all going to move twelve hundred miles away to Bainbridge Island, on the northwestern coast of Washington State.

Of course, my first thought was: *How am I going to see my dad again?*

I was too upset to be angry. My mother and Marc knew how important my dad was to me; I needed him. It wasn't like he could just hop on the Concorde every Friday afternoon. Or did they assume I'd buy a plane ticket? Maybe with my allowance, which was definitely enough to cover the $600 round trip. It didn't help that every single friendship that I'd had up to this point was now over. It wasn't like the few friends I had, some of whom I'd known since kindergarten, could text each other or keep in touch on Facebook, because that technology didn't exist. I thought I'd never see them again, and sure enough, I haven't.

We moved to our new home by taking the quickest, least scenic route north. Picture the scene:

MARC: Chris, have you ever seen the Golden Gate Bridge before? If you've never seen it before, it's quite impressive.

ME: No, I only saw it on that show with Michael Douglas, and the streets zigzag, and then I saw it in Vertigo when Kim Novak jumped into the water and Jimmy Stewart jumped in to save her.

MARC: Well, fifteen or twenty years from now, when you have a job and can afford your own gas, you should talk someone into lending you their convertible for the weekend and check it out. It's spectacular.

On our trip through beautiful California and the Oregon coast, we didn't see one thing I hadn't seen before. When we passed right through

Napa Valley, Marc commented, "It's pointless to visit when you've already spent so much time in the valley of the Sherman Oaks."

Maybe I didn't get to see the sights of Napa Valley that day (or for another fifteen years), but I did get to hear someone say "Sherman Oaks" with "the" at the beginning of it for the first time. Had I known that all the scenes on the planet Endor in *Return of the Jedi* were shot in the redwood forest, I would have given my fifteen-year-old testicle just to get a glimpse. But nope.

When I started at my new school, smack-dab in the middle of the semester, I was thrust into an environment where kids already had strong friendships (and enemies) from junior high. It was hard, and yet it's interesting how what felt like needlessly tough experiences at the time prepared me for future difficulties. When I joined *SNL,* it wasn't two months before the season premiere like everybody else. It wasn't even midseason, which was usually the only time somebody would join the cast during a season already in progress. No, I joined the cast six weeks before the end of the season, something that had never happened before. Not having any lead time to establish creative chemistry with other performers forces you to rely on that person you're maybe not so crazy about but who has always been there for you. Yeah. Yourself.

At Bainbridge High, I went from being alone to being a loner. Believe it or not, there was one kid at Bainbridge High who I knew from Mount Baldy, though we hadn't been friends. What I remembered most about "Josh" was that he was always laughing or giggling, even when he was alone. Whether he was stuffing his mouth with food so he could pretend he was throwing up at the dinner table or pinning someone down so he could fart on their face, Josh always knew how to have a good time. Of course, that had been years ago, and maybe he was trying to compensate for insecurities that I didn't know about.

"Maybe you can start hanging out with him," Mom suggested.

Josh did indeed invite me to hang out with him and his friends after school. His friends were known as the cool kids, so if it all worked out, I'd be going straight to the top of the high school hierarchy. The plan was to meet on the 3:25 PM ferry and hang out at Pike Place Market over in Seattle. My mom dropped me off at the ferry terminal. But when I got on the ferry, not only was the rest of the "cool" group nowhere to be found, neither was Josh. I guess the joke was on me.

When I did make friends, it was with two girls, Kristine and Kate. There were two things I came to look forward to every day: going to study hall, where I hung out with Kristine, and going home after school to watch the previous night's episode of *Late Night with David Letterman*. It was my favorite show on television. I was in awe of Letterman's dry sense of humor and honesty during interviews with his guests. And while it may have sounded stupid to make this claim back then, watching *Letterman* gave me a comforting glimpse into my future. Maybe someday I would be able to make people laugh the way Letterman could. I have so many vivid memories of watching *Letterman* back then. Even Teri Garr week—which I doubt anyone else really remembers—where they played back-to-back episodes of every show Teri Garr was ever on—was a highlight for me. And they did it not to promote anything, but out of the sheer love the show had for Teri Garr.

At some point, I had an epiphany: If I wanted to improve my chances of gaining any social status or confidence (or girlfriends), I'd need to use my one and only gift. I got up for school two hours earlier than usual the next day, I felt so determined. And so that morning I went straight to the principal's office and asked if the high school had a theater, and if so were there productions coming up, and if so when would the auditions be?

Sadly, there were no plays in production, nor were there any plans for any future plays to be in production. What a fucking shame! How was I ever going to get a chance to make my mark by playing Hamlet? Or more realistically, gentle Puck in *A Midsummer Night's Dream*? I was desperate to perform, but at the time the island school just didn't provide an outlet for any performance that wasn't sports related.

Then one day a helpful team captain came up to me and said, in a gesture of friendship toward the new kid, "There will be a pep assembly on Thursday right after third period for the football game on Friday night. Are you interested in becoming a cheer captain?"

"A cheer captain?" I asked.

Before he could answer, I remembered the politically incorrect term that male cheerleaders were often known by in those days: "Cheer Queer." That just wouldn't sit right for a scrawny freshman newbie trying to make a social breakthrough.

"Is it possible for me to do a sketch during the pep assembly?" I asked.

Pep assemblies at our school had a reputation as "not cool." While the cheerleaders stacked on top of each other or did some impressive high kicks, the other students sat up on the bleachers looking bored.

(By the way, our team was the Spartans. Yep, the Bainbridge Spartans. Just like Will and Cheri's Spartan Cheerleaders. Not funny but true.)

The captain wasn't sure, so I went straight to the pep assembly organizers and asked if I could do an impression of Pee-wee Herman and interact with the potentially disinterested crowd. I don't think there were auditions; they just agreed to let me do it.

When the day came, I wore a gray Gap jacket and matching jeans. A bow tie, obviously. I scotch-taped my nose up and threw Tootsie Rolls into the bleachers. I did the same bit Paul Reubens first did back in the Groundlings.

The response was "lit." Does that word even work? Anyway, it was a hit.

That pep assembly changed my life. It was my first performance in front of a live audience, and the attention from my peers was immediate. I officially became known as the "funny guy who did the Pee-wee Herman bit." I guess that was also my first experience with being known more for a character I played than for myself.

High school improved a lot after that. And when I first saw *Ferris Bueller's Day Off* after it was released during the summer of '86, I found a new role model. I wanted to be that guy, that rebellious, funny, charming punk who could get away with shit, the one the girls all loved. Bueller went around saying things like, "Life moves pretty fast. If you don't stop and look around once in a while, you could miss it" and "The question isn't 'What are we going to do,' the question is 'What *aren't* we going to do?'" I mean come on! I wanted so badly to be perceived as Ferris Bueller in high school—and in many ways, I was looked at as a Ferris Bueller type during my junior and senior years. At least that's what two girls told me after I kept asking them over and over if it was true.

Of course, being like Bueller meant I had to be able to drive myself around, so when I was sixteen, I got my license right away. Unfortunately, my vehicle was nothing like the iconic 1961 Ferrari 250 GT SWB California Spider owned by the father of Ferris's friend, Cameron. Instead, my stepdad gave me his mom's car, which she was now too old to drive. He told me that "it was the perfect car to start with," and he was right. It was a 1975, four-door, mold-colored Datsun originally driven in the streets of Puerto Vallarta, which was where his mom had retired. (She'd also lived across the street from Richard Burton and Elizabeth Taylor during their second marriage, which I always thought was cool.)

The car was . . . well, let's just say it wasn't in the best shape. The left side had a hole in the door that had been fixed by some Puerto Vallartan mechanic who had the genius idea of repairing the damage by filling the hole with concrete grout and then spray-painting over it. Not only did it look embarrassing, but it also added a considerable amount of weight to the right side of the car, causing it to veer that way constantly. Even when it was parked, it would lean over.

What I loved about the car was that it had a stick shift, so when I drove my friends around (girls of course), I could do this thing I called "car dancing." First, I'd put on a CD and play a specific song, "Suicide Blonde" by INXS, for example. Then I would use the brakes and shift gears to the beat of the music. As Charlie Musselwhite broke out his harmonica in the song's opener, I'd shift into first and go forward with the procession of the tune, then I'd shift into reverse and go backwards. Then when there was a pause, I'd slam the brakes so everyone in the car jerked backwards, then shift forward again. Obviously it's the kind of thing you have to experience to truly appreciate, but if I were to break it down . . . First gear, Michael Hutchence would belt out the catchy "you wanna make her, suicide blonde," then reverse, "love devastation, suicide blonde," then back to first gear. I had no idea it would fuck up the transmission.

Because of my love for films, Bueller included, one of my first jobs on Bainbridge was working at a video store creatively titled Bainbridge Island Cinemas. Compared to today's insane convenience, with

Hulu and Netflix that cost something like ten dollars a month, renting movies on tapes was a total pain in the ass. Yet just like checking out a book at the local library, there was something exciting about going to a video store and choosing a movie from a collection of titles. Sure, a new release may be unavailable and already rented out that night, but you could always put your name on a list and wait two weeks or so before finally watching it. In the meantime, you'd rent a different movie for five bucks (and these were '80s dollars, kids), and if you happened to forget to return it on time, you'd be charged a late fee. Ahh, the good old days of home entertainment . . .

VHS was more popular, but I was a Betamax man myself since the quality was better (and no, I don't have time to explain the differences between the two—half of you don't even know what a videotape looks like anyway). By the age of nineteen, I would end up building a pretty impressive collection of movies on Beta. Instead of a quarter-inch hard drive, my collection took up a whole goddamn wall. I remember wanting to own the movie *Gremlins*, so I saved up and I paid (I'm not kidding) ninety frickin' dollars for it. That's how much it was, retail.

And of course, before there was Rotten Tomatoes, there was my dad's beloved *Leonard Maltin's Movie Guide,* the big, fat pocket-sized book, updated every year, that basically reviewed every movie ever made—Hollywood, indie, foreign, you name it—on a one- to four-star basis. Since my dad lived by this book, I promised myself at one point that I would watch a four-star movie every night for the rest of my time in high school, and I nearly fulfilled that promise. I was introduced to the brilliance of Scorsese, Fellini, Coppola, Truffaut, Capra, Sturges, Kazan, Kubrick, Tati, Polanski, Lean, Wilder, Brooks, Welles, Hitchcock, Lubitsch, Powell and Pressburger, Huston, Lang, Malick, Cukor, Cassavetes, Stone, Hawks, and more.

Eventually I got a job working at Lynwood Theatre on Bainbridge Island. The Lynwood Theatre was an art-house theater built back in 1936. Like most landmarks that you grow up near, I didn't have any interest in its history until years later when I came back to reminisce . . . okay, fine, it was when I just wrote this paragraph. It was the first theater on Bainbridge Island to show "talkies." At least that's what the website I just looked at said.

The job was perfect for me. It was the first time I worked doing something I loved. After working in the front box office, I moved up to being a cashier and popcorn maker. Eventually the manager gave me the keys to the building so I could open and close the theater myself. In retrospect, this may have been a mistake.

One night I invited some friends to the theater after it closed to drink and watch a movie. I already knew how to run a projector, so we watched *Dirty Dancing*. We never vandalized the property nor did we pillage or steal any cash. I did crawl into the popcorn machine, however. It was funny because I could actually fit my entire body into the machine with a bunch of popcorn still in there. Unfortunately, somehow the manager found out about our wild night and let me go. I was crushed; I loved that job. I told my mom and stepdad, and for once they actually understood where I was coming from, and they asked the owners to consider giving me my job back. The owners, too, understood where I was coming from, but I was still fired.

I had started to have actual romantic relationships with girls, my crushes turning into deep infatuations as I tried to woo them with letters and poems. As usual, I was a hit with parents, mostly because I made them laugh, and all through high school the parents of whatever girl I was going out with loved having me around. That is, as long as I showed respect, which mostly meant not flirting with their daughter in front of them or showing any signs that I was only there to pick her up and wanted to leave as soon as possible. Here's important dating advice for young men: Make it seem like you've come over to visit everyone. It really is true that if the mom loves you, you're halfway there. It's nice if the dad likes you, too, but if there's friction with the father, your girlfriend will usually find it attractive. (Or maybe I just dated girls with daddy issues—who knows.)

The first girl I went out with was Ellen. Like everybody else at school, we would usually sneak out at lunchtime or in the afternoon to go back to one of our houses and screw around. Sex was pretty much a given when you were going out with someone, at least in my high school. I do not have any children, and I'm proud to say I don't hang out on high school campuses anymore, so I don't know if it's the same with kids today.

Another girl I went out with, we'll call her "J," had the distinction of being the first person who asked me to keep my eyes open while we were having sex. She would place her hands along the sides of my face with what I would describe as a pretty firm grip, and then with my eyes wide open, we would physically and most importantly psychologically time it so that we had our orgasms at the same moment. And man, I'm telling you, it scared the shit out of me! Of course it was amazing. There's no question. But that's why I was so fucking scared. Being vulnerable at that age isn't the easiest thing, especially when you've spent years either alone on a mountain or building up walls to protect yourself. I'd only seen this level of intimacy in movies that earned a four-star rating from Leonard Maltin. Was I expected to remain at this level of vulnerability from here on out? Only a few years earlier I'd still had a crush on Smurfette, for

God's sake. Eventually I had to tell J that I felt like our relationship was going a little too fast.

One girl I spent a lot of time with for years, hoping my feelings would at some point be reciprocated, was Patty. On the surface, she was quiet and kind, and she hid behind her hair half the time. But inside, she had a unique radiance that was nothing short of mystical. She introduced me to the beauty of insecurity, if there is such a thing.

Patty and I were just friends, but I was infatuated with her and did anything I could to be near her, eagerly performing any task or favor she might need, which was something of a recurring theme for me when it came to girls I had crushes on. On her birthday, as a token of my love, I gave her this sweet silver bracelet that had two tiny bells on it so that whenever she walked down the school hallways, I could hear her coming.

That year, I was beside myself when Patty asked me to be her date for Tolo (that's Pacific Northwestern for Sadie Hawkins). It was the first time I'd ever worn a tuxedo, and 'scuse my French, but I looked pretty fuckin' suave. As with any other school dance on Bainbridge, the routine after the dance was to head to the house of someone whose parents were gone for the night to drink beer and hopefully make out and then . . . oh, I don't know. Needless to say, I was hoping it would be a night to remember.

The party at the house was in full swing—"full swing" being six people counting myself and the stereo—when we ran out of beer. I volunteered to go get more, and just as I was leaving, this kid named Peter showed up out of nowhere. Peter was Patty's ex-boyfriend from back in junior high.

I managed to talk my mom into buying me a case of Rainier Beer at the Jiffy Mart. Rainier Beer was a local brand, named after Mount Rainier of course, and the commercial was on the air a lot back then, featuring a guy on a motorcycle with someone singing "raiiiinnnn-nmmmmmmeeeeeeeerrr beeeeeeeeeeeerrrrrrrrrr" to simulate the sound of the engine. It tasted exactly as cheap as it was (which was very).

Half an hour later, I walked back into the party carrying the case of Jiffy Mart's finest, and not that I expected a crowd of people to greet me cheering, "Yay! Rainier Beer! Kattan, you're fantastic!" or anything, but there wasn't anybody around at all. No Patty . . . and no Peter.

As I set the beer on the kitchen counter, I heard the sound of those sweet little silver bells coming from Patty's bracelet off in the distance. It seemed to be coming from upstairs. I followed the sound, and as I approached a closed bedroom door on the second floor, I remember stopping and actually saying out loud a classic 1960s television-style "Naaaah." Finally, I opened the door—just wide enough to see those silver bells bouncing up and down on Patty's wrist as Peter lay on the bed underneath her.

So I guess it was a night to remember, just not in the way that I'd hoped. Patty was my first official heartbreak, but we remained friends off and on, and a little part of me will always belong to her. All in all, my high school romances taught me something most of the world already knew: Lots of girls *love* funny guys. At least up to a point.

Chapter 10

BELOW THE BELT

few days before Christmas in 1996, I was home visiting family over the three-week hiatus from *SNL*. I was in a bit of a funk as this was during the period when I wasn't getting much material on the show. In the kitchen, my mom answered a phone call and then held the receiver to her chest and said to me in the loudest whisper you can imagine: "It's Lorne Michaels!"

She presented me with the phone like it was a very fragile Holy Grail. I ran into the nearest room that afforded any privacy—the bathroom.

With the door locked, I sat on the lid of the toilet, holding the receiver to my ear. "Chris, I have Lorne Michaels for you," said a perky young female voice. "He's calling from his home in Amagansett." For a few moments, there was silence. Then, in an unfamiliarly welcoming tone, Lorne's voice said, "Hello Chris." For some reason, he sounded more like

Dana Carvey's impression of him than he did himself. But maybe it was just because I so rarely heard him speak.

Unsurprisingly, that was it for small talk. If he wanted to talk to you, Lorne always had a reason and got right to it, which I grew to prefer. It's easier to have a conversation when there's a point to it. This time, the point was something I could not have predicted.

"Amy Heckerling wants to do a movie about the Roxbury Guys," he said.

Heckerling, the director of Fast Times at Ridgemont High *and* Clueless, *wants to do a movie with us?*

Yeah, I was both stunned and confused.

"Really?" I asked. "They don't even speak. I'd think they'd make a movie about the Cheerleaders before a Roxbury Guys film."

Silence. It's very possible that Lorne felt the same. Nonetheless, he was obviously open to the idea, making this call one of the greatest Christmas gifts I had ever received. He told me to call Will and discuss it with him, and that we'd all talk after the break.

"Enjoy the holidays," Lorne said before hanging up.

I called Will, who was spending his holidays in Roanoke Rapids, North Carolina, where his mom lived. He had already spoken with Lorne. We were both giddy and agreed that we'd be stupid to say no. Sure, there was the Amy Heckerling factor, but there was also the exciting prospect of getting paid to have fun with each other all summer while filming.

After I hung up with Will, a feeling came over me that I can only describe as devilish glee. Sort of like that feeling you get when you're sixteen and sneaking off to smoke a joint just off the school grounds or sneaking off to masturbate in the bathroom. (I do hope someone reading knows exactly what I'm talking about because I really didn't have to write that.) Then I felt guilty for feeling wicked, because a movie offer immediately made me feel more secure about my status on *SNL*, and that kind of security was something almost no other cast member got to feel back then. Later, it was completely different—Bill Hader was already in pre-production for *Superbad* when he joined *SNL*. But then I realized that Will had every reason to feel just as guilty as I did—we were in this together, and while I still may have felt a little like a black sheep, he was universally beloved on the show. I quit second-guessing and let myself be happy. In that moment, I felt this calming sense of stability. The anxiety I had been carrying about not getting enough material on the air that season began to diminish.

After the pitch meeting our first night back at 30 Rock, as scheduled, Will and I met with Lorne in his office to talk about the film. He said he'd be in LA during the next break, which was coming up in a few weeks, and that it would be a good idea if we were there as well so we could have a meeting with Amy at the studio.

So, a few weeks later, Will and I were in LA. The first order of business was to have dinner with Lorne at The Ivy on Robertson. The charming landmark was known for its star-studded crowd and the paparazzi waiting just outside to take as many pictures as possible while stars quickly saunter towards the valet. Will and I both felt a little nervous about not having the faintest idea of what type of questions we might need to come up with creative answers to during dinner, so we decided to drive together. Lorne arrived about fifteen minutes after us, which allowed me enough time to order one of the gimlets that the restaurant was famous for. I sat on one of the very rickety "original" chipped wooden chairs, fidgeted with my silverware, and questioned my decision to spray myself liberally with Polo cologne, something I hadn't done in years, before I'd left to pick Will up.

Dinner not only turned out to be a lot less nerve-wracking than expected, it was surprisingly comforting. This wasn't the intimidatingly distant Lorne we had both grown used to. It was a much warmer, amiable Lorne that dined with us that evening.

Any conversation with Lorne usually involves him reminiscing, and in this case, not only was it interesting, but the situation required it. Will and I would be co-writing the script, and we were starved for direction, and we welcomed any advice at all. Lorne told us a little about how he'd worked with previous *SNL* comedic duos like Mike and Dana on both *Wayne's World* movies and with Farley and Spade on their films. We didn't come away with all the information we needed to create a story concept that everyone would agree on or to begin writing an actual movie script for a major studio. But we did get a lot of helpful background, as well as two pieces of information that Lorne seemed to think were especially important to underline.

The first piece was about the poster. This may seem a little premature, but whatever. We learned that Lorne liked to use a blue sky with fluffy white clouds as the background for movie posters. He did this for *Wayne's World*s, *Tommy Boy* and *Black Sheep*, for *¡Three Amigos!* and *Coneheads*. Why is it important for a movie poster to have a blue sky with clouds in the background? How should I know? But for some reason, it really did work. We also learned that the reason the poster for *It's Pat* didn't have a sky-clouds background was because it wasn't his film. And *Stuart Saves His Family?* didn't have the sky background because director Harold Ramis wanted that poster of Al Franken holding up the world. But neither of those films did well at the box office.

As it happened, the poster for *Night at the Roxbury* ended up having neither a blue sky nor fluffy white clouds as the background but instead a very colorful depiction of a busy nightclub-hopping Sunset Strip photographed by the great David LaChapelle. But for the films that followed, Lorne returned to his standard blue sky with clouds background with the posters for *Superstar*, *The Ladies Man*, and *MacGruber*.

The second important piece of information Lorne gave us at dinner came with a big buildup after the main course. "This doesn't leave the table," he began, then, after what felt like a two-hour director's cut version of the five-second scene of us sitting on the edge of our shabby-chic pillows on our shabby-chic chairs waiting for the space shuttle to finally take off, he said: "Jack Nicholson wants to do the movie."

Later that week, we headed to Lorne's newly minted office on the Paramount lot to meet with Amy. The first time you receive your very own drive-on parking pass is so exciting. Lyle and Erin, who worked in Lorne's office in New York, would now be assisting Lorne during the production in LA, and when Will and I walked in, they were in the middle of putting up posters of past films Lorne had produced with Paramount while taking down the *Crocodile Dundee* posters left by the office's prior tenant, Paul "Now *that's* a knife" Hogan. It felt like the first day of school for us as Will and I sat anxiously holding binders filled with (blank) paper and freshly sharpened pencils. Lorne was busy on the phone with Paramount's CEO at the time, Sherry Lansing, responsible for six of the ten highest-grossing Paramount films ever, including *Forrest Gump* and *Titanic*. I could tell Lorne had a good relationship with Sherry when I heard him say "Aww, honey," while on the phone with her. After he hung up, Lorne grabbed his coat and instructed Will and me to wait while he went over to Sherry's office alone. Forty-five minutes later, Lorne returned and told us that before Will and I met with Sherry, the next step would be for the three of us to solidify Amy's commitment to the film. As far as we knew, Amy wanted to direct. But judging from Lorne's demeanor, that didn't seem quite as definite as we had been led to believe.

In the beginning, Will and I would often talk with Erin, who had worked with Lorne on *Tommy Boy* and *Black Sheep*. She was really the only person around capable of explaining not just the process of writing and starring in a studio film, but more importantly the process of working with Lorne on a studio film. Most of the time when Will and I were alone, we'd just look at each other, overwhelmed and clueless about what to do. I couldn't imagine doing this without him. Having Will reflect what I was feeling was beyond comforting.

These were pre-internet times, and neither of us had any idea what Amy looked like until she walked into Lorne's office the following week. Her voice was soft and low with a Brooklyn accent as robust as what I was hearing back east. She wore a fire-engine red cardigan buttoned over a white shirt with a fitted black skirt and black tights. Even though she had every reason to be confident, she came across as shy and reserved, and her hiding place was behind her strands of dark hair that curled out of a top bun and nearly covered her face.

Amy spoke first, explaining that she pictured the two brothers still living at home with their wealthy parents in Beverly Hills. Lorne saw it as two brothers living at home as well, not in Beverly Hills but in Brooklyn. He pictured a "bridge-and-tunnel" movie like *Saturday Night Fever*. It's very possible the reason for this difference was that they each wanted the location for the film to be closest to their home to avoid having to travel between coasts. What was finally agreed upon was that Will, Steve Koren (who would write the script with us), and I would come up with the overall plot before the next meeting with her, but after Amy left we agreed it was crucial to keep her happy.

A couple of days later, Will, Lorne, and I finally went to meet with Sherry Lansing, but for some reason she wasn't there. Instead, we met with Jonathan Goldwyn—who, by the way, now heads Broadway Video, Lorne's production company. At the time, Jonathan, who is actor Tony Goldwyn's brother, was the head of comedy at Paramount. He was a very happy person. Every time I saw him, he was in a good mood.

We met in Sherry's beautifully capacious, flawlessly pristine office. Where everything—from floor to ceiling, furniture, desk, bouquets, every single item—was white. The only thing that wasn't white was the green *Variety* magazine logo on the front page of the trades spread on her linen-white coffee table. All that was missing was Kubrick's monolith from *2001: A Space Odyssey*. The four of us sat not in the center but off to the side near the entrance, for some reason. Will and I sat on what was a very small Roman bench for such a big room. Perhaps Jonathan thought that it would be disrespectful to sit at Sherry's desk. Maybe he prefers to hear movies pitched from no further than a yard's distance. Who knows. Point is, it wasn't very comfortable. Then, Jonathan started with a very enthusiastic, "So, let's see these guys!"

Will and I stared at each other, dumbfounded. Then we started improvising dialogue for our one-dimensional characters who had never before done anything but bop their heads and enthusiastically hump any females who unwittingly danced in between them.

"What's up?" I asked, in the voice that would become Doug Butabi's, one I had literally given no thought to before that moment. "Not much," said Will, "What's up with you?" And that's as far as we got.

We sounded more like two surfer dudes than a couple of night-club hoppers. But for whatever reason, an excited and now almost *too* rosy-cheeked Jonathan Goldwyn enthused, "Great! I love it!" Before Will and I had time to form the thought *What just happened?* Lorne expertly dove in with, "I see it as a bridge-and-tunnel story, but Amy sees it set in LA."

Walking back to his office, Lorne asked if Will or I had seen a certain cast member—who out of respect shall remain nameless—on *Leno* the night before. Both of us had. "Career ender," Lorne murmured. Will and I stopped cold. I realized right then that Lorne's opinion had the power to completely taint somebody. And that was fucking scary. He could be having lunch with the head of HBO or Judd Apatow and casually say to them what he'd just said to us. What I'd seen on *Leno* wasn't anything like a "career ender." The nameless cast member didn't bring the house down but certainly wasn't terrible. It was their first time on, and it can be nerve-wracking. But Lorne could say whatever he wanted, whenever he wanted, to whomever he wanted, and even if he was absolutely incorrect, the person would respond with, "Really? Wow. I didn't know that. Thanks for telling me. Now I know." Lorne's opinion wasn't questioned, which made it something to fear.

When I came back to Los Angeles—now the agreed-upon setting for the Butabi brothers—to start filming *A Night at the Roxbury* in the summer of 1997, my relationship with Jennifer Coolidge began to deteriorate. You'd think it would have been better, now that we were in the same city full-time, but being apart and bicoastal for so long had changed the dynamic between us, and my schedule didn't exactly leave much time for reconnecting. Every day that summer, I was submerged in work on something movie related—rehearsing, rewriting, blocking scenes, and (this was pretty surreal for me, and I know Will felt the same way) auditioning other actors as they read for roles in the film. The hardest auditions were those of friends from the Groundlings.

Top Left: My beautiful mother in the early 1960s.

Top Right: My dad, Kip King, playing a crucial role in *Breakfast at Tiffany's*.

Bottom: My parents' Zen wedding.

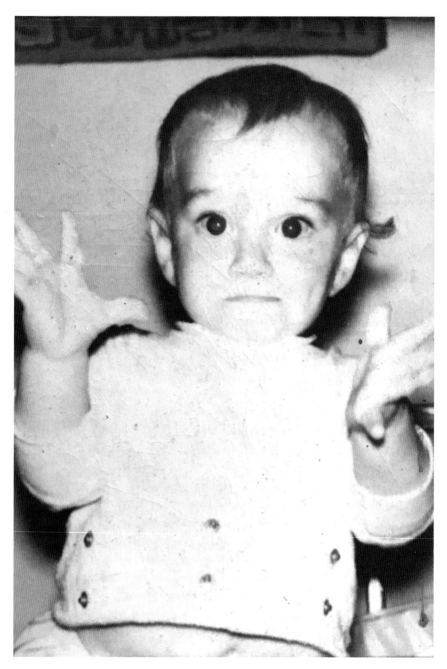

I still have the same face . . .

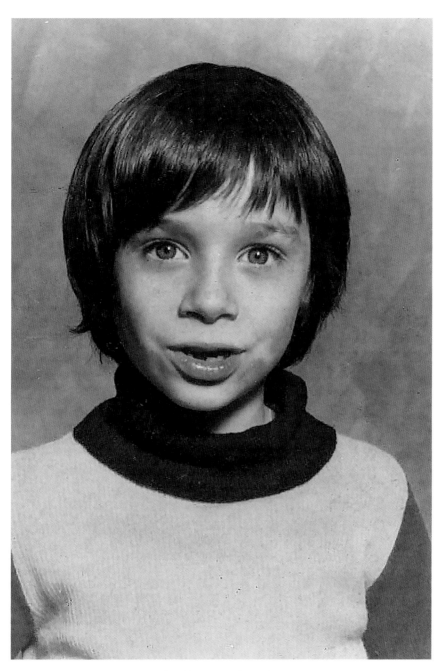

Me in second grade.

Debuting my Pee-wee Herman routine at a Bainbridge High Pep Rally.

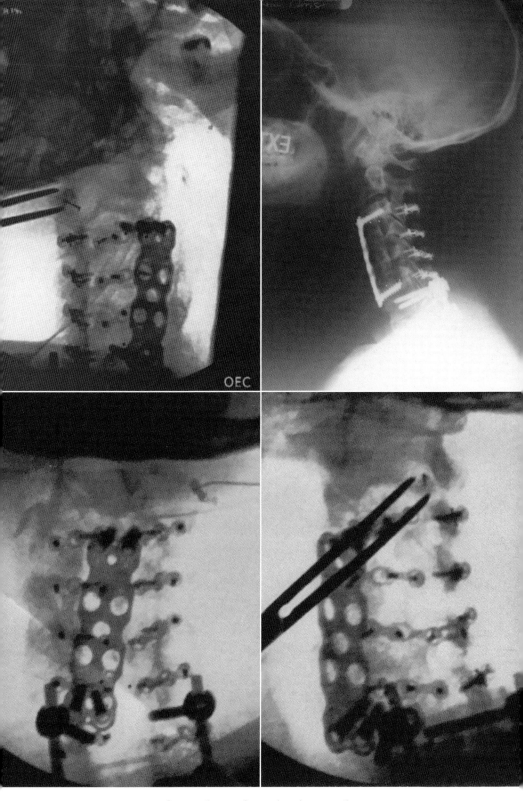

Some shots of my titanium neck.

Top: Behind the scenes . . .

Bottom: Professionals hard at work.

Top: Tina and Jimmy.

Bottom: There's something about Cameron.

With Eddie Murphy, my hero.

One day, after an afternoon of casting, Amy offered to drive Will and me home. The three of us had a great time in her BMW listening to some new songs I thought would be perfect for *Roxbury*. On the way to my apartment, after Will had been dropped off, Amy turned to me at a stoplight and in the shyest tone, asked something very blunt: "Are we gonna have sex?"

I was shocked. Was she joking? Did she mean today, *right there in the car,* or sometime in the future? I had no idea how to respond. We weren't formal with each other or anything, but she was still basically my boss, and aside from the usual playfulness you'd expect from a couple of comedians and a director working together on a comedy, everything had been professional between us up to that point. I tried to keep it light. "I don't know," I said. "I can't believe you just said that." The conversation ended there. But while I had never thought about it before, now that it was out there, I couldn't stop thinking about it.

The following day I was at Coolidge's apartment when I got a call from Lorne. He sounded furious.

"Amy doesn't want to direct the film," he said.

When I asked why, he began to yell, shouting at me that Paramount would only do the movie if Amy signed on as director, not as producer—a screen credit Lorne wasn't interested in sharing. And if I wanted to make sure the movie happened, then I had to keep Amy happy. *Why me?* I thought. *How is this my responsibility?*

"Chris, I'm not saying you have to fuck her, but it wouldn't hurt," Lorne said.

What the fuck was that supposed to mean? I mean, what was this, my casting couch moment? I had no idea what Amy had actually said to Lorne, or how much was being assumed. Was I really supposed to be a reason for Amy to direct the movie? That seemed insane. *And why wasn't Will on this call?* I thought. He was my partner—he should be hearing this. I started to say that I need to talk to Will, but Lorne cut me off, telling me that this conversation didn't concern Will or anybody else, and it was best if I didn't mention it.

There wasn't a thing about this conversation that didn't make me uncomfortable. I couldn't call *Will?* Was Lorne kidding me? Will and I had come into this together, and now I was being asked to keep something from him? *Fuck that, that's not the person I am*, I thought, *I'm calling him.* But in the end, I didn't. I was too scared. I thought that maybe I could tell Will and make him promise to keep it secret from Lorne, but that seemed risky, too. The last thing I wanted was to have someone hear Lorne say "career ender" about me. To this day, whenever I think about that conversation with Lorne, I still feel repellingly pathetic.

After I hung up, I walked back into the other room where Jennifer was. She could tell something was going on and looked at me, waiting for me to fill her in. I realized that I couldn't tell her, either. I was suddenly carrying this weight of guilt. The fact that I felt instant guilt about something I hadn't even done told me it was wrong, but also indicated that it was only a matter of time.

A few days later, Amy called and invited me to a party at the home of Jonathan Goldwyn and his wife at the time, actress Colleen Camp. I assumed it would be all the *Roxbury* people, but when we arrived, it turned out that we were the only ones there from the movie. No Will, no Lorne, no Steve . . . were they not invited? Why was I? Was it because Amy was invited, and I was her date? It did seem like a dinner party. When I asked her about it, she said that she didn't know if they would be coming or not, but, to me, things just didn't feel right. Amy knew Jennifer was my girlfriend. But I was green and trying to please everyone, and Amy and Lorne were more than just my coworkers—one was the head of a studio and the other a major director/writer, so I chose to keep breathing with my mouth shut.

After the party, I drove Amy home, and when I dropped her off, she leaned in and kissed me softly on the lips. The thing is, I *was* attracted to her. She was powerful, intelligent, and fascinating to talk to. She was passionate about everything, and our conversations were stimulating and educational. That in itself was intoxicating, and naturally, I felt thrilled that a woman of her stature was interested in me. But as much as I enjoyed that moment, I remained weighed down by guilt over this unfolding secret I was withholding from everyone who mattered to me.

That week, I told Jennifer that I thought it would be a good idea if I took her up on her previous suggestion to separate. I could tell she was surprised, but her feelings hadn't really changed, and I'd been the one pushing to stay together, so she agreed. We'd known each other so long that there was no ill will, but I think there were still some hurt feelings and resentments on both sides. It probably didn't help that I was so preoccupied with the events that were happening around the movie that I didn't give that breakup the time and mourning it deserved. It wasn't a surprise later to find out the way I handled it was seen as insensitive and dickish by a lot of Groundling friends, especially Will.

I saw Amy a few days later when we were rehearsing at Paramount, and we both acted as if the kiss had never happened. But a few weeks after that, after a night of scene blocking at Paramount, she asked if I wanted to stay. She thought it would be fun to have sex on Lorne's desk. Wow, what a great idea! Jesus Christ. I said a polite "Fuck, no!" to that, so we ended up going to her office and having sex on . . . yep, you guessed it, the "casting couch." Afterward, I was so nervous about anyone seeing us late at night on the Paramount lot that I asked her if it would be all right if we walked out separately.

I really thought that would be it. I wasn't looking to jump into any sort of relationship, especially with someone I was just getting to know and working with. By now, too, Amy had joined the project as a producer, working with John Fortenberry—he'd directed a lot of Amy's *Clueless* TV spin-off—who came on as the credited director. I was attracted to Amy, but at the same time very afraid of the power she and Lorne wielded over my career.

Even though Jennifer and I had broken up, we still lived together for a few more weeks. I didn't own a lot of stuff at the time, so moving out would be relatively easy; the hard part was finding the time to do it. But eventually I managed to relocate—back to my dad's house in good ol' Sherman Oaks.

Amy had started calling, wanting me to come over. It was clear that this wasn't going to be a one-time thing after all. Like gangrene, guilt returned to eat away at me, and this time he brought along his always reliable friend shame, who gave me a sharp punch right in the balls. Unfortunately, none of this stopped me from seeing Amy. She never flirted on set, and I didn't tell anyone. I thought if I could just maintain in the face of this stressful shitstorm a bit longer, everyone would be happy and everything would work out. I'd been focused on keeping people happy my whole life, starting with my dad, and in this case the mix of professional and personal relationships involved made the stakes seem higher.

About a quarter of the way through the ten weeks of shooting, I got a call from Steve Koren, wanting to know if Amy and I had been hooking up and, if so, what it was like to sleep with someone like Amy Heckerling.

I don't know if it was the casual, unaffected way he broached the subject or what, but I was emotionally screaming for someone to talk to about what was going on, so I told him. I had to. The whole thing was eating away at me, and I don't just mean psychologically—it was physical. My hands developed such intense eczema that the palms would often bleed. Finally being open about the situation was such a huge fucking relief. I even told Steve about Lorne not wanting me to tell Will; I'd later find out that Lorne himself had told Will, unbeknownst to me.

But as good as it felt to open up, I ended up more vulnerable. Evidently there was a lot of gossip and speculation about Amy and me floating around, and Steve had decided to find out the truth.

On set the next morning, I stepped up into the hair/makeup trailer as Will was having his wig fitted, and it seemed like the temperature between the two of us had changed. I decided to brush it off, not knowing how right I was—or that it was already too late. I had inadvertently pulled the pin out of a grenade that was soaring over my current and future life. It wasn't a question of *if*, but rather *when* that grenade would explode.

I was newly single and sleeping with the director of the movie I was filming. Meanwhile, I was falling for the actress who played my love interest in the film, Elisa Donovan, a beautiful redhead known for her role in *Clueless*. Being attracted to Elisa felt natural, especially since it helped add visual chemistry to our characters and their storyline. Best of all, because our attraction to each other wasn't secretive, it actually felt healthy—and thank God, it was something I could be honest with Will about. One of the great things about having a friend, today known as a "bro," is being able to share that boyish excitement of falling for someone. Will first met his wife, Viveca Paulin, at an auction house in Hollywood called Butterfield & Butterfield where he was working part-time while we were in the Groundlings, and every day he would tell me about little moments, like how nervous he got when she passed by his desk, or even glanced at him.

I was literally counting the days until the movie wrapped, so I could enjoy pursuing Elisa before heading back to New York without feeling dishonorable. Considering everything going on, my feelings for Elisa probably seemed foolhardy, but I couldn't help them. Whenever I fell for someone, I fell hard. But sometimes I felt like I couldn't get what I wanted without hurting someone else. If Amy and I had met and started seeing each other without all the added confusion and pressure I felt, things might have been different. But as it was, our relationship was never given the chance to be something healthy, and finally, I had no choice but to be honest with her. When Amy reassured me that things were okay between us, I felt it was safe to admit to her that I had developed feelings for Elisa.

In retrospect, when it came to the Amy situation, I was in completely over my head. When you are working on a movie with someone, you can spend so much time together, and (depending on the role you play) the chemistry between two characters can sometimes be such an intense experience that it is no wonder that personal relationships develop out of professional ones, but all the power dynamics involved blur the lines for everyone. It was still the beginning of my career, and it was just too much for me to handle. So unfortunately, I ended up handling everything wrong.

At the wrap party for *Roxbury*, I spent most of my time hanging out with Elisa. I think we barely even sat down to eat with everybody because we were too busy running around wooing each other. Our new romance was intoxicatingly free of secrets or hidden motives. When I stopped at Will's table to say hi to his family, I asked if he was going to stay in LA for the last few weeks before *SNL* started, and he told me he was going back to New York to film commercial parodies for the new season.

SNL shot most of the show's commercial parodies three weeks before the season began, and most of the cast was back in New York by then in case they were written into one. I had already decided not to go back for another few weeks, not just because of my new relationship with Elisa, but because I was rarely cast in commercial parodies anyway. Actually, I'd been in one commercial that Adam McKay wrote when I first got on the show, but that was it. So I thought: *Fuck it. I'll stay here with my dad.* I told Shoemaker that if he did cast me, I'd fly back immediately.

I hadn't yet received the expected pre-season phone call from the show with the details of my starting date, and when I called my agent, he informed me that as of that moment, my contract had not been picked up. I waited through the next few days, trying to stop myself from drowning in my always freshly filled pool of anxiety and panic. That's when I found out that I was literally the only regular cast member whose contract hadn't been picked up yet.

Someone I trusted and who was always honest with me told me once: "I don't know what it is, but Lorne just really doesn't like you." Was that the truth? It didn't feel like a huge improbability. For whatever reason, I never felt like he was that fond of me. When I first got on the show, it was very clear that Lorne had my back, but then something that summer, whatever it was, changed that. So now my contract had not been renewed. And yet, Will and I had been told how important it was that we start promoting the movie during this upcoming season. Even my agent and my manager thought it was crazy. What lesson was I supposed to learn from this? So, I was advised to get an entertainment lawyer. Something I'd never really wanted or imagined I'd ever need.

Finally, a convenient mere days before the season started, my contract was renewed. Forty-eight hours later, I flew back to New York. I was so overwhelmingly relieved to officially be back on the show that there really wasn't any room for me to be angry. I was excited about the lineup of guests, about seeing the writers and the rest of the cast. Elisa and I broke it off—we tried to make it work, but for some reason this long distance relationship proved harder than most. I had made some absolutely terrible fucking choices over the summer, absolutely awful. But I thought the shitstorm had passed.

Drama aside, working with Will to create *Roxbury* had been exciting, and sometimes an absolute blast. But making a movie had a steep learning curve.

When Will and I saw a rough cut of the film—not the final cut that was eventually locked and released, but the very first cut—we were worried. Even with months of post-production, with the timing of the jokes being fixed and the best takes chosen and reworked in editing, you can't always guarantee that something will turn out the way you envisioned it.

When it was time to do press for the movie, there was a lot of stuff Paramount asked of us that Will chose not to do. He didn't want to go out on the road with me or become heavily involved with the publicity. He seemed to detach himself from the project. We never talked about it, but I always thought he blamed me and the situation with Amy.

Shortly after Season 23 of *SNL* started, in September 1997, I finally realized just how irrevocably things had changed between Will and me. The last time we'd seen or spoken to each other had been at the *Roxbury* wrap party in LA. I'd left him a few messages, and he hadn't returned my calls. This wasn't at all like Will.

On the first Monday of the new season, with the pitch meeting coming up in a few hours, a lot of the cast members, including myself, were making the rounds, checking in with various writers to catch up and see if they wanted to collaborate on ideas we'd thought up over the summer. Sylvester Stallone was guest hosting that week, and my first priority was to see if he was as short as everyone said. The good news . . . he was shorter.

I then headed over to Dennis McNicholas's office to say hello and see if he was interested in doing a "Goth Talk." I thought Stallone dressed in goth makeup would be a pretty funny visual.

I walked through the writers' room and down the hallway next to the research department, and just as I was about to knock on Dennis's door, it opened and there stood Will. I smiled at him. "There you are!" I said.

I'd been feeling apprehensive about running into Will for the first time, obsessing over why he hadn't returned my calls. (I tended to obsess over pointless and unproductive things. Eventually, a few years later, I was prescribed Cymbalta, which helped. Just a fascinating celebrity trivia tidbit to put in your back pocket.)

Will placed his hand over my shoulder, looked straight at me, and calmly said, "We need to talk." Immediately, a wave of undefined guilt slid over me, followed by the ever-popular "knot in the stomach" feeling. I followed Will to the other side of the seventeenth floor, toward my office. Will peeked in and saw my office mate, Colin, at his desk listening to doo-wop music, and who would want to interrupt that? (Yes, it's true . . . Colin Quinn loves doo-wop music, and I loved Dion and the Belmonts, so we got along just fine. Now you know.) He moved on, looking into various offices, and I realized he was trying to find an empty one where we could "talk." It was amazing how similar this felt to being sent to the principal's office.

Finally, we found an unoccupied office—Shoemaker's—and Will shut the door behind us and sat down across from me.

"So, I got all your messages, but I didn't call you back because I didn't want to talk to you," he said.

Not surprisingly, the knot in my stomach started to twist.

"I don't understand."

"I'm done," he said simply. "I don't want to be your friend anymore. I'm going to be professional and still work with you on the show, but that's it."

"Can we talk about this?"

"No. That's it. I'm serious. I'm done."

I felt as if I'd been in a car accident that was my fault; I found it impossible to speak, like someone had dumped a ton of sand into the basin of my stomach, preventing me from explaining myself. It wasn't like Will was being cold; he was just being honest. He was hurt, and I was devastated. Devastated because I knew how seriously I had fucked up. I had tried to hide my relationship with Amy, not realizing how obvious it had been to everyone else, including Will (not to mention that Lorne had told him about it in the first place).

At first, I'd thought I had good reasons for what I'd done, but in the end the reasons didn't matter. I didn't know or hadn't let myself see until that moment that although the situation with Amy hadn't *directly* involved Will, my actions and dishonesty had made him feel deceived and betrayed. And now everything Will and I had done and shared—everything that made us feel like a team, that incredible amount of trust that had been built up—was broken.

Will didn't come right out and say it; in fact, he didn't say anything about how he felt. He didn't really have to. We were soul brothers. My friendship with Will was the closest and most important friendship I ever had.

We still worked together on the show after that. And we still laughed when we worked together. We continued doing a lot of sketches. He cast me in "More Cowbell" and "Old Prospector." I felt that we still loved each other. But some damage can't be undone.

There's a line in *A Night at the Roxbury* . . . and no, I don't often quote that film, okay? But anyway, there's a line near the end of the film, when my character, Doug Butabi, interrupts the wedding of his brother, Steve Butabi—Will's character. There had been a falling out, and as the brothers finally reconcile, I apologize for my actions, telling Steve/Will this:

"You don't drag me down. I drag me down."

Then I say the famous *Jerry Maguire* line about him completing me, and we have a moving moment set to a Bruce Springsteen song.

That pretty much sums it up. The *Roxbury* movie was supposed to be our big adventure; I never imagined that when it was over I would have lost my best friend.

The last time I worked with Will was on *Saturday Night Live* in 2002; I've always wanted to work with him again, but it's never happened. Has he forgiven me? I don't know. But as I reflect on all of this, I still feel sick about everything that happened that summer, and I probably always will.

Chapter 11

YOU CAN'T HAVE-A DA MANGO

The twenty-third season of *SNL* was only a few minutes old, and I was already in drag and kissing Sylvester Stallone. It was the opening monologue, and Stallone, a.k.a. Rocky Balboa, was on the show promoting his latest film, *Cop Land*. I, of course, was Adrian; Jim Breuer was playing Rocky's trainer, Mickey; and Tracy Morgan was "I pity the fool" Mr. T. It wasn't until I read Tina Fey's memoir, *Bossypants*, that I remembered doing the Rocky/Adrian bit. Tina wrote that Cheri really wanted the Adrian part since she was petite and from Philadelphia and could do a good impression of Talia Shire.

"Instead, somebody thought it would be funnier to put her co-star Chris Kattan in a dress," Tina wrote. "I remember thinking that was kind of bullshit."

When I first read this, my heart stopped. *Tina! But we were friends!* Then I continued reading: "no offense to Kattan, whom I love . . ." and my heart started beating again.

That night, Will and I also performed a Roxbury Guys sketch with Stallone at Lorne's request, or more specifically at Paramount's request, to promote the upcoming release of the *Roxbury* movie. Since Stallone was having a difficult time with the head bop, we wrote a bit where he basically punched me in the face because he didn't know how to bop his head. It wasn't the best of the Roxbury sketches, but I remember Stallone being a very nice guy. Plus, it's always comforting to be around someone who's shorter than me.

When Chris Farley hosted *SNL* a month later, we *almost* got a chance to do a Roxbury sketch with him. Farley was a self-deprecating sweetheart, and he gave so much to his performances. I'll never forget the read through that week. When Farley stood up next to Lorne during the reading and started to bop his head to "What Is Love," he bopped it so hard that a small amount of what looked like blood flew out of his nose. Not one person said a word about it; head writer Paula Pell just handed him a Kleenex. It wasn't a surprise to find out that the sketch didn't make the lineup. I always thought it could have been the best Roxbury aside from the Jim Carrey one, but it probably wasn't safe for Farley to do it.

Anyway, as that season began, I knew we were running out of steam when it came to ideas for Roxbury sketches, and I was very aware of the overall importance of having go-to recurring characters on the show, so

I came up with an entirely new persona. I'd never tried anything quite this . . . *colorful* before, even at the Groundlings.

Contrary to what many people believed, Mango was not based on a gay male character. In fact, there were four distinct sources of inspiration for Mango, none of them gay, none of them male, and only two of them human.

Mango was based in part on a girl I met in Russia as a teenager on a community theater exchange trip. (A girl also known as my first wife—but more on that later.) She had this sexy, dramatic aura about her, a "come-hither—go away!" sort of thing. She spoke in broken English, and whenever she got mad at me, she'd shout, "Kattan, I kill you!" while she stomped her foot, which only made her look more adorable. Mango was also inspired by Winni, my Dalmatian back on Mount Baldy. Winni would play this game where she'd stand turned away from you, so that you were facing her ass straight on, and then she'd look back in a fashion I'd later see eerily reflected in my aforementioned Russian girlfriend: *Leave me alone . . . but come here!*

The third bit of inspiration for Mango came from the time I was at a strip club—one of the dancers there went by the name Mango. It struck me as such a hilariously odd choice. Why anyone would think that strutting their stuff while an announcer uttered the phrase "Give it up for MANGO!" was the way to give patrons erections and really get the dollar bills flying mystifies me.

The final source of inspiration for my own Mango came from a song I liked at the time. Like I said before, it wasn't unusual for a song to be the backbone of a sketch idea for me. In this case, that song was "Missing" by Everything but the Girl. (That would be the Todd Terry Club Mix to be exact, since I know you're planning on downloading the song now to listen to as you read the rest of the chapter.)

Thinking through the character and sketch possibilities, I reimagined Marlene Dietrich in her famous role from the 1930 movie *The Blue Angel*. In the film, Dietrich sang and stripped in this underground nightclub and mesmerized the men in the process, driving them mad with lust—so crazy, in fact, that they literally turned into chickens. No, I'm not kidding. In one shot, you see a group of men in the audience reaching out and chanting "Blue Angel!" and then it cuts back to Marlene Dietrich singing in a top hat, and then back to the group of men, now dressed up as chickens. As you know, when that much lust gets pent up inside you, transforming into poultry is a real danger.

My Mango was a male exotic dancer with spit curls and an unplaceable Europeanish accent, clad in gold lamé hot pants, a shiny pink beret, pink scarf, and a vaguely fuzzy hot-pink crop top that stopped six inches above my navel. Like Blue Angel, Mango's sexual appeal was such that no one, regardless of relationship status or sexual orientation, could resist him. All were obsessed and driven wild by Mango's tantalizingly fickle demeanor; I'd stretch my arm alluringly to my latest admirer before snatching it back, inevitably ending with "No! You can't have-a da Mango!"

Mango made his *SNL* debut on the third show of the season, with guest host Brendan Fraser, who played a stereotypical husband in a sketch I wrote with Scott Wainio. The second time I did Mango, Samuel L. Jackson played a stereotypical criminal/drug dealer. But it wasn't until Mango's third appearance that the sketch really clicked. The guest host was Garth Brooks, at the time one of the most popular musicians on the planet. And this time, instead of having the host play some stereotypical character, Garth appeared as himself. Since he was such a superstar, just seeing him fall for Mango was enough to carry the sketch.

One interesting thing about Garth Brooks was his tendency to speak about himself in the third person. I remember during the pitch meeting, when someone floated an idea he didn't feel like doing, he would say, "Garth doesn't do that." He wasn't being sarcastic, either. Anyway, Garth's Mango sketch was so beloved, even by his fans, that years later he told me that at his huge, sold-out stadium shows, members of the audience would often toss mangoes onto the stage.

From then on, having the guest host appear with Mango as themselves was the standard. One of the most popular Mango sketches was in 2001 when Jennifer Lopez, a.k.a. "J. Lo," was both the guest host and musical guest. This felt more important than the other Mango sketches, perhaps because we knew there'd be so many viewers. I remember that Lorne had me come to his office to talk with J. Lo about the sketch after the read through, before the lineup was chosen. I think Lorne wanted her to understand the character a little more and how physical the sketch would be. Supposedly her famous derrière had been insured for a million dollars that very week, but that rumor didn't stop her from going full out in a bit that included us repeatedly swatting each other's butts. (For inquiring minds, let's just say that it was round, firm, and fully packed.) J. Lo was very cool and made everybody feel at ease despite being a big star. I even felt comfortable stopping by her dressing room to say hi.

The sketch featured Will as a music video director who suggests J. Lo hire Mango as a dancer.

"Listen—I think I have just the guy for you," says Will. "I caught his act at this wonderful strip club called Beefcakes. A male strip club. I went there by mistake—long story. I just fell in love with him."

"Sorry I'm late," I say as I enter in Mango's usual spangled getup. "I was just getting acupuncture on my hoo-ha."

I peel off my pink crop top and jump onto the bed where J. Lo is crouched, filming a video for "Love Don't Cost a Thing." I'm wearing long gold gloves, and I wave my arms in front of my face as I do a few pelvic thrusts . . . before turning and grinding my ass toward J. Lo's head and basically onto her shoulder.

Darrell Hammond, who is sitting next to Will, says, "This guy is good. He's making love to the camera!" Then J. Lo's song stops and Everything but the Girl begins to play.

"What the hell is going on here?" J. Lo shouts.

Will and Darrell have, naturally, already been seduced and sit there mesmerized, intoning "Mango . . . Mango."

In the next scene, in a recording studio where Mango is making an album, Will tells J. Lo they have to cancel her recording session because Mango's went long.

"Sorry, sweet cheeks," Mango crows. "Divas can't be rushed."

J. Lo looks (down) at me and says, "You are no diva!" My passions inflamed, things get heated, and I challenge her to a diva battle, shouting "Bring it on, J. *Ho!*" while Will struggles to separate us.

Jennifer Lopez really gives her all in the sketch, managing to convey the impression that she is infuriated and feeling legitimately competitive with . . . me. In the next scene, we show up wearing the same outfit, and J. Lo warns me not to get in her way.

"Can you paint a rainbow to be less beautiful?" Mango asks.

"Can you piss off a Puerto Rican and live to tell about it?" J. Lo retorts, as the audience cheers her on.

Soon we're wrestling and throwing each other into mirrors and tables; Mango even reaches out to try and squeeze J. Lo's breasts.

In its entirety, the sketch was over seven minutes long, and almost a full minute of this was a video of Mango in a limo, dancing and singing with several ladies to a version of Madonna's "Music," with the lyric "music" changed to "Mango."

Mango appeared in sixteen shows in all, with everyone from Danny DeVito to Christopher Walken to Ellen DeGeneres. The week Gwyneth Paltrow hosted, we did a Mango sketch with her. This was also the week that I asked Matt Damon if he would do a cameo in the sketch, and he said yes, which was a pretty big deal for the show. Not just because he was a huge star and loved by everyone, but also because he had never done live television before.

We were in the studio, camera blocking a scene toward the end of the sketch where Horatio, Ana, Will, Tracy, Gwyneth, and I break into a quick musical performance of "Summer Nights" from Grease. Gwyneth, or "Gwyny Bear" as Mango endearingly called her, sat on set in her "dressing room" as Ana, playing her agent, and Will, playing her hairdresser, stood behind her. Matt was offstage, standing behind a set door, waiting for his cue to enter. At the moment, none of us were performing, just waiting for our director Beth to say, "All right, let's take it from the top of the song" so we could continue blocking.

Then Gwyneth called someone over, and they exchanged some words. I won't name this person or say what he did on the show, but he wasn't in the cast nor was he a writer. I had no idea what they were talking about, but it wasn't my business, nor did I really care.

A few hours later, after we were done, I went over to the control booth and asked if I could watch the videotape of the sketch so I could see how it worked on camera. Writers and cast members did this all the time—it was extremely helpful if you wanted to improve on a sketch before Saturday night. Actually, let me explain: in any television studio, there's a feed of whatever is happening "live" on camera in the studio that you can watch from any monitor in any dressing room or office. For example, you can watch the feed of the *Today* show an hour before going to air and see the hosts going over their notes without makeup on. Or, at 5 PM, you can watch *NBC News* with Tom Brokaw at his desk in a sweatshirt with his glasses on. In every show's control booth, there is tape that's recording the feed just in case . . . I don't know. But basically, if something is happening on set, even a rehearsal, someone is recording it.

So, I was in my dressing room, watching the tape of the rehearsal for the Mango sketch, and I was at the point where we were about to start singing about "summer lovin'" when Gwyneth called the unnamed person over. This time I could hear everything they were saying.

"Since Matt's here, can we get him in the monologue?" Gwyneth asked.

Which was a good idea. As long as he's here for a sketch, why *not* use him in the opening monologue? The one reason not to have a guest in the monologue is that it can spoil the "surprise" part of a "surprise cameo," but that doesn't always matter. But instead of saying, "Well, the only reason he's even here is because Kattan asked him to do a Mango sketch," or, "Hey, that's a good idea; let's ask Kattan," this person replied:

"Well, what I'm hoping for is that *this* sketch, the Mango sketch, tanks. Then we can have Matt in the monologue." Suddenly, the volume in the tape cut out. I didn't get to hear the rest of the exchange.

The hardest part of overhearing that conversation was that this person was someone I trusted and considered a close friend. I never confronted him about it. If I had, what good would it have done? Instead I simply decided to forgive him. On Saturday night, Matt didn't do the monologue and, as planned, he did do the Mango sketch, which was a hit. His appearance was one of my favorite cameos ever. Unfortunately, you can't watch it because for whatever reason it's not available on the *SNL* app. You used to be able to find it on YouTube, but it was recently taken down by NBC. Who knows—maybe they have big plans for it!

My last Mango sketch was with Winona Ryder, who was just coming off her arrest for shoplifting. She was fine with joking about the situation, so in the sketch Mango is shopping with Winona, who of course plays herself. Winona had to check the content of the sketch with her lawyer, and a few things ended up getting nixed for legal reasons. A pre-tape that didn't air had musical guest Moby wearing a "FREE WINONA" T-shirt while she wore one that said "FREE MOBY."

I made an appearance on Bill Maher once, and all the questions about gay issues were directed at me, which I found very strange; I just didn't realize people thought I was gay. In fact, throughout my run at *SNL*, I was dogged by gay rumors. It didn't bother me except for the fact that I started getting typecast outside of the show as a gay character. Actually, I shouldn't have minded at all—I think the whole gay thing helped get me laid because women saw me as nonthreatening.

Of course, part of this was Mango's fault; when an actor does any character so often and so completely, people begin to assume that's who you are. The rumors were also probably a result of the many female impersonations I did, such as Anne Heche and Kerri Strug and Queen Elizabeth. Then, of course, there was Gay Hitler. Obviously, that might have made a few people stop and wonder. *Deep down, is Chris Kattan . . . a Nazi?*

Gay Hitler was a favorite of mine, despite the fact that he wasn't a character I'd created on my own. Michael Schur, the head writer of "Weekend Update" and one of the creators behind *The Office*, *Parks and Recreation*, and *Brooklyn Nine-Nine*, came up with him for me. A book had come out claiming that Hitler was gay, and Schur thought it would be hilarious if I came out onstage as Gay Hitler for "Weekend Update." Schur came up with the line, "*Sprechen Sie Dick?*" and I came up with the bit where I'd do the Nazi salute but then trail it off with a limp-wristed flutter. I spontaneously added the bit where I'd say, "Hi, Tina," all friendly, and then "Hi, Jimmy," as if there were some sort of animosity between us. There was no reason or explanation for it, it just worked.

That segment was popular enough that they brought it back for the end-of-season finale, recapping all of the biggest hits from "Weekend Update." Will was there as Neil Diamond and, of course, he wound up making out with Gay Hitler. Will was always making out with somebody. It was fun to play a character so popular that it came up in all the end-of-season retrospectives that year, but I suppose it probably didn't help tamp down the rumors that were swirling about me.

Perhaps Mango and those rumors contributed in some way to something I'd discover over the seasons, namely the fact that some of the male hosts liked to get rough with me.

Take for instance when Dylan McDermott hosted. We did a Mango sketch in which McDermott slapped me, and I swear I had the imprint of his hand on my ass for two weeks straight. He was a really nice guy, so there was nothing malicious about it, but he hit me *hard*. Ben Affleck, the future Dark Knight, did a sketch called "Who Wants to Be Groped by an Eleven-Thousand-Aire?" with him as a white-trash trucker, and me as the lone male among the finalists, the others being played by Ana and Cheri.

At the end of the sketch, Affleck wrestles with me in a car, and during dress rehearsal, he grabbed my thighs so tight he truly hurt me. He was being all caveman violent, growling and rubbing me with his chin, and all I could think was *What the fuck is happening?* While doing our Mango sketch, David Duchovny, too, grabbed me a little too hard and spanked me just a bit too roughly. He was otherwise great—I'd done an impression of him, but he didn't hold it against me (unlike some). Sometimes later I'd run into him with Téa Leoni and their kids, and he was always smiling. He would jokingly ask me to come spend the night with him and Téa. He told me he'd tickle me, but I couldn't have sex with Téa.

Anyway, the rough stuff was definitely a trend among a certain type of male guest, mostly the tall, dark, and handsome ones who seemed like they might have been prom king. It's always been one of those things I wondered about. I never spent any time in locker rooms, so maybe this was some kind of locker room boys-being-boys humor. Maybe they all played football or something like that. Or maybe they were just really excited to have a chance to play with Mango.

Chapter 12

FROM RUSSIA AND THE WEST SIDE

I n high school, my humor was not always as well received by the teach-ers as it was by my classmates. My math teacher, Mr. Quistorff, was probably the least of my fans, but what could I do? He was just beg-ging to be made fun of. Like a lot of the teachers, he had to repeat the same information six times a day for his six classes, and maybe that's why he had a tendency to mumble his way through the lesson. When-ever somebody raised their hand and said, "I'm sorry, I can't understand what you're saying," Mr. Quistorff would respond with a loud, overly enunciated, "Well, maybe I should *articulate* for you!" It probably goes without saying that Mr. Quistorff inspired a certain popular character of mine.

But I did have a fantastic English teacher, Mr. Bob McAllister. And so when Mr. McAllister decided to get the school's theater program up and running again, I auditioned immediately. Mr. McAllister served as the director, and he cast me twice in a row as the lead bad guy—first as the Reverend Parris in *The Crucible* and then as the innkeeper in the musical *Man of La Mancha*. I believe I sang two lines. The number of lines didn't matter to me, though; I just loved having the responsibility of a role that was so important to the story. I would have been overjoyed to have been cast as the plant in *Little Shop of Horrors*, for instance.

So it came as a shock when my director reprimanded me.

"You're very funny, Chris. That's the problem. You're *too* funny."

Now how could that possibly be?

"You're great," he explained. "But we'll never be able to open on time because you're also distracting. You're funny, and that's very appealing to other people, but that means they're being distracted. They're laughing and they're fucking around and you're fucking around and people are more attracted to fucking around than to starting the fucking play."

I thought: *I don't want to be that person. Fuck.*

I felt like I was getting closer and closer to finding out what made me who I was, and I was pretty sure that making people laugh was part of it. But I also wanted to be a professional, and to do that, I realized I had to *be* professional. I didn't want to be just a distraction. This was the first time I grasped what being professional meant.

It was good timing, as I had just joined a local theater troupe called Greasepaint. Most of the actors in Greasepaint were young and in high school, but there were adults there, too, who did this in their free time. It was a step up from high school theater. At least, in some ways.

One of my first roles was as A-rab, in *West Side Story*, one of the Jets. I'd loved *West Side Story* as a kid, so when I learned Greasepaint would be performing it, I was thrilled. Then I heard the director's vision for the production.

"I want to do an apocalyptic version," he told us. "I want all of you to prepare by watching *The Warriors* and *Escape from New York*."

How in the hell were we going to prepare for a play about star-crossed lovers by watching an eye patch–wearing bounty hunter named "Snake" rescue the president from future Manhattan, which just so happened to be a gigantic *prison*? How might we better understand the mindset of our hero when he sang, "There's a place for us, somewhere a place for us" by watching an antihero say, "Listen to me. The president is dead, you got that? Somebody's had him for dinner!"

It was hard to take this seriously, but everyone was *very serious* in community theater. We got deep into character. We did trust falls, and we massaged each other's shoulders to de-stress before curtain time. So we dug in and got excited, as if we were all saying, "Let's make this the best apocalyptic *West Side Story* ever!"

If I thought the concept was ridiculous before, seeing the costumes didn't help. The poor wardrobe department was like one lady who worked at the Sunglass Hut at the mall in Silverdale and came after her shift to beat her head against the wall making these fucking apocalyptic outfits. Our Sharks and Jets had bats and chains. There were people in *RoboCop*-like costumes with tights.

The director's spin on the Officer Krupke character had a touch of a *1984* "big brother is watching you" thing going on. Our Officer Krupke was supposedly watching us from a TV monitor that sat onstage. Of course, we didn't actually have him on a monitor, but rather he spoke from a box that had a lightbulb in it. The guy playing Krupke worked at the ferry during the day and happened to be a bit of a drinker. During the performance, he sat in a booth in the theater, reading from his script into a microphone.

"Yeah, you kids," he would say, in character, but then, "Hold on a second" and over the mic we'd hear the sounds of paper shuffling while he found his place, or sometimes the clink of a glass spilling.

My dad came up to see me in Bainbridge, and he visited the set to watch us act out our timeless story of love and the coming apocalypse. I got to introduce my father to the rest of the cast, and it was a big deal for everyone to see a real Hollywood actor and comedian who I could tell them played "Tailor Smurf." At the time, I was slightly embarrassed by the play and having my father see me in it, and I only had a few lines. But when I asked Dad what he thought of the show, he was kind and encouraging. We joked about other apocalyptic versions of famous plays that could be made. How about a *Death of a Salesman* where maybe Willy Loman turned into a zombie? Or an apocalyptic version of *My Fair Lady*!

It was 1988, so the Cold War was still going on—communism still ruled the Soviet Union, the arms race had everybody freaked out, and the world was nervously watching negotiations unfold between President Reagan and Mikhail Gorbachev. One of the producers on the board of the Bainbridge Performing Arts organization knew someone in Russia, and an idea was concocted to have Greasepaint go over and visit a similar theater troupe in this Russian city, an idea we all thought was really cool. Together we would do a play in both English and Russian, working together, and no doubt bring about world peace.

The Russian group was in Novosibirsk, Siberia, at the time one of the most miserable places in the world. The adults responsible for this joint venture did it for nothing but the love of the craft, and in retrospect, they honestly took on *way* too much. For a seventeen- or eighteen-year-old, however, it was an incredible adventure. There were fifteen of us and fifteen of them. They knew very little English and none of us knew Russian, so it was a real foreign exchange. The whole enterprise was pretty amazing, especially with no ulterior plans to make money or some secret drug deal going down. For the three to four weeks we were there, our worlds were expanded.

My mom had encouraged me to go since she had grown up in hardship in Hungary and wanted me to get a picture of it. She got her wish. Siberia looked like pictures I'd seen of the Great Depression. The state-run markets were tiny, and you'd walk in and find two heads of lettuce and a fish lying on the floor. Long lines of poverty-stricken men and women stood waiting to buy the meager items on their grocery lists. Witnessing these conditions was depressing and shocking, especially for me as an American teenager. Reading about something is one thing, but seeing it for myself made it very real.

There were no direct flights into Novosibirsk, so we'd flown into Russia and then taken a train on the longest railway in the world. At nighttime, I stuck my head out the open train window next to my bunk and fell asleep. A few days later, I felt a cold sore in my mouth. Then it rapidly became difficult to swallow or even to breathe without pain. Before long it felt like having a hundred fucking cold sores burning on my tongue and gums and on the sides and back of my throat. I don't know if it was the soot in the air from the open window on the train, but whatever the cause, a pus-filled mass had developed in my mouth. From Russia with love!

The woman producing our play owned the theater we were performing in and was the wife of Novosibirsk's sheriff. She also happened to be a hardcore Communist, powerful and influential enough to be friends with Gorbachev. When she saw how bad my infection had become, she took me behind the Iron Curtain to see a doctor. Crossing into the Communist part of the city, the streets and buildings suddenly became brighter and cleaner and bigger. Those in the Communist Party were given more, from the places they lived and shopped at to the doctors they visited.

I was brought into an office, and a woman entered speaking Russian. That's all I remember for a while—I was in so much pain I blacked out. I woke up in some medical building that was sterile and beautiful; everybody wore masks and white uniforms. They put me in a chair and slipped glasses over my eyes, and they then told me to open my mouth right before they shot a laser into it. For 1988, this was incredibly advanced. The whole experience was weird and surreal, and yet I was incredibly grateful to the woman who'd brought me there. Whatever special procedure had been done on the other side of that Iron Curtain, it took care of the abscess, and I started to feel normal again.

Which was a good thing, as we still had a show to put on. The play was called *Lullaby for Tomorrow*, and our group all played various characters from children's stories, everyone from Wonder Woman to the Seven Dwarfs. I was Pinocchio, a role I was destined to play—my dad had always said I looked like him when I was a kid, and he wasn't wrong.

Our Russian counterparts would be performing their own version of the story, with favorite Russian children's characters, and I was soon captivated by the girl who played the Firebird, a mythical bird popular in Russian folklore. The Firebird, or "*Zhar-ptitsa*" had influenced many artists. The great Russian composer and pianist Igor Stravinsky had been so inspired by the character that he wrote a ballet score titled *The Firebird*. My Firebird's name was Vita, and she was gorgeous, beyond beautiful in a way that's difficult to explain. She wore a red-and-gold outfit and performed ballet in her role, and being such a romantic at the time, it's not really surprising that I fell under Vita's spell.

Vita would sit beside me when we got our notes on our performances during rehearsals. Everything in Novosibirsk was BIG, including the massive stage where we rehearsed. Now imagine me as Pinocchio—a legendarily sexy character—sitting next to a beautiful red-and-gold creature called the Firebird. Really though, we were just two high school students who couldn't understand each other. I flirted with Vita, which felt something like William Hurt trying to court Marlee Matlin in *Children of a Lesser God*. I'd point to a piece of furniture and name it, and Vita would say "table" with her adorably thick Russian accent.

Our group was focused and talented, and all of us cared deeply about the project. Nobody got pregnant, and there were only a few nights when we snuck out and got drunk. We were there because we loved theater. I didn't have a very big part, but it didn't matter. I was in Russia, spending my time putting on a play and falling for this incredible young woman. Our friendship was very sweet and innocent. We never even kissed while I was there.

I fell in love with Vita on that trip, though at the time, she was going out with some guy who looked like Marlon Brando in *A Streetcar Named Desire*. When it was time to leave and go back home to America, I was heartbroken. Once I was back home, we wrote letters back and forth to each other. This was pre-internet, when international calls cost something like fifteen dollars a minute. A letter might take a month to reach her.

After our trip to Siberia, someone had the idea to bring the Russian group over to do something similar at small theaters in the Seattle area. We raised money, and the group eventually came to Bainbridge. Each of the Russian kids in the show was assigned to stay with one of the kids in Greasepaint. Vita wasn't staying with me; she stayed with another girl in our group, but at last I got to see her again. By the time Vita came to the United States, she knew a little more English. We could say we loved each other and know exactly what it meant. I felt like I'd met "the one." We grew very attached in our few weeks together, and watching her leave was devastating.

I graduated from high school, and moved in with my dad to begin training with the Groundlings in LA. Vita and I continued to write to each other, talking about some future when we could be together. I was about to move on from the basic improv class to the intermediate level when Mindy Sterling decided to hold me back.

"I want you to wait a year," she told me. "You're so young. There's never been somebody your age in the Groundlings." I was nineteen.

I didn't know what to do, so I decided to take some classes at Cal State, Northridge. But it was impossible to concentrate—all I wanted was two things: to be a Groundling, and to be with Vita. Eventually, we saved up enough money to buy a ticket so Vita could fly to LA and move in with me and my father. For a while, life was good and normal. I worked at a video rental store and Vita gave piano lessons. She was an amazing pianist and hung out with some amazing musical people. I'd pick her up every night and hear about people she'd met or what had happened during her day.

A few years later, on January 17, 1994, a magnitude 6.7 earthquake rocked the San Fernando Valley at around 4:30 AM. Vita and I were asleep in my bedroom at my father's house when I woke up feeling like I was hitting my head in a car accident. I found myself lying on the floor next to Vita with the mattress on top of us.

As the violent shaking continued, we crawled out from underneath the mattress and ran into my dad's bedroom. I remember thinking we were either being bombed or it was simply the end of the world. Dad's mattress was overturned, too. I didn't know he was underneath it until I heard him say, "I love you guys."

He crawled out, and the three of us ran toward the kitchen. When we reached it, the cabinet doors flew open, and much like in the opening scene of *Raiders of the Lost Ark*, plates started flying toward us. We tried to dodge them, like heroes ducking and avoiding poisonous darts, and I remember thinking something random like: *Finally, I'm Indiana Jones! As long as that huge fucking ball doesn't come rolling down behind us . . .* and then, as we stood in the front doorway, just as I remembered being taught in fifth grade when preparing for an earthquake (or "The Big One" as it was usually called), the three of us said our goodbyes to each other.

After the longest twenty seconds ever, the ground beneath our feet stopped rolling, the cracks in the pavement stopped trying to make their way to the street, and the pool was almost completely empty of water. We stood there like we were the last survivors of an apocalypse, grateful to still have one another.

Initially, Vita and I lived off romance, not worried about staying in my dad's spare bedroom or the fact that I didn't have much of a job. I went back to the Groundlings, and eventually made it into the Sunday show. But something happened during this time. Maybe I grew up. I just know something changed inside of me. I felt like I had become a different person, almost without noticing it happening.

"I think I'm falling out of love with you," I told Vita. "I also don't want to lose you."

I meant both statements. I felt terrible.

Vita still loved me, but if I was honest, love and romance had taken a back seat to my career. I knew exactly where I wanted to go, and that it would require everything I had. If you have huge dreams and aspirations, then you can't fuck around. And you can't set someone up for betrayal if your true goal and desire is somewhere else. But how could I live with the fact that I had invited her to come to America and move in with me, only to then tell her it wasn't working out? She didn't have her green card, and Vita ending up back in Russia would have been a travesty. She deserved every opportunity she could get. So I did the most natural thing a guy can do when breaking up with a woman: I suggested we get married.

A marriage would allow Vita to earn her green card. So we did it. We went to the courthouse and made it official. Vita had become close to my family, who'd fallen in love with her as well. I told my mom, Marc, and my dad why we were getting married, and they were totally behind it. If I hadn't told them the truth, I would have lost respect for myself.

For a while Vita and I continued to live together, and then she moved next door. I still paid her rent, feeling responsible. I loved her, and I wanted her to be able to pursue her own dreams and goals. Her talent eventually led to a music scholarship from UCLA, and she would go on to have musicians like violinist Joshua Bell interested in working with her. In time she began to date other people, and met Teddy, a drummer from the Groundlings. They married and moved to New York. Teddy had grand plans, too, and joined a fledgling company as its music director and in-house composer. That company turned out to be Sirius radio.

I will always feel lucky to have had the opportunity to know someone like Vita. She was and is exceptional, and the relationship that began in Novosibirsk when we were so young and that carried us into the early part of our adulthoods will always be precious to me. I understood how sacred love was, having grown up receiving it from my parents, and it was something I didn't take for granted. Intimacy with another was something that you had to be responsible about, and in my case, that meant being honest about what I wanted to do. For me, it was time to direct all my energy and passion toward the one great love of my life: comedy.

Chapter 13

CHARLIE'S ANGELS

The first time I seductively opened up my silky, black, button-down dress shirt to reveal all eight of the coiled hairs on my pale chest, there were girls in the audience actually hollering. No hoots, mind you, just hollering . . . maybe a couple of whistles. I was like, *Ummm . . . Whoa. What's happening?* Then I thought: *So that's what a girl feels like when she's catcalled on the street.* It was October 1998, and I was on the *SNL* floor, playing Antonio Banderas as a talk show host in a sketch called "How Do You Say? Ah Yes, Show."

I would dress in black with a *Mask of Zorro*–era flowing black wig and greet the audience from my sofa, accompanied by three guitar-playing, maraca-shaking musicians—a.k.a. Jimmy Fallon, Darrell Hammond, and *SNL* music supervisor John Zonars (or, the first time around, Horatio Sanz). In an improbable Spanish accent, I would "interview" the female guest until the room grew so heated from (my) pent-up sexiness that I was forced to undress. The unsuspecting couch guest was first played by Lucy Lawless, and later Jennifer Love Hewitt and Amy Poehler each took a turn. When Drew Barrymore hosted *SNL* in March 1999, she told me that her then boyfriend, later her husband, comedian Tom Green, had suggested that she work with me. "You can trust him," Green told her. This was the perfect opportunity to have Drew appear in the sketch as Melanie Griffith, who at the time of course was married to Antonio Banderas.

We were pretty rough on Melanie in the sketch, with me saying things like, "Please, no kissy the face. Not now. For your lips are like two Mexican slugs covered with the Mentholatum." Drew plays along like a pro. "I love you," she says, in role as Melanie, to which I reply: "Yes, you do." At one point, she points to her breasts and says, "You're so hot! You wanna play bunny in the sailor?"

"No talky," Antonio says back to Melanie. "Please. I do not like the voice. It is like a slow, painful leak from a little Spanish tire."

Cue jokes about Antonio's aversion to hearing the name of Melanie's ex—"No! Never again. Never bring up the *Miami* man with the Johnson who shoots the coke dudes with a black man with-a no socks!"—which she interprets as foreplay; then some brilliantly frenetic guitar playing courtesy of Fallon and team, and off comes my shirt.

Lorne tried to get Antonio on for the twenty-fifth anniversary show back in 1999, but it didn't happen. Then, a couple years after I left *SNL,* Antonio Banderas was hosting, so I decided to call the show's head writer, Tina Fey, and try to get the sketch on again.

I was flown out to New York for the episode. The sketch I'd be doing wasn't actually with Antonio, though; Tina wrote it as a "Weekend Update" feature.

I played myself, and similar to true events, asked Tina if I could do an Antonio Banderas "Ah Yes, Show" sketch, since he was hosting. Tina responds: "Kattan . . . What makes you think you can just come on the show and do your Antonio Banderas sketch?" I make a pissy face and leave, and Tina says, "Chris Kattan, everybody!"

Was it more original than doing a sketch with Antonio? Yes. Was it funnier? I don't know. Was it better for the show? Maybe. Did I have a good time that night? Of course. Was Antonio Banderas not a fan of the "How Do You Say . . ." sketches? I wasn't sure.

As I walked out of the studio and toward my dressing room, I heard the soundproofed heels of an NBC page shuffling behind me, and then: "Mr. Kattan! Mr. Banderas would like to say hello to you."

Antonio and Melanie Griffith were still married at the time, and when I entered his dressing room, she was sitting on an Art Deco bar stool, one leg crossing the other as her red-painted nails pinched the end of a Marlboro. Because there didn't seem to be an ashtray on the table in front of her, I remember thinking: *Where is she ashing?* On the other side of the couch, pulling up his pants while looking in the mirror, stood Antonio.

As if he was reading lines from an "Ah Yes Show. . ." sketch, he said: "Chris. Oh, my God. You are so de funny. Really. No joke. I'm so de serious right now."

"Yeah," said Melanie. "We love the sketch. You got him dooown, honey." Then, with a tap of her cigarette, an ash fell, bounced off her stiletto heel and onto the rug.

"But why this . . . this other thing?" Antonio wanted to know. "Why not the sketch? Why not doing this tonight?"

I gave him the only answer I had: "This . . . I don't know."

In September of 1998, Will and I were dressed in Roxbury attire shooting a ten-second promo for the season premiere of *SNL* with the hottest woman in the world, guest host Cameron Diaz. While Will and I were bopping her back and forth between us, there was a moment where she started straddling me, and I couldn't help but wonder: *Is Cameron Diaz flirting with me?*

Her line was: "Hi, I'm Cameron Diaz, and I'm hosting the season premiere of *Saturday Night Live* with musical guest the Smashing Pumpkins." Then with three seconds remaining in the spot, she really got into the bopping back and forth, specifically with me. Probably mostly because I was shorter than Will, but still. I remember looking at Marci Klein to see if she was seeing this, and later she told me, "If she likes you, she has an interesting way of showing it."

No actress has come closer to being the embodiment of my childhood idol Marilyn Monroe and having that sort of effect on me than Cameron Diaz. My reaction to seeing her for the first time in *The Mask* was honestly a lot like Jim Carrey's over-the-top animated Tex Avery–styled "AaaaOooooogga!"

That show's Roxbury sketch featured the Smashing Pumpkins and a surprise appearance by the Festrunk Brothers—Steve Martin and Dan Aykroyd's "wild and crazy guys," who also try to work their magic on Cameron.

"Where do you live, Kattan?" Cameron, wearing sky-blue eye shadow and a dress of the same color, asked me during the after-show party. She said that we should hang out, and she gave me her phone number.

I held on to that number as if it were the Ark of the Covenant. Cameron left me this hilarious eight-minute message, and for immediate affirmation I played it for Molly, who said, "Oh, yeah, she definitely likes you."

"Like" can be such a lame word, but that "like," when Molly said it, couldn't have sounded more passionate.

I went to LA to promote *Roxbury*, and Paramount put me up at the Four Seasons. I had called Cameron, who said she'd pick me up on the night I arrived. I think I changed my outfit and brushed my teeth and cut my fingernails five times before she got there. Like a Vargas model riding a silver bullet, she pulled up in a sporty two-door silver convertible Mercedes. I remember actually blushing as I stepped out of the lobby that warm LA night, which felt more like the Miami strip. I climbed into the car, and before I had a chance to reach for my seat belt, she had already peeled out. I don't know what the speed limit was on Robertson, but with the top down it felt like we were going 70 mph. I honestly felt like I was in a romantic comedy. And what was really cool was that wrapped around her neck was the longest pashmina scarf that flapped in the wind, just like when Snoopy's alter ego, the Red Baron, was flying his doghouse.

Cameron introduced me to her friends at a club on Beverly, next door to Jerry's Deli, and they eventually became the first and only group of outside friends I'd had since I started the show. One was Cameron's makeup artist, a girl named Gucci, who coincidentally shared the same birthday with me (October 19, 1970); another was her best friend, Jennifer, this absolutely stunning woman from Argentina who Cameron knew from her days as a runway model.

After we all started hanging out, every now and then someone would seem to wonder why I was always around Cameron, and I could see them looking at the two of us and asking *Why are they even friends?* Ben Stiller was one of those people.

About a month after Cameron guest-hosted *SNL*, Ben did as well, in October 1998, and I remember the parting gift he left for me. It wasn't customary, but sometimes the guest host would give out gifts or notes to the cast members at the end of the show. For example, Charlize Theron gave out rocks with messages written on them. Ben Stiller gave everybody Curious George thank-you cards, and the note in mine was short and sweet:

"Chris, Fuck You."

I wasn't sure if he was joking or not. I thought it was maybe a bit passive-aggressive, since it wasn't just aggressive—otherwise he wouldn't have even given me a card, right? Not long after that, he left a message on my answering machine and pitched me an idea for a comedy he wanted to do about horse jockeys, one of which I would play, along with Rob Schneider. Just like with the card, I wasn't quite sure if he was serious or not. The movie idea did sound funny, but was I supposed to be offended by the jockey part? I was just confused. Horse jockey movie and a card that said "Fuck you." Anyway, it was years ago. We were kids back then. Kids who were almost thirty years old.

Obviously, Cameron and Ben knew each other from *There's Something About Mary*. One night, we hung out with Ben at the beautiful and impressive penthouse he had at the time. Cameron had a place in the same building, the famous El Royale. The twelve-story, white concrete building was constructed two years before the stock market crash of 1929, and its famous occupants have included Clark Gable and William Faulkner, along with Judd Apatow, Jack Black, and Uma Thurman. Ben's suite was on the top floor, and when I arrived with Cameron and her friend Jennifer, Ben was very kind, but there was this hint in the air of a little, let's say, *something*. Something that whispered: *What the hell is he doing here?*

Ben never expressed anything remotely like that, though. He gave us a guided tour of the apartment, and I could tell he was enamored with the grandeur and the history of the place, although Cameron, Jennifer, and I were acting like fourth graders, laughing while the teacher talked about science. Ben showed me the impressive collection of original black-and-white photos of '60s and '70s rock bands that he had all across the walls. Then we went through the living room and eventually into this lounge/den/library/nightcap room that had a fireplace. All the while, I knew my host couldn't quite understand why I was still there with Cameron, and to be honest, I wasn't exactly sure why she had taken me under her wing. I guess I should be more clear. We weren't dating or anything like that. I didn't push for clarification, since I loved hanging around with her and was comfortable just being friends. But now and then, even I couldn't help but wonder what exactly *was* going on.

At one point in the evening, Stiller came up to me and walked me back into the living room to ask me a favor.

"Hey, man. Why don't you go down to my car and grab some CDs?" (Yep, we couldn't simply touch a screen and hear whatever album we wanted just yet; we still had old-school compact discs.)

Even though he already had some smooth tunes playing, he wanted me to take the elevator twelve stories down to the parking lot where his Porsche sat and rummage around for . . . I wasn't sure what, exactly. Nor did I know how to respond, so I simply said, "Yeah, sure."

In the elevator, it dawned on me how odd the request happened to be. Were these special albums he carried around in a deluxe carrying case? How many CDs was I supposed to grab? What if he had fifty albums? Should I take *Yanni Live at the Acropolis* and leave behind TLC? Maybe grab En Vogue and forget about Fatboy Slim? And if I couldn't find the perfect choice right off, should I search through the glove compartment and the back seats for some Eagle-Eye Cherry? Maybe Limp Bizkit? (I could keep going.)

While gathering the few albums he had in his sports car, I realized Ben simply wanted to get me out of his place. Not because he didn't like me. Not necessarily. He just wanted Cameron all to himself, which I didn't blame him for. I actually rushed back to get into the elevator. When I got upstairs, Cameron and Jennifer were sitting on the couch across from Stiller, who was laid back in his beanbag with his sweater pulled up and his hand rubbing his six-pack. He gave me an "Already? You're back? Come on!" sort of look. Was he expecting that I'd take an hour to choose the perfect album?

"Here are your CDs," I said, holding out the stack and feeling like a Girl Scout selling Samoas.

Hanging around Cameron and her friends was the beginning of my having a social life outside of anything work related. This steady group of friends became reliable, caring, and even helped me become more responsible; Cameron hooked me up with her accountant, and even her money manager, Dana Giacchetto—who was a well-known investor and close friends with celebrities like Leo DiCaprio, Alanis Morissette, Ben Affleck, and Michael Stipe. Giacchetto seemed like the smartest person to make my first investment with . . . until a few weeks later, when Cameron called me in a panic and said to drop him immediately because he was going to prison for securities fraud and stealing over ten million dollars from his clients. Luckily I came out unscathed.

During this time, I decided to move out of my father's house. One of Cameron's friends who I'd gotten to know was this very cool woman named Stacey Sher. When I met her, she had already worked as a producer on films like *Pulp Fiction, The Fisher King,* and *Reality Bites* as one of the heads of Jersey Films along with Danny DeVito, and I ended up moving into Stacey and her boyfriend Kari's guesthouse on Oriole Drive, just north of the Sunset Strip. I'd describe it as being very similar to the Fonz's guesthouse above the Cunningham's garage in *Happy Days.* The lush property with its pool and outdoor fireplace felt more like a resort getaway than a residence. The guesthouse didn't have a kitchen, so I would go over and use theirs, where I would usually run into a variety of industry people.

Since Stacey had worked with director Steven Soderbergh on *Out of Sight* and other films, one week I got to see them prepping for *Erin Brockovich,* writing at the dining room table along with Richard LaGravenese, who wrote the screenplay for *The Fisher King.* Once while I was back in New York and up on the seventeenth floor, Stacey called me and said to come down to 8H to meet Miloš Forman! That afternoon, I got to watch the great Czech filmmaker direct Jim Carrey channeling Andy Kaufman in the Mighty Mouse scene from *SNL* for *Man on the Moon.*

I felt like I was becoming part of this amazingly creative, often brilliant family while living in that guesthouse. Not just in Stacey's world but the neighborhood in general. Jennifer Aniston lived right around the corner, and I would often see her on Oriole Drive doing her daily run. Lionel Richie lived across the street, and Leo DiCaprio lived at the end of the block. I later began dating Cameron's friend, Jennifer, and we stayed together in the guesthouse. Jennifer was a lot taller than me, exotic, and our relationship, short-lived.

One year, Cameron invited me to celebrate New Year's Eve with her. It wasn't some big extravaganza, just a small dinner party. Robert Downey Jr. was there, wearing a cowboy hat and sunglasses, looking like a trendy space cowboy. He's always a sweetheart of a guy; he came with

Jared Leto, who I remember not being such a sweetheart to me, a little standoffish. And watching Cameron flirting and having fun with someone as pretty as Jared Leto was starting to make me feel jealous.

Cameron and Jared started dating while he was filming *Requiem for a Dream,* which for those who don't know is that sweet family film about heroin addicts who see their lives fall apart. During this time, I went out to dinner with Cameron and Jared and a few others in the West Village in New York. What was funny about that night was that for the entire evening, Leto was doing his method approach and locked into his Brooklyn-based character from *Requiem,* so whenever he would order something, he would speak in a thick Brooklyn accent. "Yeah . . . uh, gimme the salad with croutons and uhh, gimme the hot tea. Thanks babe." Out of respect to Cameron, I wasn't going to start making fun of her boyfriend, even though this behavior was practically screaming "Please make fun of me. I'm begging you!"

Then at one point, while trying to move a little closer to Cameron, Jared accidentally lifted his chair up as he scooted over a few inches and landed right on her toe. Since she was wearing open-toed sandals, not surprisingly she screamed. Then Leto, still in character and sporting that crazy accent that sounded more like Travolta's character in *Welcome Back, Kotter* than anything else, responded by saying: "Hey—come on. It was a joke. Whaddya want?" Which made sense since every actor knows, no matter what happens . . . always stay in character.

Eventually I became acquainted with the third member of the *Charlie's Angels* trio. When Lucy Liu hosted in December of 2000, she took photographs during the week on an actual camera, and after the show she gave cast members the photos she'd taken of them as gifts. At the after-party

I asked if she'd like to hang out when we were both back in LA, and we
exchanged phone numbers. When I finally got up the courage to give her
a call, I found out that the phone number she had given me belonged to
her assistant.

At the time, Lucy was busy filming the second *Charlie's Angels* along
with Cameron and Drew, but somehow she found time to meet. When she
drove up in a Porsche convertible, she sported a leather jacket, yoga pants,
and a Hermès scarf around her neck, and for our destination she similarly
chose only the finest: 7 AM breakfast at Du-par's on Ventura Boulevard. I
tried to convince myself that pancakes and coffee could be categorized as
a date. Especially when it costs eleven dollars, which I insisted on paying,
of course. Ah, *ma chérie,* the morning is young!

Chapter 14

YEAH, BUT HAVE YOU SEEN THEM LIVE?

When I first heard the last half of "New Year's Day" on a local Seattle radio station, I was immediately infatuated with the sound of a little band called U2. Then I heard "With or Without You," and I was obsessed. I spent many of my high school nights sitting in my car at the pier with the engine off, overlooking the still waters of Puget Sound; the rain would continuously knock on the hood of the car, and I would turn on my Kenwood CD player, the one with the detachable face, to play "40" from their *War* album.

It wasn't just that I became a big fan, it was much more significant and emotional. As if psychologically, and I know this sounds corny, *The Joshua Tree* became the sound of my youth. A bit like the character in Edgar Wright's *Baby Driver*, U2 provided the soundtrack to my high school years.

When I saw Bono's emotional performance of "Bad" at Live Aid, I couldn't believe how his physical performance combined with the band's music to give him so much control over the audience. He was one of the few performers (other than Bruce Springsteen and Freddie Mercury) who seemed to have an almost sexual command of the entire stadium. I would save up money and buy overpriced VHS bootlegs and study terribly videotaped concerts of U2's *The Joshua Tree* and *Zoo TV* tours. In the process of finding my so-called "self" by performing at pep assemblies in high school, I once sang "With or Without You." Because I didn't dare do an impression of Bono outright, my impression was Bono via Bobcat Goldthwait's impression at the first Comic Relief benefit, where he ran from one end of the stage to the other in a leather vest, hair tied back while holding up a white flag.

So when U2 came on the show in December 2000, I knew I had to try to get Bono to do a sketch. I wanted him to do a Mango cameo; they showed Bono a tape of Mango in action, and he decided he didn't want to do the cameo or any other sketches. He recognized I was a big fan, though, and invited me to his dressing room after the show. The whole band was there, along with Tom Cruise, Nicole Kidman, and the legendary Joey Ramone.

I sat down across from Bono. He had orange-tinted shades covering his wise, weathered eyes and was sipping from the nearly empty bottle of Heineken in his hand. We talked about his physical performance and his connection to the audience. Bono told me, "When you're singing and you get to that level of control and one with the audience, you say:

"I love you, I love you,

Fuck you, fuck you,

Wait, I'm sorry, I love you, I love you,

Fuck you, seriously. Fuck off.

Wait. Come back, I'm sorry."

Brilliant.

At the end he said, "Come see us," and surprisingly he followed through. They put aside some front-row tickets for a U2 show in Toronto while I was filming the movie *Undercover Brother* with Denise Richards, who I took to the show. I was so excited to see them live, to have front-row floor seats no less, and then Bono started singing "With or Without You"—my song, my anthem, my soundtrack. It was just like the movies; I turned and looked into Denise's bright blue eyes and yelled as loud as Bono was singing so I could be heard.

"Denise! Kiss me! You have to kiss me. This is a moment."

She shook her head and shouted, "No! Absolutely not."

". . . *nothing to win, and nothing left to lose.*"

"Come on! He's singing like three yards away from us—it's a moment!"

"Stop talking!" she screamed.

When you give yourself away, it doesn't always mean someone wants you.

During the next year or so I got into "the scene," frequenting the club at the Roosevelt Hotel, named Teddy's in honor of the late director Ted Demme. Teddy's was always packed, and you could always count on seeing the regulars like Lindsay Lohan, Paris Hilton, and Kate Hudson, but one night in 2002 I ran into Bono there, wearing dark shades and a cowboy hat. He had just been featured on the cover of *Time* magazine with a headline saying: "Can Bono Save the World?" He was becoming involved with the (RED) campaign for AIDS and was coming from an ANC meeting with President George W. Bush. When I walked up to him, Bono immediately remembered me, and we talked for a while. But at the end of the conversation—that is, when I ran out of interesting things to say—I said "Goodbye, Bono." And he pulled down his shades to look at me, and said, "Goodbye, Jimmy!"

Then, to add insult to injury, I got a call from Fallon a couple of days later.

"Hey, um, did you talk to Bono the other day?"

"Yeah. Why?"

"Well, he just invited me to his birthday party."

Fucking A!

In the beginning of Season 25, the musical guest was one of my absolute favorite musicians—and most likely one of yours—the incomparable David Bowie. It was one of the few times I asked a guest on the show for an autograph, and he kindly obliged. I didn't do it that often because I was slightly embarrassed at the time, but today I'm happy I did, like with Bruce Springsteen and Tom Petty. And hey, I didn't do it with the group All Saints or Natalie Imbruglia. I stopped after Jimmy saw me at the page desk asking one of them to ask Janet Reno if she would sign my *SNL* book, and he gave me a "that's not cool, pal" look.

Anyway, back to Bowie. Instead of asking Marci or someone who worked in Talent if I could meet him, I decided to go to his dressing room, and when I got there, the door was wide open and he was just sitting in a leather armchair with one leg over the armrest, swinging his foot back and forth. He was such a rock star.

I said, "Hi. I'm so sorry to bother you. I'm Chris."

Like a six-year-old boy seeing Santa Claus for the first time, Bowie jumped up and with the utmost grace and what I can only describe as an elegant curtsy came to shake my hand.

This was the first time I noticed how clear blue the color of his right eye was compared to the moody black color of his left eye. Later I learned that the hypnotic, beautiful color difference of his eyes was actually the appearance of one pupil being larger than the other, a condition called "anisocoria."

Later, when David Bowie and his band finished rehearsing the single "Little Wonder" for camera blocking, I yelled, "Sing 'Ashes to Ashes!'" And you know what? They did. It was absolutely insane, and finally my movie moment!

One of the kindest musical guests was Lenny Kravitz, who hosted in January 2001. He brought his dad with him, and they wore matching wool sweaters.

But some were not so cordial, like the lead singer of Jamiroquai, Jay Kay. When he and his band were headed to their dressing room after playing their set in September 1997, I said "Great job" as I walked by, and he replied "Fucking rubbish."

In a similar circumstance, while I was briskly passing Sir Liam Gallagher, the lead singer of the band Oasis—by the way I'm almost positive he wasn't knighted, but he sure acted like he was—I said "Hello," and he answered "Oh, come off it!"

Probably the most fun I ever had with a band wasn't actually on the show. One night at a star-packed VH1 benefit for the survivors of 9/11 at Madison Square Garden, I met Destiny's Child when they asked me to introduce them before they sang the hit song "Say My Name." A few months later, I saw them again when we were on the same six-hour flight from New York to Seattle. I was going to see family, and they were on tour, and for about three of the six hours in the air, Michelle, Kelly, Beyoncé, and I played games while seated with our seat belts on. We played charades. We played Heads Up! And we played a game we made up ourselves, where we basically threw pretzels at each other from across the aisle. But the best game was a scavenger hunt, which lasted almost an hour because poor Beyoncé had to search the entire cabin while trying to find the hidden treasure.

For the Christmas episode in 1998, legendary operatic tenor Luciano Pavarotti was the musical guest. Between dress and air, I was in the makeup room getting all dolled up for camera, and I noticed in the mirror that, directly behind me, sitting in a makeup chair, was Pavarotti—with extremely dark eyebrows. When my makeup artist waved me to get out of the chair since she was done, I asked if I could put on some ChapStick for another minute since I wanted so badly to keep watching Pavarotti.

"You're all done, Mr. Pavarotti," said his makeup artist. Pavarotti grabbed the eyebrow pencil, held the head of it to his eyebrow, and pleaded to her, with an Italian roll of the tongue on the *Rs*: "More! More!"

"Of course," she said, applying more dark pencil to what already looked very similar to the eyebrows of an *Angry Birds* character.

"How's that?" she asked. "We good?"

Pavarotti took one more look in the mirror and said, "More. Please, more. More!"

"You never know what people will talk about," Christopher Walken said in a *Rolling Stone* interview when asked about the popularity of the infamous "More Cowbell" sketch. "I've made so many movies, movies that I've never even seen. It's just as hard to make a movie that doesn't succeed as it is to make one that does. Things just happen a little mysteriously."

Walken was right. Nobody realized how popular the sketch would become when it aired on April 8, 2000.

(No, this book is not missing a page, we are jumping right into the "Cowbell" sketch; I just don't know what else to say about my Pavarotti experience. Moving on . . .)

Will said the idea came from hearing the cowbell in the background of the Blue Öyster Cult song "(Don't Fear) The Reaper." He wrote the sketch with Chris Parnell and first pitched it to Norm Macdonald when he hosted. But no go. Submitted a second time for host Alec Baldwin, but rejected again. Normally two strikes would kill a sketch idea, but in this case the third time really was charmed. Walken hosted, and it was finally chosen.

Between dress and air the night we did the sketch, instead of wearing the shirt he wore in rehearsal, Will asked wardrobe if they had a much smaller one. Wearing a shirt three sizes too small, the bottom half of his orange-haired belly was unmasked, and you could see his appendix scar. Will wasn't afraid to expose anything, and I always admired that. One time I walked into the office he shared with Parnell and he asked me if I wanted to see his "taint." Which, for those who don't know, is the smooth hairless area between the testicles and the anus. I passed, but I'm sure if I'd said, "Yes, I would very much like to see your taint," he'd probably have been okay with it.

Just a few seconds before going live, while holding the drumstick in one hand and the cowbell in the other, Will whispered to me, "When you push me and say, 'Don't blow this for us Gene!' . . . go ahead and push me as hard as you can. Just shove me."

So, in the sketch when I shouted, "Don't blow this for us, Gene!' I literally shoved him as hard as I could, and I don't think Will expected it. He lost his balance, almost fell over, his tight shirt slid up his chest, his belly spilled out, and—a little surprised by my adrenaline-fueled push—Will started laughing.

Then Jimmy broke, of course. Jimmy always was the first one to break.

I still love this exchange between Walken and me:

CHRISTOPHER WALKEN AS BRUCE DICKINSON: Babies, before we're done here, y'all be wearing gold-plated diapers.

ME AS GUITAR PLAYER BUCK DHARMA, GIVING HIM A "WTF?" LOOK: What does that mean?

None of us had any idea that almost two decades later, those five minutes would remain one of the all-time favorite moments of *Saturday Night Live.*

Chapter 15

"YOU GUYS WANT SOME COOKIES?"

Whenever people tell me they loved *Corky Romano,* I usually don't believe them, and the reason isn't as obvious as you might think. It's not because of scenes like the one where I'm driving an orange Fiat and singing "Take on Me" by a-ha. It's because making the film was painful and creatively damaging.

After *A Night at the Roxbury* came out, Will and I became stronger critics and wanted to make movies we could be proud of. When someone like the late, great Roger Ebert writes "Sometimes a movie is so witless that I abandon any attempt to think up clever lines for my review" about a film you've just made, you're going to think long and hard about follow-up movies you might do. I made a conscious effort to be cautious about making a studio film with a script that needed a lot of work.

My agent at the time, Adam Venit, was one of the few reps who would invite me to his home for dinner with his wife as well as to quite a few lunches where he actually opened up about his life outside of the business. I figured that if you were in the industry and confident enough to be yourself in a conversation instead of limiting yourself to small, unimportant talk, then you were usually one of the more powerful and legitimate players. It helped that his list of clients included people like Sandler, Farley, Sacha Baron Cohen, Steve Martin, and Dustin Hoffman.

We had connected during my first season on *SNL*, when I received a letter from Venit and his then partner Doug Robinson at Endeavor, before Endeavor joined up with William Morris. They wrote: "We have Farley, Sandler, and Spade, and we want you."

In my first gig for the *SNL* summer hiatus of 1999, Venit set up a meeting with Bob Simonds, who was supposedly persistent about having me star in my own movie, which he would produce for Disney where he was under contract. His deal with Disney was to make at least three comedies a year within a budget of $12 to $14 million. Simonds had been on a roll with Sandler after producing *The Wedding Singer* for $18 million, making $80 million, followed by *The Waterboy*, which was made for $23 million and earned a whoppin' $161 million! Before Sandler and his writing partner, *SNL*'s Tim Herlihy, came to Simonds with their pitch for *Billy Madison*, Simonds had made a few not-so-good comedies, like *Problem Child*. (By the way, Herlihy also helped write "Southern Lawyer," the Suel Forrester sketch that took place in a courtroom.)

Simonds had three scripts finished and ready for me to choose from. One of them was *Bubble Boy*, which I passed on and Jake Gyllenhaal did later. But the best script was titled *Corky Romano*. Even though it needed a lot of work, the plot was totally original (I say sarcastically): "The loser son of the head of the mob must go undercover for the FBI." Hey now, I'm laughing just thinking about it. With a plot that's been done many times before, a movie had better be funny; that way, instead of being panned for repeating the same formula again, reviewers would hopefully say "because it's absolutely hilarious, and Kattan's character glows, you forget the story has been done a thousand times before."

The cool thing was that Venit got my quote up to $1 million to star in the movie, and $600,000 to rewrite it. Three times more than what I'd earned on *Roxbury*. I was still concerned that the story needed a lot of help, which is not terribly easy to accomplish, especially when we were going to begin shooting in two months. Even though they agreed it could use some good jokes and a couple of set pieces, everyone on Simonds's team was already happy with the script, but Simonds wanted to make sure that *I* was happy with the script as well, so he let me hire two *SNL* writers and friends of mine, Matt Piedmont and Scott Wainio, to do rewrites. I knew they would come up with some ideas, but at the time none of us were really that skilled at story structure. Simonds suggested that maybe I could ask someone more experienced to take a look at it, and I lucked out big-time when friends Richard LaGravenese and Paul Thomas Anderson (writer and director of *Boogie Nights*, *Magnolia*, *There Will Be Blood*, and *The Master*) offered to help. I mean, Paul fuckin' Thomas fuckin' Anderson? If only I could tell every critic who gave *Corky* a bad review, "Oh, yeah? Well, Paul Thomas Anderson helped write it, dickhead!"

Then, during rewrites, casting began. And names like Peter Falk, the late Chris Penn, Peter Berg, and Vinessa Shaw, who I'd had a crush on since Kubrick's *Eyes Wide Shut,* were all joining the cast.

One thing I remember: seeing how important it was to be off book during an audition. When you're reading with someone, and you look down at your "sides," you can lose the connection that you have. It made me realize I probably should have memorized the lines for all the auditions I'd done in the past. Especially when, and this is true, I was auditioning for Francis Coppola's *Bram Stoker's Dracula* in the role of Dutch student #3, in a scene with Anthony Hopkins as Professor Van Helsing. I didn't get the part. I know, great story. It was very exciting for me at the time.

After we wrapped on our second day of shooting, I was asked to watch the dailies. Nowadays, you're sent an email with a link, but back in ye olden days, at the turn of the last century, in order to watch the dailies we had to go into a projection room. Anyway, everybody just *loved* the dailies. Even I, always ready to dislike everything I did, was laughing at almost every take. But what made me happiest was that my instinct to play the character of Corky Romano as a human being rather than an unrealistic caricature was actually working. Even Simonds, the producer, was as giddy as a schoolboy, laughing his ass off.

I know this may sound stupid, but making movies can be a lot of fun! A few weeks later, when things were still going along "easy peasy," our friend Mickey Mouse came by the editing room one afternoon and brought his playful dog, Pluto. Well, that crazy Pluto shot out a big turd across the room and it hit . . . well, you guessed it, the fan. In other words, Peter Schneider, a top executive at the Walt Disney Company, was hearing such great feedback that he decided—with just a few hours' notice—to come by after lunch and watch a rough ensemble, even though we didn't have anything edited yet, nor were the sound or music mixes properly done. So after having a splendid brunch that may have included a few cocktails, Peter showed up with a few of his buddies. He sat down, and a few minutes into watching a twelve-minute, unapproved, and beyond rough-cut ensemble of *Corky Romano*, Pete Schneider fell asleep.

Now I don't actually know if Mr. Schneider was one to enjoy a drink or four before his afternoon nap, but it really didn't matter. All that mattered was that he fell asleep watching the dailies. Bob Simonds flipped out and turned into Cruella de Vil. He'd suddenly changed his mind—he no longer loved my performance; instead, he decided nothing was funny. But he came up with a solution. Not that we'd have to do some reshoots, no: We had to reshoot *every single scene* we'd already shot. Usually, if a scene didn't work no matter how hard you tried in editing, you would reshoot after you wrapped production. But because the budget of the film was so tight, and everyone including the crew already had commitments immediately after, we had no choice but to reshoot three weeks' worth of work *while we continued to shoot the rest of the film*. So, every time we finished a scene, while the crew was setting up for the next scene, a second unit would set up a scene we had to reshoot, and I would be rushed over to that set for the do-over. Then, as soon as we finished reshooting a scene, I was rushed back to the first unit to continue shooting new scenes. This went on every single day for the rest of the shoot. All because Peter Schneider fell asleep. What's really fucked up is that after *Corky* finally wrapped production, Peter Schneider left Disney.

Having to reshoot all the previously done scenes while shooting the film forward was not pleasant, to say the least. And Bob bouncing off the walls twenty-four hours a day didn't help. But the worst part was that Bob's new idea of funny was to make the Corky character more of a happy-go-lucky cartoon than a human being.

"You need to smile all the time," he explained. "What I want and the studio wants to see is that 'Chris' that we all love, who walks into a room smiling."

"Yeah, but real people don't smile *all* the time," I said. "Especially when they're alone."

But I was exhausted, and for the first time, I stopped listening to my instincts and simply followed orders. Maybe everything they were saying was right and everything that I'd been thinking was wrong.

I told myself: *Bob must know what he's doing and the studio knows what they want, so I have no other choice but to trust the system.* I pushed for showing moments of the character's vulnerability, especially in the scenes with Vinessa, but it was the fart jokes that seemed most important to Bob.

Zach Galifianakis had a small part in the film where he played Dexter, the computer hacker. When they shot the scene, Zach was having trouble acting frightened while Pete Berg and Chris Penn yelled orders at him, and Simonds got so frustrated at Zach that he stepped in and started screaming at Zach over and over. Although it did make it easier for poor Zach to reach a level where he was sweating, nervous, and truly scared, it was still uncomfortable to watch Simonds literally scream in Zach's ear, toss papers around, and even grab and shake the computer desk. Zach eventually included a story in his stand-up routine about this experience, and he made *Corky* sound like the biggest piece of shit he ever made.

When we finally wrapped, I sat in the editing room, cringing at how far my performance was from what I had originally intended. I remember thinking: SNL *is going to have a field day making fun of this when they see it.*

That summer filming *Corky* was the hardest I had ever worked on anything in my life. I was pulling fifteen-hour days, and after work every night

I would come home to, well, this: a gorgeous woman, like someone you would find in a Federico Fellini film, her face inflamed and dotted with sweat, her voluptuous lips quivering as she held a kitchen knife out at me. My home life had started to play out like an episode of a show on the *ID* channel. I call it "My Introduction to Dating a Hot Mess."

This may have been The Kattan Curse my dad had warned me about. My girlfriend was like an exotic "Sybil." Every night, another personality would appear and magically create an argument out of nowhere. She yelled at me about everything and nothing, yet always honestly seemed to believe she had every reason to. Sometimes she would greet me with a charming, "Oh. Okay. *Now* you're home!"

"Why didn't you call me back?" she would shout. "I called you like . . . forty times! Not once did you pick up!"

I usually just let it go. When you're exhausted, you don't want to pick a fight.

One evening after a very long day, I opened the fridge to see it completely empty except for one beer on the bottom shelf.

"Didn't I just buy two cases of beer?" I made the mistake of asking her.

"Uh, no. Why?"

"Because there's only one beer left now."

From that point on, she yelled every word she said.

"Oh! So you're saying I drank them all?!"

Then came the final act, when she threatened me with a knife, then changed her mind, shouting, "That's it! I'm gonna call the cops and tell them you stabbed me!"

So this is the full story of what my life was like while working on *Corky Romano*. At the time, I had no idea that my girlfriend of two years was doing drugs behind my back. I had no point of reference for this relationship, nor any idea how a person doing blow even behaved. She did eventually turn her life around and became a success story. I won't mention this woman's name, but I will tell you she was taller than me.

I understand now that she couldn't help it. She was battling a disease. At the time, I actually believed her anger was somehow my fault and that she was rightfully furious with me. My dad's words of wisdom: "Is the fucking you're getting worth the fucking you're getting?"

Months after shooting concluded, *Corky Romano* was audience tested in theaters and got a positive response, even the agonizing scene with an overly long fart joke. *Corky* was now "locked" and ready for final editing. When I met with Disney's marketing department, it was encouraging to see how excited they were about the movie, and their reaction made the rest of the studio even more excited. Their ad campaign was a big picture of my very worried-looking face with the tagline "Who is Corky?" slapped right above it, or below it, or beside it, depending on . . . whatever. The image was all over the place. It was on billboards, buildings, streets, newspapers. There was even a huge Corky face on the pavement directly in front of the Disney offices in Burbank. I mean huge, as in three stories huge. "Who is Corky?" was working. The brilliant thing about it all was that the tagline really didn't have much to do with the film. It was its own machine. With the exception of my face, there wasn't any relevance to the movie at all. It was really quite brilliant.

When it came time for me to do press, a few weeks before opening weekend, Disney kept me very busy. I had appearances on *Letterman*, *Leno*, and plenty of other shows lined up, including one that was more in line with our audience demographic, MTV's *Total Request Live*, which taped in

New York. A week before the movie opened, the premiere took place at Universal CityWalk, and when I was asked to say something before the film began, I kept it very short and simply said that, being a comedy, this movie was exactly what the country could use right now.

I was being honest. The September 11 attacks were just a few weeks behind us, and the country was badly in need of a laugh. When I returned to my seat, my agent, Adam, who was sitting just to the right of me, gave me more encouraging news about the movie, including box office predictions for a strong opening weekend. Things were looking good. And then, about ten minutes into the film, Adam fell asleep.

There was an *SNL* taping the week of the opening, and Lorne was kind enough to let me do press as long as I was back at 30 Rock for the read through and scheduled rehearsals. That week, on Tuesday afternoon, an announcement was broadcast on all media outlets, saying that on Friday, the day *Corky* was scheduled to open, the entire country would likely be put on the "highest state of alert." According to then mayor Giuliani, this was in response to threats indicating terrorists might attack at least one major city. I was too shocked to be scared. Then Giuliani said something else, something that almost made it feel like the terrorists might actually be trying to stop *Corky Romano* from having a successful opening weekend. "This weekend," he said, "please stay at home with your families and do not go out." Specifically, he urged people to "avoid shopping malls and going to the movies."

I called Bob Simonds right after the announcements and asked—actually, I pleaded—if he could please push the national release date another week, even though the opening was now three days away. He actually said, "I'll check." Why I thought delaying opening day was even a possibility, I have no idea.

Needless to say, the terrorists did not attack again that weekend. *Corky* opened as scheduled. There were two other films opening that Friday, and *Corky* was the only comedy. That same Friday, I was rehearsing an *SNL* sketch, and although it didn't make it to air, it was pretty damn funny. This was Will's now famous "Old Prospector" sketch, and I played an officer addressing a room full of people that included most of the *SNL* cast. When I walked onto set for camera blocking, everyone, about twenty people, was wearing a Corky Romano mask. I have Horatio to thank for the idea of having the cast do the entire scene while wearing a cutout of my face with that tormenting smile, which I admit was funny, even though at the time I didn't think so at all. Another thing Horatio did that Friday, because he was so excited to share my work with everybody, was something that he'd never done for anyone else in the cast: he bought a bunch, I'm guessing maybe a dozen, bootleg copies of *Corky Romano* off the street for everyone to watch at work.

There's a scene in *Corky Romano* where I visit my crime family's mansion while undercover. That scene, me standing on the front stoop disguised as a Girl Scout, pressing the doorbell, and then asking in falsetto, "You guys want some cookies?" ended up being, I think, the best moment in the film. *Corky* was the third-highest grossing movie that weekend, making just over $9 million; its box office career landed at around $24 million. Even though the film earned nearly double its production budget, it was considered a flop. (Adam Sandler's first starring vehicle for a studio was *Billy Madison*, which also grossed around $24 million but *wasn't* considered a flop. Go figure.)

Leonard Maltin, the critic whose movie reviews I grew up with and believed were more valid then anyone else's, had this to say about *Corky Romano*:

> *Dreadful comedy from the "idiot as hero" genre. Hyperkinetic Kattan (funny only in small doses) plays the wayward son of a Mob family who's forced to infiltrate the FBI to destroy evidence that would convict his father, Pops Romano (Falk). Clumsy in every department.*

Chapter 16

BROKEN

There's a scene toward the end of *Million Dollar Baby* that's not easy for me to watch. For those who haven't seen the film, consider this a spoiler alert. Don't think I don't take you into consideration, dear reader, because I do. I care.

Anyway, Hilary Swank plays a welterweight boxer named Maggie, and in the climax of the film, when she's just about to win the big "million-dollar" boxing match, her asshole opponent knocks her out with an illegal sucker punch right after the last round. Before her coach, played by Clint Eastwood, has the chance to move a small, stupidly placed corner stool out of the way, Maggie falls right on it. When she lands, her head hits the top of the stool, and the side of her neck lands directly on the edge of it. The impact breaks her neck. After a few weeks in the hospital, because of the specific area she injured, the nervous system in her neck stops functioning, causing her arms and legs to atrophy and eventually making her a ventilator-dependent quadriplegic for the rest of her life, which ends up being only a few months.

The scene isn't easy for anyone to watch. But it has a particularly significant meaning for me, dating back to May 12, 2001.

Lara Flynn Boyle was the guest host that week and at the height of her career. At that time, Tina Fey was one of the head writers, plus she did "Weekend Update" with Jimmy. If Tina cast you in one of her sketches, you were lucky, because no matter how they did during read through, if she wrote it, it would always make it in the show.

That week, Tina had written a parody of *MSNBC Investigates.* Almost everyone in the cast was in it—Will, Maya, Chris Parnell, Ana, plus Lara—but the focus of the "investigation" centered around Jimmy, Tracy, Horatio, and me, playing a group of men who would secretly get together in a kitchen to enjoy tea, bake a pie, and dress up as *The Golden Girls.* In the last scene of the sketch, while sitting at the kitchen table, I choke to death eating a piece of the pie that Horatio baked.

Now, as I've said before, when a sketch you wrote makes it into the lineup, you automatically become the producer or "showrunner" of that sketch, which meant that for the *MSNBC Investigates* parody, Tina was the showrunner. Thursday afternoon when we blocked the sketch, in order to make my "choking to death" as funny as possible, she suggested that after I say my line and take a bite of the pie, before I fall out of the chair, we needed to see on camera that I was choking. When we blocked the scene a second time, I was told the choking hadn't worked on camera, which made sense because as I was choking, I fell off the chair to my left. That move may have been safe, but unfortunately it wasn't reading funny.

After watching the sketch being camera blocked from the control booth, Tina suggested that instead of falling out of the chair to my left, it might work if I fell backwards instead. Standing on set, I looked at the chair and noticed that it wasn't a breakaway (a prop chair specifically built to collapse to prevent any injury); instead it was a regular tacky, trailer-park kitchen chair, made completely of chrome steel. I questioned the safety of falling backwards from this chrome chair, but nobody in stunts or in props asked if I needed a thick floor mat, off camera, to fall on. Then again, I didn't ask for anything at that point, either.

For the run-through Saturday afternoon, the four of us—complete in *Golden Girls* attire—were on set, sitting at the kitchen table goofing off in our blouses and wigs, waiting to rehearse. Then I remembered the choking bit, and that I needed to fall backwards instead of out of my chair to the left for the camera to see me and get laughs. The only way to do that was to be seated with my back flush against the chair and to take the chair with me when I fell. In order to save my best for the show, just as Phil Hartman had once advised me, I decided that since there wasn't an audience for run-through, I'd be safe and not do a proper fall, then at dress rehearsal, I'd give my performance eighty percent, and go for it 100 percent for the live show.

When I did the stunt at dress and fell backwards, everybody in the booth said it looked hilarious because when I took the chair with me, my feet and arms were flailing and stretched way out in the air. The only problem was that in order for me to get my arms and feet as high as possible for the cameras to see, instead of pushing myself with my feet, I had to literally throw myself backwards using my entire body—which was fine, and I was happy to have a solution; I just had no idea how I was going to land when I did the stunt full out. Honestly, I did not like this chair. This chair was not my friend. These were probably real trailer-park chairs and looked great for the scene, but they were not safe enough to land on. Right after dress, I asked props if they could "please get me another chair instead of this one, because I do not want to break my neck."

A few sketches into the live show, we heard Jenna's voice on every speaker in the studio: "Thirty seconds to air. Thirty seconds to air! Cast for '*MSNBC Investigates*,' please set yourselves!"

As we were running towards set, I could see ahead that the steel chairs facing me on the camera side of the kitchen table were the exact same chairs that they'd used during dress rehearsal. That was fine, because my chair was on the other side, where the camera could barely see it. I walked onto set, walked around to the other side of the table, and looked at my chair. It was the *same fucking chair* as all the other fucking chairs. WTF?! The props crew was almost always on top of it. They never, ever, ever fucked up. I mean *SNL* has won an Emmy every year for Best Props, for fuck's sake. (It is Best Props, right? Best Props on a Show? Okay, maybe it's the Production Design Award, I don't know. Whatever it is, they win it.) Anyway, so I stood there like a frustrated little lamb hoping that someone from props might come running over within the next ten seconds before we went to air.

Suddenly, one of the prop guys veered around the set background towards me and asked, "You okay?"

"No, I'm not. What happened with the chair?"

"We couldn't find four other chairs that matched in time."

"Five seconds!"

"It doesn't matter if it matches. It's not safe. That's why I asked."

"Two seconds!"

"Sorry, Kattan."

"Fuck, man."

Fuckin' production design and their fuckin' yearly Emmy-winning streak. This was one of the few times I wished the show wasn't so god-damn professional—I had no choice but to change my thought process and decide: *As long as it's funny, I'll be fine. That's what's most important.*

So, the sketch was going great and I said my line—". . . he looked beautiful in the St. Jorgen's Day Punch Bowl"—started choking, and then threw myself forward as far as I could to gain enough momentum to then launch myself backwards. Which I did.

When I hit the ground, I waited a few seconds before getting up. My first concern was hearing whether I was getting laughs or not, and thank fuckin' God I was, because when you're given a good joke, especially from Tina, you had better deliver. My second concern was seeing if I'd injured anything. The only thing that really hurt was the back of my head, which was expected, considering I'd slammed it against the floor. When I stood up, I felt an unfamiliar pain in my neck—probably a little whiplash from throwing myself backwards—and a strange, slight numbness in my left arm and fingers and, for some weird reason, the toes on my left foot. But I didn't think anything of it.

A few days later, my head felt fine, but I had a sharp pain that started in my left shoulder and traveled down my arm to the tips of my fingers, which once again started to feel numb. But like most pain I've experienced, I assumed it would just go away in a day or two. I'd been accustomed to dealing with pain from injuries since my physical escapades growing up on Mount Baldy.

Not long after that, someone from the talent department came down with a copy of *Entertainment Weekly* and asked if I had seen the latest issue. What I thought would be a small blurb in a hard-to-find section of the magazine turned out to be one of the top stories, four pages in and two full pages long. I don't remember exactly what the title of the article was, but I believe it was something like, "Kattan Injured Live on a Saturday Night." What I do remember was at the bottom of the spread, pictures were laid out shot by shot, similar to the Zapruder photographs of President Kennedy getting shot in the motorcade in 1963. Or, as Kevin Costner put it in Oliver Stone's *JFK*: "Back and to the left. Back and to the left." Someone had taken a series of photos of a television screen showing me during the *Golden Girls* scene in the "*MSNBC*" sketch. In the first photo, I was sitting down and hunched forward over the table. In the second photo, I was bent over backwards. In the third photo, the only parts of me you could see were my hands and my feet up in the air as I was falling backwards heading towards the floor.

How was this one of the more important stories of the week? I didn't even know that I really was injured, especially enough for it to be written up for publication. I mean, nobody on the show really even asked me if I was okay after the stunt. And who at the show told the magazine that I was injured when I'd never even complained about any physical discomfort to anyone? None of it made sense. This was the first time I considered that maybe I really had been injured, and that this was a much bigger deal than I'd thought. And that maybe my continuing pain was going to, well, continue. Long before writing this chapter, I hunted around for a copy of that issue of *Entertainment Weekly*, but I couldn't find it. Nor could I find it online in the *EW* archives. Finally, I found a copy for sale on eBay. When it arrived, the article about me was missing. A few months later, I found another seller, and again the issue didn't include the article. Could it be that NBC and the powers that be were terrified that I was going to sue them or something? The thing is, that's just not who I am. I always felt that suing someone was more about wanting to take advantage of a situation and being a scuzzy opportunist.

A few days after the accident, I went out to dinner with a friend on the Lower East Side, and while we were sitting there, I raised my left arm and felt the same piercing pain again, except this time it felt like someone was really stabbing me in the shoulder. An unfamiliar burning sensation flared between my neck and my shoulders. Then the real pain started—in my neck. And the fingers on my left hand, my left leg, and my foot tingled until they became so numb and so heavy that I had trouble lifting them. I am left-handed, and because I couldn't hold my fork, I kept dropping it. I didn't say anything about what was happening to avoid embarrassment, and I just got through the evening somehow. But every morning after that, I felt fine the second I woke up, but once I stood up on my feet, the numbness and pain would start up again, and throughout the day the pain became more and more intense. Within a week, the numbness was so intense that it became visibly obvious. My left arm from my shoulder down to my wrist was now beginning to atrophy. My chiropractor was the first to tell me something was not right, and that whatever was creating the pain and causing the atrophy was something she couldn't fix—and something not to be ignored.

I became very self-conscious about the atrophy of my left arm, not just because of how I might appear while trying to conceal my pain, but because my left arm looked so much skinnier than my right. I didn't want to tell anyone, because I was embarrassed and the last thing I wanted was to appear weak. Or, as I saw it, to act like a "victim" as my father habitually had. No one respected that trait of his. My stepfather had raised me never to be "the boy who cried wolf." I didn't want to be that boy, although there were times I would be walking down the hallway on the seventeenth floor and all at once my neck would be in excruciating pain. The moment nobody was around, I would run somewhere private like a vacant office so I couldn't be seen, and by using the office wall I would stretch my shoulder, my neck, even my leg, as instructed by my physical therapist, trying to alleviate some of the pain, even if for just a few seconds.

By the time I did a Peepers sketch almost a year later with Cameron Diaz, when she hosted in April 2002, my left arm had terrible atrophy and looked almost half the thickness of my right. I still hadn't told anyone on the show about my injury and had done a pretty good job of hiding it. My balance, coordination, and pretty much everything I did physically with my upper body had become limited, especially so because, as I mentioned, I am left-handed. What I envisioned in my head for the character's physical comedy was no longer matching the reality of my physical condition. It was like thinking I was driving a Ferrari when in truth it was actually a Dodge Dart. Since Mr. Peepers was 80 percent naked, I was afraid my injury would be obvious. If you watch the sketch today, you can see the difference in my arms, although I tried my best to hide it by keeping my left arm from being on camera. Who knows—maybe the writers were right. Maybe I should have ended Mr. Peepers earlier.

Even though the pain and weakness was becoming more and more debilitating, I tricked myself into believing the pain would eventually go away and that my arm would grow to look normal again. After my chiropractor saying, "This is serious. You need to get this checked out" three too many times, I finally went to the person I most feared would judge me for having a problem that might prevent me from performing like any normal functioning human being on the show: Lorne. He wasn't able to meet with me that week to discuss it, but he did give me a recommendation for one of the top doctors in New York City. The doctor recommended that I have a CAT scan.

Producer Ken Aymong was (and is) one of the kindest people on the show, and in charge of the show's budgeting, and so on. After he learned of my injury and the chair not being replaced, he would check in from time to time and was the first person to actually say something to me about the accident, and I note, with honest sympathy.

"Whatever you end up deciding to do," Ken said. "We'll take care of it."

For some reason, even though it was never verbally stated to me, I had a strong impression that they wanted me to keep quiet about the situation. And why wouldn't I think that was the best advice? *SNL* wasn't just a job; *SNL* was family. In most cases, if you were shooting a movie and got injured on set, you would call your union—the Screen Actors Guild, or in this case AFTRA for television. But bringing in the union, I thought, would create a wedge between me and the show—or the network. The way I saw it, that wouldn't help the show, and it especially wouldn't help my future in the business. I mean, honestly, would you really sue your family? The last thing I wanted to do was carry a lawsuit around while on the show. That's just not how I was brought up.

Then Lorne's doctor gave me the news: "You basically broke your neck. You're going to have to have surgery."

"I broke my neck?"

"Yes."

"How is that possible?"

"It's very possible."

Immediately, I thought of my father, who had once been fired from a sitcom because he told the show he couldn't perform a particular feat jumping on a trampoline. This was just another reason why I needed to be quiet about this and not create any drama or put any focus on myself by telling people about the doctor's results. I was known for my physical comedy, and I didn't want anything to jeopardize my career. So, instead of reaching out to the people I worked with and hung around with, and since Ken already had confirmed that *SNL* would take care of medical costs, I kept the injury to myself—for a very, very long time.

"You could become paralyzed if you don't have surgery soon," the doctors told me.

I chose to have a minor procedure performed by a doctor known for his noninvasive technique. I refused the thought of putting anything in my spine. "I'm not putting metal or parts inside my back," I told the doctors. "I'm not a car."

For the surgery, they would fuse tissue at three levels in my neck, harvesting bone tissue from one part of my spine where the nerves were being compressed and placing it at the site of the fusion to stabilize it. It certainly didn't feel like a "minor" surgery. I spent weeks in the hospital and then started seeing a trainer, physical therapist, and chiropractor on a regular basis. The pain in my neck did go away at first. What I didn't realize was that the pain had lessened in part because many of the nerves in my neck were dead.

I spent the early summer of 2002 in isolation, recovering and continuing to remain silent about the surgery. My agent and my manager didn't know, nor did most of the people in my life. I only saw a handful of people during that time and lied to the rest about how I was doing. The doctors told me to take half a year to recover, but I only spent a couple of months recuperating before going back to work.

Over time, people noticed that something was different. I tried to keep my scars hidden and my posture straight, but some people wondered if I was ill or taking drugs. My silence remained stronger than my body as the numbness in my fingers and toes came back. The doctors said that the blood was not reaching the ends of my nerves. I just kept forcing myself to get through the next episode, to remain strong, to not stop.

As a physical comedian, I had always been worried about waking up with a whole different body one day. That fear became my reality. After those forty-five seconds on the *SNL* stage in May of 2001, my body would never, ever be the same.

Chapter 17

THIS LOVE

Zooey Deschanel appeared in two very brief scenes in the movie *Almost Famous*, and she was so likable that in less than a minute of screen time, you could tell that someday she would be a star. Jimmy and I became big fans of Zooey D. because of those two scenes. Then, in 2002, Carmen Cuba—one of my dearest friends, now a successful casting director for *Stranger Things*, as well as films by Steven Soderbergh and Ridley Scott—thought Zooey and I would be a good match and set us up.

By the way, I met Carmen through her cousin, Ariel Ashe. When Ariel was nineteen years old, she worked in the *SNL* art department. Every Wednesday night when all the sketches had been chosen after read through, as I walked to the elevators to go home, I'd pass Ariel kneeling on the floor, spreading out the blueprint set-design drawings for each of the sketches. After weeks of flirting with each other, Ariel and I became good friends. Ariel had grown up with Jake Gyllenhaal on Martha's Vineyard. When the Gyllenhaals weren't staying on the Vineyard, they were living in LA, where Jake and his sister, Maggie, both attended a private school called Harvard-Westlake, which Zooey had attended as well (as did Jane Herman and Adam Levine—more about them later). Oh! Also, Ariel's sister Alexi came to my wedding in 2008, and that's where she met Seth Meyers; now they're married with two kids.

Now, back to Zooey. When Zooey and I first met, she was exactly how I'd thought she'd be. Every day we spent together after that felt like I was falling in love with her again and again. She was beautiful, free-spirited, intelligent, and she played the ukulele. She was probably the easiest person to fall in love with. And like any normal human being, because I was so in love with her, I couldn't wait to introduce her to my friends. So of course, I had to introduce her to Will. Things had never been the same between Will and me after *Roxbury*, but they were better than they had been—every once in a while we still got together outside of *SNL*, and he was still the person I most wanted to tell when I was falling for someone new.

So one night in LA, when *SNL* was on summer hiatus, Zooey and I met up with Will at this dive bar called the Snake Pit on Melrose. And at one point, when Zooey went to the bathroom, I candidly said to Will, "I know it's early and yes, she is young, but in, I don't know, a couple years . . . she could be the one."

I couldn't spend a day without her. We went to Disneyland, saw Radiohead at the Hollywood Bowl, watched old movies. Once we went up to Big Sur for the weekend, and in the car she sang Billie Holiday songs, and then I'd sing Sam Cooke songs on key but with exceptionally bad vibrato. Her voice wasn't just beautiful; it was powerfully nostalgic.

Zooey was twenty-one years old, nine years younger than me. She was in the beginning of her career, and it was in her blood; *everyone* in her family was talented and in show business. Zooey still lived with her parents and her sister, Emily, who later starred in the series *Bones* on Fox. Their father, Caleb Deschanel, was an amazing cinematographer who shot *The Right Stuff*, *The Passion of the Christ*, and *Being There*. I remember when I first went to their house, he had the *Being There* slate board in their guest bathroom. Caleb had met Zooey's mom, Mary Jo, another great actress, on the set of *The Right Stuff*, in which she played the mute wife of John Glenn, portrayed by Ed Harris.

When *SNL* started up again, Zooey and I were still together, and I'd go back to LA whenever I had a week off. She booked a movie called *All the Real Girls* that was going to shoot in Alabama, meaning she was going to be down there for a few months. I thought: *Okay, fine, long distance. I've done it before, and I don't want to lose her.*

Then, a few days before she was set to fly out for the movie, Zooey told me that she thought we should take a break from each other while she was doing the film. She said that since the movie was a love story, as an actress she felt she should do the film with an open mind. I was devastated. Why the fuck did I fall in love with a twenty-one-year-old actress?

Back in New York, I couldn't stop obsessing. I phoned her. I left messages. We had the same publicist, and I asked if *she* could give Zooey messages. This is when I was prescribed antidepressants, but they didn't stop me from being obsessed and miserable. After weeks of this, I knew I had to do something. So what did I do? I did cocaine for the first time. It was something I had sworn I would never do, but I did it and, sadly, it helped me forget about her. Unfortunately, I became an addict.

I remember Jackie Chan, when he hosted *SNL* in May 2000, once saying he never even took aspirin for his pain, stating how easy it might be to become dependent on something. This was the same belief system I'd always had. I wish I'd been able to stick to it.

I remember 2003 as the year of Jane.

Jane Herman often thought of herself as a "plain Jane," but she was far from it. She was beautiful, smart, funny, driven, independent, and the quality that can be most terrifying in a relationship: healthy. It was late in the fall of 2002 when we met, just after Zooey and I had broken up; Jane was a senior at New York University, and her inspirations were Bob Dylan and Joan Didion. I've often had friends tell me that Jane was "the one that got away," a comment that's always encouraging to hear. Just a few months into the relationship, she moved in with me. But she brought baggage, though she didn't realize it.

Her ex was a musician named Adam. Prior to meeting me, Jane left Adam and moved to New York, but before she officially moved on, she agreed to let Adam and his band use her first name as the inspiration and focus for their album, *Songs About Jane*. An album nobody would ever hear, right? Except everybody heard it, and it eventually won a Grammy. It wasn't the best news to hear that my girlfriend was the muse for all the songs on her ex's album, but I didn't let my insecurity get the best of me.

Until one day, while in the children's books section at Borders in New York, I recognized Adam's voice playing over the speakers. He was singing:

I tried my best to feed her appetite.
Keep her coming every night.
So hard to keep her satisfied.

This was the second single off their album, and it was just the beginning. I didn't need to ask Jane about Adam; I heard it all in his lyrics:

This love has taken its toll on me

She said goodbye too many times before.

On my week off, I'd be at a Whole Foods in LA, shopping for some in-season produce, and suddenly hear Adam's tiny voice:

Remember how my body tastes.

Or sitting in the waiting room at Just Tires:

I've had you so many times

But somehow I want more.

Was this a way for Adam to express that art would soon imitate life and that he wasn't done? Was it possible that *People* magazine's future "Sexiest Man Alive" was going to try to get Jane back through the power of suggestive lyrics? Whatever the case, those fucking Maroon 5 songs played everywhere for months, one after the other.

Halfway through the 2002–03 season, I made the decision to leave *SNL*. I'd always felt I'd made it onto the show and had the success I did because of the physical antics of the characters I had created, and now I felt like they'd had their run. The other motivation for my departure was more practical: I was about to have a second, more intensive surgery. The fusion procedure I'd undergone had only been partially successful in improving my pain, and the effects were temporary. The specialist I was seeing, neurosurgeon Carl Lauryssen, leveled with me about the reality of my situation.

"You came very close to being paralyzed for the rest of your life," he told me. "When you broke your neck, your nerve endings were cut off. If you don't have another surgery, one that addresses the problem more completely, your left arm will continue to atrophy. And if you don't use that arm, you're going to lose it."

After hearing that I was leaving, Mike Shoemaker told me how much he'd miss me, and said that the show didn't want to lose me. "We don't want you to go," he said.

"Is this coming from you or Lorne?" I asked, because it was important for me to know what Lorne thought, as codependent as that may sound.

"Of course it's from Lorne," Shoemaker said. "Yeah, it's from everyone."

It was good to hear, but no one made an effort to get me to stay. It wasn't as if Lorne got on the phone with my agent and tried to figure out a way to keep me on the show. Dennis McNicholas said to me, "Now? Why would you want to leave now? Just when the writers want to write for you!"

I couldn't help but think to myself: *Did it really have to take this long?* Not that there weren't some great sketches written for me throughout the seasons; there were. But all of this made me remember something Vince Vaughn had told me when he hosted the show in December 1998, a couple of years after I joined the cast. He and I were in his dressing room on Saturday afternoon going over a few changes in the Peepers sketch. This version was a parody of the movie *Swingers*. To show Peepers a good time, like Vince's character Trent had done with Mike (played by Jon Favreau) in the movie, Vince took Mr. Peepers on a trip to Vegas, and he eventually used his famous catchphrase: "You're so money, Peepers. You're so money!"

At one point that afternoon, Vince asked me to close the door, and as he sat on the couch, he said something totally unexpected.

"Kattan. You need to look out for yourself."

For a moment, I wondered if he was being serious. It really did sound like a "You're so money" pep talk at first.

"I've seen it all week," Vince continued. "Nobody's looking out for you, so you have to fight for yourself."

I was shocked, but appreciative. It was true that I often felt uncertain of my place on the show. I had joined *SNL* feeling like an underdog, and after a brief golden period that first season or so, I had gone right back to feeling that way, but I never knew how much of that was in my own head. In a way, it was a relief to have someone else notice. But what could I do?

Even when I was leaving the show, Lorne's opinion mattered to me, and I didn't feel any more sure of what that opinion was than I ever had. On the one hand, honestly, Lorne had been very generous to me throughout the years. On the other hand . . . well. Lorne once told me: "I don't completely trust you until you're on camera. When we're live, I know I can always trust you."

I guess you could say that my relationship with *SNL* was complicated.

For the remainder of my last season, there was a nice mix of swan-song sketches featuring my recurring characters, as well as some sketches where the writers cast me in a way that said, "Aww, I'll miss you!"—"Aww, you'll miss me? Aww, come on now, everybody!" Those last months all felt like a sweet and perfect goodbye.

For the final show of Season 28, Jimmy had planned on doing a "To Be Continued Next Season" cliffhanger bit with Tina for their last "Weekend Update," which they'd done with good effect at the end of the season before. But they generously volunteered to scratch that for the tribute to me. It would be one last "terrible reenactment" of all the memorable characters I had ever done on *SNL*, with balloons, confetti, and a lot of love.

But it wasn't just me saying goodbye to *SNL*. It was Tracy Morgan's last show as well, and when I finally realized this, I felt guilty for not remembering. When I apologized and asked why he wasn't receiving a proper send-off, he replied, "Well, that's because I'm doing a show with Lorne right after this."

I'd forgotten. Tracy had a pilot picked up for his own series, which Lorne was producing. Meanwhile, I would be going back to California to have surgery number two for my broken neck . . . quietly. Nobody would be sending me balloons or lots of get-well love, simply because almost nobody would know. Nobody except for Jane—and my family of course.

The eight-hour surgery would be done through my throat, and they'd have to push my larynx over to the side of my neck in order to get to the back of my spine where they would be operating. The doctors asked me if I wanted them to videotape it so I could see it. Like I was going to fucking watch that—and I didn't really want them adding me to their home movie collection either, no matter how much they wanted to show off their expertise. I could imagine them in the sixth hour, pawing around inside me while saying, "What should we watch tonight? A videotape of Chris Kattan lying on his face unconscious while we cut a fifteen-inch-long slit in his back, or the original *Jumanji*?"

After the surgery, it was four weeks before I was even allowed to move around with a walker. I couldn't simply leap out of bed after having bolts drilled into my back. The recovery process was painful and tedious, and it took a major toll on my life, including both my career and my relationship with Jane. There's nothing more vulnerable and humiliating than having to ask someone to carry you into a bathtub, wash you, and put your clothes on every morning for a month. Needless to say, my self-esteem began to suffer.

That next season, *SNL* occasionally asked me to come back to do something on a show. The timing worked perfectly because I was a few months post-op, and even though I didn't look healthy, I was at least able to walk. The most memorable cameo was on Episode 8, in December, when Elijah Wood hosted to promote the last in the *Lord of the Rings* movies, *The Return of the King,* and I got to do my impression of Gollum for a second time. Doing Gollum didn't exactly demand that I be in great physical shape.

These brief stints only reminded me of the *SNL* family I had already left. That year, cast members would call me often to see how I was, to say hello and tell me they missed me. Sometimes they would get together and sing to me over the phone. Poehler was so sweet, telling me, "It's not the same around here." When Fallon called to check in, he always wanted to know what I had planned; he seemed to understand the psychological side of leaving a show like *SNL*.

"I want to make sure you're keeping that creative mind going," he said.

I had accomplished so much and learned so much about my craft in the past decade. I had learned how to use my body as an instrument for my humor. Now I wasn't that person anymore. I grew self-conscious and began to lose my appetite for performing. Physical pain and the effects of my pain medication didn't exactly help my motivation.

Every so often I'd fly out to see someone. I visited Tina and her husband after they had their first kid. Maya was probably my closest friend on the show, and I'd see her or Amy or Jimmy and know they could hear the pain in my voice and were concerned. Of course, worried my career would be affected, I just lied, saying things were fine.

My surgery in 2003 became the second of five surgeries stemming from my neck injury. Each time, I was afraid to tell the people that I worked with and hoped to continue working with about my ongoing injury. The surgeries put me out of commission for months each time—and those months were beyond frustrating because I couldn't do a fucking thing. God forbid I would go to Rite Aid to pick up pain medication or visit my physical therapist—someone would be there with a camera. I tried to appear healthy and ready to work every second of the day, only to have TMZ tape me and make me out to be drugged out and decrepit. Once, TMZ filmed me outside of a Rite Aid while I was putting groceries into my car. On camera, the reporter asked why I looked like a hunchback. Even years later, after catching up to me in an airport, one of their taglines read: "Chris Kattan: 'I'm Not a Drug Addict, I Just Have a Bad Back.'" I tried to let everyone's opinion and all the comments slide off my broken back so I could have a career, but inside I was screaming, "Fuck you, TMZ!"

Six years later, during my time on ABC's sitcom, *The Middle* with Patricia Heaton, I still couldn't open my left hand. Any movie or TV show or public appearance I did, my left arm and sometimes even my left leg wouldn't respond normally due to all the nerve damage. There were a number of jobs I didn't get because I became top-heavy in my physical appearance. "Stiff" was the word that my agent would use to tell me why I didn't get the part (or "hunchbacked," as TMZ so kindly put it).

Even today as I write this book, I still can't open my hand wide enough to use my fingers normally on the keyboard.

The impact that my injury and subsequent surgeries had on my career was immense, but more importantly, the fallout proved to be devastating to some of the closest relationships in my life. Jane had moved out to LA to be with me, and ended up less my girlfriend than my caretaker. And while I certainly couldn't help the physical stuff, I could have spent less time feeling sorry for myself and more time paying attention to the woman I loved.

Later that year, Jane put me in rehab for being addicted to cocaine and pain meds. I had been introduced to cocaine by a friend I no longer talk to since our friendship centered on drugs—somehow he was able to hide his drug use and remain extremely successful. As I've already mentioned, I used cocaine for the first time after Zooey left me, and I attempted to treat the downward spiral of my broken heart with a dab here and there of self-destruction. It wasn't like I was Tony Montana in *Scarface* with a big mound of blow on my desk that I'd bury my face in, but cocaine eased the constant nerve pain I was experiencing and lifted my self-doubt, which helped me become more social and get back in front of the camera.

I stopped doing cocaine after rehab but continued taking pain medication. It was prescribed to me after each surgery, and I had to take it in order to heal and function. I needed a way to manage the pain that came with my mangled spine and one procedure after another to fix it, but in retrospect, becoming addicted was a predictable side effect. It's painful to admit or write about, but I struggled with this addiction for years, until shortly after my final surgery.

Even though you're supposed to go into rehab for yourself, I went into rehab for Jane. I remember when I first walked into the facility, a pair of big-name celebrities were walking out, like I had just wandered into a *Vanity Fair* Oscars after-party instead of a drug treatment center. I didn't like being there, though I got adept at participating in the group talks. During my time at Promises in Malibu, every Sunday was family day, and

Jane promised to be there for me since she was my main support. The third week into my rehab, she didn't show up, nor did she come the week after. I can remember completely breaking down and lying down on the floor and having people simply walk by, ignoring me, their expressions saying, "Let him have his time." When I left after my four weeks, I went back to my house, and everything belonging to Jane was gone. She had moved back into her parents' house, and then a few months after that she moved back to New York and was out of the relationship for good.

I still blame myself for her leaving, and I know I can't be angry for how things turned out. Jane had been a great partner. It was one of those relationships that made me think: *I really screwed that one up, didn't I?* I know that when you turn to drugs, you're being selfish. I was the reason Jane moved to LA, and I should have been more prepared to give her what she needed and wanted. I just hadn't quite figured out how to do that. Maybe a part of me deep down believed that I never could.

Chris Rock once confided in me that some of the hardest years of his life were right after he left the cast of *SNL*. After you leave, he said, you have a lot more time on your hands. During the show, you're so busy in every single way. Suddenly, you're not busy at all. The adjustment wasn't easy, Rock told me, and as the months wore on, I had learned the hard way that everything he'd said was true for me as well. I was realizing how important to my mental health it was to have a job. For so long, ever since starting in the Groundlings, I had been focused on one thing: getting on *SNL*. I had been so hungry to do it and make it happen, and it finally did. Now I found myself at a point where I was asking, "Now what?"

The same went for my personal life. I had rarely been single. Since high school I'd had a series of relationships that were emotionally draining and heartbreaking. It had started to become a cycle that I wanted and needed to break. It would take a long time before I was actually strong enough to do that.

Chapter 18

COUPLING, COMPLICATIONS, AND WILL YOU BE MY VALENTINE, TOM CRUISE?

met my future wife, Sunshine Deia Tutt, in LA in spring 2005. After surgery, rehab, and losing Jane, I was on top of my physical therapy, doing Pilates, and finally working. I was beginning to feel normal and alive again.

I first crossed paths with Sunshine at a party. She was beautiful, funny, and we had instant chemistry. For our first official date, we went to the Coachella music festival. After that, we began to spend all our time together, and something happened that had never happened before: I began to hang out at my own place a lot—and host parties there.

My house in the Hollywood Hills had been built in 1924 and felt more like a secluded getaway than a residence, with bungalow-style buildings interspersed with trees and gardens. I bought it in September 2001; the previous owner, Danny DeVito, had infamous parties there during his days on the show *Taxi*. He and his wife, Rhea Perlman, who was on *Cheers* at the time, would have a lot of the cast from their shows over, along with John Belushi and other *SNL* cast members who were on hiatus. The grotto-style pool and bordello-like vibe felt private and inviting at the same time; it was the perfect place to relax and mingle.

As beautiful as the house was, it had a strange kind of energy. Whenever I threw a party, it usually began in early evening, but for whatever reason—I don't think it was me, honestly, I think the house was to blame—people wouldn't end up leaving until the following morning or afternoon.

Actually, I rarely threw a party on purpose—usually, I just invited a few friends back to the house. At this time in LA, a lot of celebrities hung around at Teddy's bar in the Roosevelt Hotel, and late on a Friday or Saturday night after it closed, I'd suggest my place to someone, and somehow end up with twenty or thirty people at my house. Paris Hilton would be buzzing at the gate to come in; Samantha Ronson would show up to be the DJ. There was something about this house; when people came over, they wouldn't want to leave. When I went to bed, around 3 AM, I'd try—usually unsuccessfully—to kick everybody out. Some would still be at the pool when I woke up the next morning.

Sunshine and I got close fast. I felt like I could relax around her in a way that was totally new to me. We were always laughing. For her birthday, I made her a ten-minute movie starring Pepper, her Chihuahua. The plot was a day in the life of Pepper, and I gave her the voice of a whiny, older Jewish woman from New York. I actually did a pretty good job, considering I was holding Pepper while moving her arms or her legs. The movie opened on Pepper waking up in bed with the alarm going off, and we see her paw knock the clock over. Then she's brushing her teeth in the bathroom. Then taking a shower, and after that there's a long, white string hanging down between her legs while she bitches, "I'm in a shit mood. Yeah, ya heard me. Did I stutter?" Then Pepper's driving a Mercedes with her shades on—and her paws on the steering wheel. Then she's out dancing with some of Sunshine's friends at a club and doing shots . . . you get the idea.

Sunshine was laughing hysterically watching this, but then, about four minutes in, she started to cry. I mean *really* cry. So I asked her, in a tone that reeked of insecurity, "Why are you crying? You don't think it's funny?" And she said, "Yes! Of course, it's funny. I just . . . nobody has ever done something this nice for me before. Ever."

It was rare for me to be the person giving something to someone instead of needing things from them. I think that's what bonded us.

I proposed to Sunshine on Christmas Eve of 2006. It seems like, in the entertainment business, once you're engaged to somebody or get married and have kids, you are suddenly seen as an adult. To many people, it appears as if you're finally growing up. Your social life changes, and you end up hanging out with other couples. My friend, the writer Chris Henchy, was married to Brooke Shields by that time, and they had two children. Henchy helped create the website Funny or Die along with Will Ferrell and Adam McKay, and he is now partners with Will and Adam at Gary Sanchez Productions. Henchy, Sunshine, and I would have barbecues with Chris and Brooke and talk about things like the best wines. It was a new "adult" way of life, and, in my midthirties, a first for me. Chris and Brooke really were the perfect couple, and highly respected by other couples, and not only did they support and encourage our engagement, but they treated us with kindness and love. Sunshine and Brooke would walk out to the deck and talk about things women talk about when they're alone, whatever those may be. And Henchy and I would stay in the kitchen, talking about cabernets and sports. I knew nothing about sports, but that was fine. Henchy was a great example of the perfect husband with a perfect life and was becoming the perfect friend.

It all looked like this was going to be the lifestyle I was meant for, since I was an adult heading in that direction. I was finally becoming someone who was healthy, happy, and working. And I was excited about this new course for my life. The great Garry Shandling came over on a Sunday evening and joined us for a barbecue. He was a neighbor and also part of the basketball team Chris played on. A lot of industry people, celebrities, and comedians would play basketball and form teams. I was never asked because, well, probably because I never really learned how to properly play basketball. Maybe in the future my child would be on the same soccer team as the kids of my other industry friends.

One afternoon, Brooke called me at home and invited Sunshine and me over for a special Valentine's Day dinner. We would be joined by two other couples: J. J. Abrams and his wife, Katie McGrath, and *Tom Cruise and Katie Holmes*. And yes, the moment I heard who was coming, I did say what just about any human being would have said: "Are you fucking kidding me?"

Everyone knew that Tom Cruise had made a huge effort to befriend Brooke after a highly publicized feud when he publicly criticized her for taking prescription medication for postpartum depression. Whether his comments were encouraged by the Scientology club, I don't know, but I'm guessing they were. Brooke then gave a ballsy reply to Tom in an interview, saying, "Tom should stick to saving the world from aliens and let women who are experiencing postpartum depression decide what treatment options are best for them." Damn! You go girl!

So then Tom, being Tom Cruise, who always needed cleanliness and absolute perfection in his on- and off-screen resume, apologized to Brooke. Only he didn't just apologize in words, he also did it through his actions, which I have to give him credit for. He invited Brooke and Henchy to his and Katie's wedding in Italy.

But I had no idea why Sunshine and I were invited to Brooke's Valentine's Day dinner with Tom and Katie. We tried to figure out why we'd been chosen. Of course we were going to *go*, are you kidding me? Brooke had probably suggested us, and they'd approved. Tom and Katie had probably conducted the standard background checkups on us to see if we were appropriate to have dinner with. While a team of professional Scientologists probed our lives to examine pretty much everything we had ever done.

Sunshine and I arrived at Brooke's house about twenty minutes early the night of the dinner, which I'm embarrassed to say is a triumph since

I'm always a little late. When we got there, I could tell Brooke was a little nervous. I kept obsessing over questions like *How does Tom Cruise want to be served?* and *How does he unfold a napkin?* and *Will there be people coming along with him?*

J. J., Katie, Sunshine, and I all sat down while Brooke was nervously setting the table and having a time wondering which of her embroidered napkins Tom and Katie would prefer. As we waited for the iconic couple, we were all becoming nervous, too. *How should I sit?* I wondered. *Did the Scientologists tell Tom that I'm funny, and does that mean I have to be funny the whole evening?*

Chris, Brooke, and Sunshine had a few glasses of cabernet, but I was hesitant. I felt like if I had a glass of wine or two, it might be something Tom Cruise would judge me for. The wine would certainly have helped ease the anxiety building for the moment when *he* would arrive. *If* he would arrive. Just the thought of him sitting with us at the same table was stressful. The moment I started to think *they're probably not going to show up*, Katie arrived, but without Tom. Thinking that he might not actually make it gave me a tremendous amount of relief.

"Tom is on his way," Katie said. "He just wrapped working, so he'll be here soon."

Shit. I guess now I'll have a glass of wine.

Everyone sat at the table waiting for Tom, which also meant waiting to eat. J. J. was seated to my left, and we talked about *Star Wars* like *Star Wars* nerds do. This was actually before he had any idea he would be chosen to start the franchise again with *The Force Awakens*.

Suddenly, I realized that maybe I did know why Tom and Katie were fine with us coming to this dinner. The second time I met Tom (the first time was at *SNL* in Bono's dressing room) was at an Emmys after-party at a small but trendy restaurant on Sunset Boulevard. Nearly everyone who'd been at the awards show was there. Since *30 Rock* was the big winner of the night, a lot of very happy *SNL*'ers were in attendance, so I felt comfortable going. Alec Baldwin was especially happy, running around with his Emmy in his hand. Justin Timberlake was there; he had just broken up with Cameron and was trying his best to be incognito when he met up with his soon-to-be new girlfriend, Jessica Biel. I had a conversation with the legendary Warren Beatty, who was tipsy and fun to talk to. After giving up on waiting for Lorne to finish talking to someone so I could say hello, I spotted Tom and Katie chatting with CAA power agent Kevin Huvane. Because she'd hosted *SNL*, I felt comfortable going over to Katie to congratulate them as newlyweds. This was the only thing I could think of that might have made the couple comfortable with me attending this Valentine's dinner.

After three glasses of wine and no longer feeling anxiety—because it looked like Tom probably wasn't going to show—I felt a slight breeze hit the back of my neck. I thought the sound of the front door closing would follow, but there was only silence. And no Tom. It was probably the woman I'd seen helping Brooke in the kitchen. Two minutes later, there he was, standing right next to me, just as short as I was. The one and only Tom Cruise, sporting that beautiful smile with his perfectly arranged teeth. But when did he arrive? Where did he enter from? Could he have magically appeared by using some Scientological transporter? Could it be that Tom Cruise was an apparition? Maybe he was joining us tonight as a hologram?

At the moment, it didn't matter. What was important was that he was standing next to me, his beautiful hair tossed with the perfect amount of hair gel. For a second, I actually felt jealous of all the men who were rumored to have slept with him. Like the lead singer of the band Matchbox Twenty. I remembered hearing that one.

Suddenly, the amiable smile disappeared, and he drove his hands dramatically through his hair, saying, "Sorry I'm late. I was just finishing up a scene with Meryl."

He walked toward his seat at the other end of the table just across from me, stopping for a second to kiss Katie's head before arriving at his chair between her and Brooke. Then, as he stood there, he took off his tailor-fit bomber jacket in a way I'd never seen anybody take off a jacket before. He wasn't awkward, using two hands like everybody else and sliding it off with one arm and then using that arm to grab the other sleeve to pull it off. Nor did he shake his wrist on one arm while the other arm was behind his back, then grab the loose end of his sleeve to pull it off. Tom Cruise didn't do either of these things.

He used one hand and quickly peeled the sleeve off the other arm and then whipped the jacket over one shoulder. Exactly as a runway model would while working the catwalk.

It was the most graceful "taking off of a jacket" I had ever seen in my life.

In every second of the five hours I spent with Tom Cruise, everything he said or did physically was so polished that it seemed rehearsed and camera ready. When he listened to me, it was a perfect "take." Picking up his fork: "Tom, the first take was gold. Let's move on to the next shot!"

When he spoke to me or whenever I was talking, he always, always looked me straight in the eye and never blinked. As polite as Tom was, this still made me feel pressure that, when it was my time to speak, it had better be good. The only other person who was like this when I talked to them was the musician Beck.

I'd guessed correctly; Tom told us he'd wanted Sunshine and me to come to dinner because of the night at the Emmys after-party. He liked the fact that I hadn't been afraid of just coming up to them to talk. Tom had thought it was so great to be congratulated on their engagement. Then Katie mentioned the *SNL* show we had done together in 2001.

"I played a monkey," I said with a grin.

Katie lit up and smiled that beautiful, crooked smile as she talked about the memories of our Mr. Peepers sketch.

"I know, I know about it," Tom said.

During dinner, Henchy asked about my engagement to Sunshine, so I was able to tell the story of how I popped the question.

"Well, I proposed to Sunshine on Christmas morning at her grand-parents' house. I gave her a box that she opened to reveal another wrapped box to open. Then there was another smaller one, and so on for two more boxes until the ring was in the last and smallest box."

Proposing to her in front of her family in Gainesville, Texas, was a good idea but it wasn't mine. I did it because she once told me that if I proposed to her, this was exactly how she wanted it to happen. Having me propose in front of her family was just as important to her as getting married and having a big wedding that everyone would know about.

"I didn't want to do the whole propose-by-the-Eiffel-Tower-under-the-glow-of-Paris sort of clichéd thing," I said. "It's beautiful but not that original."

Suddenly, everyone at the table including Tom became very quiet. Because my peripheral vision isn't the best, at first I didn't notice Henchy waving his fork to get my attention so I could stop talking. But what did I say?

Finally jumping in to save me, Henchy said, "Um, Tom actually pro-posed to Katie in Paris at the Eiffel Tower."

Oh, shit.

Tom took a moment, put his fork down—the most flawless "putting a fork down" ever—burst out laughing, and started ecstatically clapping. I wouldn't say it was exactly like his infamous "Happy Fit" on *Oprah*, but it was close.

Tom, I guess, loved it, or else he was just lying really well. I couldn't tell, but everyone at the table seemed to believe him, and that was good enough for me. He found it hilarious seeing me with a red face feeling like a complete moron.

After dinner, Katie gave Tom probably the best Valentine's Day gift I've ever seen. I've chosen not to put it in the book since they did allow me into their life, and exposing something about their relationship at a moment when it was pretty vulnerable would be fucked up. But I will say the gift was presentational, it involved their two-year-old daughter, Suri, and most of all, it was clear that Katie truly was in love with Tom.

Tom loved cameras, so Henchy showed him a very old Leica. Then I asked Tom if he liked the Police. This was when the group was getting back together and touring again, and they were playing two nights at Dodger Stadium.

"We should go see the Police," I said to him.

Tom smiled and looked at me for a few seconds, then said, "Hey, you know what? We should go see Prince."

Of course, I wanted to see Prince. I loved Prince, but at the time I really wanted to see the Police. They hadn't played together in over twenty years, and it was a big deal that they were on tour.

"I love Prince. But this is *the Police*! 'Roxanne' and 'Message in a Bottle.' I mean, we gotta go see the Police."

"Yeah, let's go see Prince!" Tom said.

Why was he agreeing to something I didn't even suggest? I didn't get it. *Does he not like Sting? Does he not get along with the band for some reason?*

"I love Prince! But *the Police*! They're back together! This is a big deal."

"Katie, we're going to see Prince," said Tom.

Again with the Prince? *Tom, what the fuck is with you and the Police? Seriously, what did Sting do to you?*

"Yes. I agree! No question! Prince would be amazing!" I said, finally giving up.

"Great! We're going to Prince. Katie! We're going to Prince!" he said one last time.

Jesus, Tom. What is up, dude?! I couldn't wait to go home and Google "*Tom Cruise problem with the Police.*"

On the drive home that night, taking Sunset the whole way since we were coming from Brentwood, I remember feeling kinda dirty. Physically dirty, like I hadn't bathed in weeks dirty. Tom Cruise was so clean and perfect that it was impossible to compete with him. Even though we were driving home on one of the cleanest streets in LA, when I looked outside my window whenever we stopped at a red light, it seemed like skid row. Everything looked and felt dirtier than it had ever looked before. When we drove past Crescent Heights and I gazed up at the Calvin Klein and Chanel No. 5 ads on the billboards, with all these gorgeous models posing half naked, they all seemed tired and dirty. They looked so uninteresting and unmotivated.

About a month later, Brooke called me and said, "So, I just got off the phone with Katie, and she called and invited the four of us to fly out on Tom's jet to Las Vegas for the weekend so we can see Prince!"

Tom Cruise was serious? He really did want to see Prince with us! Wow!

LA is famous for people saying, "Let's get together and do something," and it almost never happens. But Tom actually kept his word. Brooke told me that he wanted to fly his plane out of Burbank with just the six of us the next Thursday. Of course, I was going to say yes. But then I realized that I couldn't fly out of Burbank that Thursday night because I was going to be in Canada shooting a really bad Christmas movie. Then, just like at Valentine's Day dinner, I was all stressed out about trying to see Tom Cruise again! The good news was that I'd gone to see the Police, so I didn't have to go through *that* fucking thing again.

I can't let Tom Cruise down! I thought. *How do I get out of work for two days that soon?*

Why would the producers even let me go? "Hey, can I get out of shooting for two days on short notice so I can go see Prince with Tom Cruise and Katie Holmes?" Are you kidding? The beginning of the following week, I asked the producers, and they said they would try their best to make it happen. The next day, Tuesday morning, they said that they were sorry, but I was in every scene Friday and they couldn't lose me. I felt like I really had let Tom Cruise down when I told Brooke the news. Tom Cruise came through, and I didn't.

The next day, Wednesday afternoon, Brooke called me again and said, "Tom said he's going to push the flight and fly out Friday night so we can go see Prince." Now I had to go! No question. Now I really couldn't let him down. I was so fucking stressed out, and now I was stressing everybody else out, especially Brooke, who at one point started to have an anxiety attack while on the phone.

I tried my best to get off the set that Friday. I begged them to let me off early to catch the last flight out to LA. And then, while I was on set, pacing around in circles and staring at the clock, hoping to make it out in time, one of the producers walked over to me and said, "Kattan! You're in the last scene of the night, but we pushed it to Monday for you."

I got to the airport, but by the time I arrived at the gate, the doors had closed, and I didn't make the flight. That Valentine's dinner was last time I talked to Tom Cruise and Katie Holmes. But you know what? I had a night that will always be remembered. And I got a fun story out of it.

Sunshine was the perfect partner in a lot of ways. I truly loved her and loved being with her. And I loved the grown-up life we had together. Yet, for whatever reason, our relationship was passionless. I'm not saying we weren't great for each other, because we were. We laughed constantly at everything, including ourselves, and we were always happy, but even though Sunshine was beautiful and sexy, our relationship had barely any physical intimacy. Sure, I was in my later thirties and had already gone through the "We just can't get enough" three-to-four-times-a-day phases in other relationships, but with my soon-to-be wife, for the majority of the time, it just was not happening. Two minutes into it, we would start laughing and just give up.

After three years spent convincing myself that sex was overrated, I went off for three months to shoot a movie and had an affair with my "as scripted" love interest and co-star. The affair lasted for the entire shoot. I felt guilty about it, but I'd also convinced myself that if I was going to enter into a passionless marriage, I might as well have one last fling. I'm a hopeless romantic, and old habits die hard: When I read a script and do the film and it's a romantic comedy, if I'm set to fall in love on the page, I'm probably going to fall in real life. I was heartbroken when Zooey D. did the same to me, but eventually I understood that impulsiveness. Karma can be a ruthless bitch.

I came home, and Sunshine and I were married in June 2008. *In Touch Weekly* magazine had approached us, wanting to take photos of the event, so after getting approvals from the guests, we participated in this gross part of showbiz. The price of the wedding was a lot more than I'd ever want to spend, but since *In Touch* was doing coverage of the wedding, they paid over half of the cost. Regardless, Sunshine was so involved in planning the wedding and it was so important to her that I couldn't say no. I've always had a problem with saying no and feeling like I was letting somebody else down.

We had our wedding in Yosemite, and even though I had a lot to do with the guest list, I can honestly say it was one of the best weddings I have ever been to. Pretty much everyone who was invited showed up, including Jimmy, Seth, Parnell, Rachel Dratch, Will, and my best man, Parker Posey, who I'd become close to while filming *Adam & Steve*. There were only a few people who couldn't make it, like Tina, Poehler, and Lorne. (Amy Sedaris didn't come either, and when I asked her why, she said, "Come on, Kattan. It's not gonna last.")

Sunshine and I had a blast, because we always did. Everything about the ceremony worked out beautifully . . . except for the forest fire that was happening at the same time just a few miles away from the bed-and-breakfast where we got married. The smoke created a lot of coughing and migraines. Whether this was foreshadowing, I have no idea.

Three days later, I checked into the hospital for the third surgery linked to my neck injury. This was another intensive operation on my back, and it was by far the most painful to recover from, taking longer to heal than any of the others. Again, I chose to keep quiet so I could still get work, which, by the way, makes for very few visitors while in the hospital. I had to lie in bed in the hospital for two and a half weeks, with morphine pumping into my body. When I got to go home, I was bedridden for another three weeks. My mother as well as my good friend Parker Posey flew in to take care of me since nobody else was there . . . including Sunshine. I had gone into our marriage with doubts, and now I knew I needed to be honest. One of the biggest problems for me was that, at the time, I didn't believe that Sunshine actually loved me for who I was. I thought she only loved the comfort I provided. This warped mind-set had come into play once she became obsessed with getting married, even before I proposed to her, after which she became somewhat of a Bridezilla. This was my personal baggage, a wall of self-doubt that I had built years before even meeting her. I already had a problem believing somebody could love me as much as I loved them. I had some things I needed to tell Sunshine, and she wanted some answers about us. A good friend advised me that when you're in the hospital being pumped full of morphine one week after surgery, it might not be the best time to hash out relationship issues. Oh well.

So while I was in bed recovering, Sunshine was getting a lawyer. When word got out what was happening, there were a lot of rumors and gossip about us. One tabloid said I cheated on her after our wedding, while other things written up about us were even more ridiculous. A friend who came to the wedding called me and asked whether the whole event had been done for publicity. "Did you just want to get photos of all of us?" Another assumption that was both hurtful and totally wrong. But I chose not to explain myself. I was exhausted.

In the end, our marriage lasted fifty-nine days.

Looking back, I wish I had realized then something that now seems obvious but takes a long time to fully accept: you can't rely on somebody else to make you happy, but you can't try to go it alone, either. I learned a lot from our relationship, especially about the difficult balance between being vulnerable and trusting and not taking responsibility for anything.

The third surgery felt the most debilitating both because it took the longest to recover from and because I wasn't sure whether it had actually helped. Advised to stay in bed for a few more months, I went back to work earlier than I should have, and that's when others really began to question my appearance. A routine visit to the grocery store could result in speculation that I was strung out on drugs and didn't know where I was, when I was simply hunched over after having bolts screwed into my back. Most of the time I couldn't feel my fingers or toes because the blood was not reaching my nerve endings. Still, I never said a word. When you give so many years to surgical work, physical therapy and being medicated, you grow accustomed to numbness.

I stupidly went to auditions and meetings consumed with pain and trying desperately to hide the atrophy that was supposed to have been solved by the first surgery but wasn't. I chose to do the "I'm going to pretend I didn't have surgery" act again without realizing how little I was succeeding at acting normal, and that keeping silent would do more harm than revealing my disability. Pain medication was just part of the deal, post-surgery, and I thought if I could control the pain, I could get back to work sooner. I never realized how out of it I looked. Honestly, I never looked worse. Because people didn't know about my broken neck and continuous surgeries, criticism and judgment came from all sides, including fans, friends, relatives, co-workers, and cast members. I can only blame myself for keeping quiet instead of sharing the truth. Every time I was in public, I appeared more and more broken.

NBC had stopped paying my medical costs after the second surgery. The *SNL* family I was part of had stopped taking care of me, and soon I wasn't able to pay for everything myself. But I never really fought for myself or demanded anything. I never thought about the potential legal ramifications of what had happened to me on the set and what was happening now. I had been brought up to be responsible for myself. I wasn't about to sue anybody. I never wanted to be that person: spending my life debilitated and fighting a network. I wanted to hide everything, pretending I was okay and in good enough shape to be go out in public and be social. That the surgeon was wrong and that I'd be healed in one month, and not six.

I learned later in my life that going it alone was my choice and my responsibility and nobody else's. I was brought up believing that when your house burns down, you rebuild it, so that's what I was trying to do, by myself. The problem was that I couldn't ever rebuild my body, and neither could anyone else.

Chapter 19

THAT'S KIP FOR YOU

My last recurring character on *SNL* was Buddy Mills, an old, washed-up, physically ailing lounge comedian who did a nightly show in the basement of the fictional Rialto Grande in Las Vegas. His partner was a senile drummer named Mackey, played perfectly by Fred Armisen, especially with his brilliantly ill-timed *ba dum tss* on the drums. Buddy told vulgar, hack jokes about his wife and then would have an emotional breakdown. The character was inspired by my real father, and my dad loved it.

"I'm trying to lose 140 pounds. *My wife!* Ha ha haaaaaa! I can't!" After saying this, I'd point to Mackey, who would do nothing. Then thirty seconds later, after my comments had turned serious, the sound of the *ba dum tss* would interrupt me midsentence.

Lorne, surprisingly, was a big fan of Buddy Mills. During every read through, at the moment we got to the part where I had the breakdown, Lorne would be laughing. I could be wrong, but I'm pretty sure it was the honesty of the character that he enjoyed. I don't know if a character who shows humanity requires more time to get there than others, but even in a show with a tight schedule, the Buddy Mills sketches would sometimes last as long as eight minutes.

Ray Liotta was the first guest to play another hack stand-up I bantered with as Buddy. Christopher Walken came next, walking onstage with his pants down around his heels and his boxers showing, asking, "Is there a draft in here or what?"

"Ha-ha-haaaaaaaaa! I can't!" I would blurt out.

"I just got back from the Virgin Islands," Walken says. "I was bringing back my ex-wife. She was so frigid, when I licked her neck, my tongue stuck to her."

"Ha ha haaaaaaaa! Wait, I don't!!"

My obnoxious, screeching laughter is followed by me explaining that Walken's character has just gotten divorced.

"I hope she finds what she wants—a vibrator with an income," Walken says.

Eventually, Walken breaks down and starts to cry, so Buddy Mills consoles him. As Walken admits how much he misses his wife, Mackey plays another awkward drum riff.

In the Season 28 finale that aired in May 2003, guest host Dan Aykroyd played another hack lounge act opposite Buddy Mills. Being that it was my last show as a cast member, my sketch-writing partner Paula Pell wrote my dad a cameo where he sat in the audience and I introduced him as my son. It was generous of Lorne and the show to let my dad and me have that moment on the night I said goodbye to *SNL*.

The sketch has some memorable lines, such as Dan's character saying, "Buddy, when I shut you out of my life, I was just too caught up in trying to be famous. You were *way* down there, and I was *way* up here. And now I'm just a tired, lonely old man who lost the only friend who really loved me. You have no idea how much that regret has eaten away the years of my life."

Once again, this touching moment is followed by the Mackey *ba dum tss!* I embrace Dan and tell him I forgive him, saying, "Love never went away." Then we break into a rendition of the Gershwin song that Sinatra and others made famous:

"The memory of all that . . . they can't take that away from me."

It was especially meaningful to share this last sketch on *SNL* with my dad since he was one of the biggest reasons I happened to be on that stage. He was and would always be my hero. The fact that his health was getting worse was another one of the reasons I decided to leave the show when I did. And naturally, when I realized he was dying seven years later, I fought as hard as I could to keep him with me. I never wanted to say goodbye. He was a father, a best friend to me, a soulmate, and, as Fallon said about losing his mom, "the best audience." Even after my dad was gone, I still couldn't let him go. Phil Hartman once told me that "When your father dies, that's when you finally become a man." Yet for the first year or two after Dad died, I couldn't even talk about what he went through.

When I began to write this book, it initially seemed like a healthy way to resolve my grief over the loss of my father and my feelings about our complex codependent relationship. I wasn't the only one who thought this. I was surrounded by encouragement. But months later, after finishing a few chapters, I started thinking about that person at the airport, grabbing the hardcover and taking it over to the cash register. Then I imagined her a hundred pages into it, and someone walking up to her and asking:

"How's the book so far?"

"Mango's dad has been dying since I started," the woman would say. "Is it funny?"

"No! Not at all."

For as long as I'd known him, my dad had been terrible at taking care of himself. Whenever the word "exercise" came up, he would immediately get defensive and say, "I exercise all the time! In fact, I walked around the block last week!" Actually, he did have an exercise regimen he followed every morning, or I should say every afternoon, which was when he woke up: He'd jump on a trampoline in his garage for four minutes. He also had some contraption called "the Gravitron," which he'd latch on to by his ankles and then use his weight to flip over backwards and hang upside down for two minutes. But four minutes on the trampoline and a few minutes hanging like a bat with a potbelly from a doorway weren't enough, especially considering that he had some terrible, self-destructive habits. People would excuse these by saying, "That's Kip for you!" It was his character and part of his charm. But in the later stages of his life, it wasn't funny anymore.

On two occasions, I was forced to intervene after I discovered that three of his doctors were either prescribing the same thing or the prescriptions were counteracting each other. My father either didn't realize what he was doing to his body or he was just lying, which he did all the way until the end. After he became sick, it was difficult to know what was truly happening. Since I was his only child, I was the one taking care of him. It required discipline, and since I had so much adoration for him, it was also emotionally exhausting.

Dad's once-imagined maladies had become actual illnesses. Sleep apnea was just one of his many ailments, and despite being among the most common, it turned out to be the most deadly in a way as well. Dad often sleepwalked, and one night he sleepwalked into the kitchen, fell, and split his head open, losing most of his blood. For months after that, he was in and out of the hospital, until one day what we thought was just another ER run turned out to be his final trip. He would never be discharged and would never see his home again.

Ba dum tss!

Hey. Not now, Mackey. I'm being serious.

Sometimes I try to walk myself through what happened, but in the end it is too complicated to retell. A scheduled blood transfusion went wrong, and things went downhill from there. There was a liver transplant, and then a stroke that left him in critical condition. He pulled through, but went on dialysis, and then he suffered a major lung infection. Then another operation on his kidney, then his gall bladder, another stroke, back to dialysis, and then his intestines got involved. At some point, Dad gave up on getting to "go home tomorrow." He couldn't leave his bed and was hooked up to endless tubes in a room crowded with machines. As his motor skills failed, he could no longer speak and had to rely on his hands to point at alphabet charts and cards with drawings in order to tell me what he felt.

As he underwent one surgery after another, it became impossible to tell whether he was being helped or not. He lost strength in his hands, and finally blinking his eyes was the only way he could communicate. His insurance ran out, so I was paying five thousand and then ten thousand dollars a day just to keep him alive. For eleven months, whenever I wasn't working, I was at the hospital with my father for hours every day and night. After everyone else that loved him or even knew him had said their goodbyes, I was still in denial. Even though the financial burden was overwhelming, I refused to give up on him. He was in a vegetative state,, but I still somehow believed he could make it home.

While I watched my dad deteriorate, I started to deteriorate as well. I was working on *The Middle*, and the producers and writers and even Patricia Heaton were running out of sympathy. My addiction to painkillers had already impacted my work, and now the situation with my father was making things even worse. Scenes with my character, Bob, became smaller and less significant. They no longer trusted me.

Then, impossible as it seemed, things got worse still . . . It was time to have another surgery on my neck. My fourth fucking surgery, which would take three months to recover from. I was in a relationship with someone, but she couldn't handle the reality of my life at the time or give me the support I needed. I was spending every minute with my dying father and about to undergo a neck surgery that would leave me helpless. Eventually she made up a story about needing to go back to Kansas to be with her grandmother—in reality, she was having an affair.

There was too much going on at once; I was losing too much all at the same time. To see the strongest man I ever knew finally give up broke me. Through the long months, my father had found the humor even in illness, since he found it in everything. But at the end, there was nothing left to do or say. I had to let go, while at the same time somehow remain strong. During the last few days I spent with my dad, the machines were the only things keeping him alive. After each of those final visits, I would feel myself die a little more sitting in the parking lot before driving home, where I would completely lose it.

The last time I saw my dad, he was already gone. His body was lifeless and cold. When I lifted his hand, it was heavy. That's when the weight of the loss came down on me full force. But it wasn't until I got sober a few years later that I realized I had been carrying that weight for years and could finally process and grieve his death.

I miss my dad, especially his laugh. One of his most memorable traits, it was something that everybody who loved him loved: that huge, crazy, infectious laugh, which sounded like a catchy, joyous cackle. No matter how funny whatever he was laughing at was, his laugh stole all the focus. The best part was at the very end of the laugh—just as he was out of breath, he would quietly gasp, "I can't!" As if to say, "I can't take how funny this is." Or "I don't!" As in, "I don't know what's going on!"

"Aaaaahhh-ah-ah-ah-aaaaahhh-ah-ah aaaaaaahhh, I can't!"

I did a sketch at the Groundlings in which I did an impression of Dad watching television, laughing very loudly, in pajamas, wearing a bad comb-over and trying to reach the remote. In the sketch, I would call out to my son, "Hey, could you do me a favor before you go to bed?" As I played my dad trying his hardest to reach out and grab the remote that was no more than six inches away, "Could you get the remote control I left on top of the TV? I'd appreciate it. Thanks." The actor playing my son would then ask, "What are you watching?" and I'd answer, "*Splash*! Ha! Haaaa! I can't!" It was the first character-driven sketch I wrote that got big laughs.

Whenever my dad came to the show and I was cackling as him onstage, he would be in the audience laughing at the exact same time and sounding just like me. If it went on for long enough, it would feel like you were in a loony bin. One review *LA Weekly* gave of the Groundlings' Sunday show titled "Green Eggs and Groundlings" read, "Kattan had the audience laughing for a solid five minutes, and I'm sure the guy in the third row is probably still rolling in the aisles."

That guy was my dad.

P.S.

LIFE IS GOOD

When they heard I was writing a book, some people told me to share my personal experiences on *SNL*, and others suggested I write about my peculiar youth growing up in a world of Leonard Cohen and Buddhism up on Mount Baldy. Patricia Heaton once told me I should write a book about my dad while he was dying, while Parker Posey told me *not* to write about my father, especially while he was dying and I was in the midst of grieving. Those who were close to me and cared for me unconditionally told me to write about the life-changing injury I suffered while on *SNL* and the pain and surgeries that followed and affected my career.

For my whole life, I've focused on being funny, but while writing *Baby, Don't Hurt Me*, I found myself wanting to recall the truth behind certain stories and experiences instead. Ultimately, I chose to write mostly about the first two seasons of my life: the first being how my father, mother, stepfather, and the environment I grew up in all led to my love for comedy and dreams of being on *Saturday Night Live*; and the second season being the time I spent on *SNL* and the complicated relationship I had with the show that I'll never fully understand. Andrew Steele, a former head writer for *SNL*, once said to me, "You're literally the only member of your cast that the show let slip through the cracks." Maybe I should have seen the writing on the wall as early as the twenty-fifth anniversary show, in 1999, when I was still a member of the cast. I didn't need to fly to New York to rehearse whatever sketch I might be cast in, since I was already there; I never left town so that I'd be available. Yet I didn't appear in the show at all. These anniversary specials focus on the history of *SNL* and the best-loved sketches of alumni through the years, so I suppose you could make the argument that not appearing in the twenty-fifth anniversary show wasn't so unusual. But fifteen years later, for the fortieth anniversary special—a three-and-a-half-hour-long extravaganza in prime time—I wasn't asked to be in a single skit. There wasn't even a quick cut to me in the audience.

After the show I kept coming across comments online that said, "Why wasn't Chris Kattan in a sketch?" and "I saw pictures of him doing the red carpet. I wonder why he wasn't in the show?" I'd tried to let it go, but seeing these questions voiced by viewers made me feel less like I was being unreasonable or paranoid, and I really wanted to know at this point, so I brought it up with friends. Their response was, "You were used in a lot of clips."

You know that feeling as a kid when you're on a team and you fuck up really bad? Then after the game, nobody says anything, but you know it's the first thing that pops up in their mind when they see you? That's how I felt at both anniversary specials, and sort of about my *SNL* alumni status in general.

I never did take Vince Vaughn's long-ago advice about sticking up for myself. Instead, for a long time, I not only accepted every negative thing occurring in my life, but I believed that I deserved them. I tried to be an anti-victim. This is something I carried from my youth, a belief that perhaps my mom and stepfather led me to embrace, maybe in part a reaction to my father, too. When it came to my neck injury, this tendency hurt me almost as much as the injury itself. While NBC paid medical costs for the initial accident, once they stopped, I spent years paying the bills for further surgeries myself, and when I finally spoke to a lawyer about the situation and asked about things like workers' compensation, I was told I couldn't get it. The fifteen-year mark had passed.

There have been some dark times over the past decade and a half, and in a way, this darkness was a blanket of protection between me and my life. I didn't have to face the future as long as I was drowning in the present. I didn't have to move forward or start a new chapter.

But my story isn't over yet. And gradually, I've been able to see the bigger picture. The nerve pain that runs from my left arm into my neck will always be there, and it's something I will always have to deal with. But while I might be limited in some ways as a result, I still have the same heart. I've had to lose a little bit of the "I must be this" mentality, yet I know I can't lose that drive that's been with me my whole career. I still am and forever will be the same Chris I always was. Nothing can ever change that.

To be honest, I wasn't even fully aware of the shift in my outlook until it was brought up at Fred Armisen's fiftieth birthday party in 2016, at the Hollywood Forever Cemetery. It was a big event with lots of people attending, and Molly Shannon came up to me and said, "You look great, Chris." I was with my friend Jennifer Schultz, and she replied, "Chris is back. He lost his hunger for a while, but he's back."

At the time, I thought, *What are you talking about?* I was embarrassed that she said this. Yet the next day, I realized that this was an amazing thing for Jennifer to say. It almost made me want to cry. And I knew she was right.

In a lot of ways, I *do* feel like I am back.

My dad loved to say, "Life is good . . . If you enjoy it." So, like I've done so many times before, I'm going to take his advice. I'm going to enjoy this season of life. And like my dad, the best way I know to do that is by continuing to make people laugh.

ACKNOWLEDGMENTS

Thank you:

To my dad, Kip (Rest in Power, Pop), for sharing his love for comedy, being my best friend, and allowing me to be the parent. To my mom, Hajni, for always being there for me, for giving me those beautiful albeit short genes, and for letting Kip think he was the funnier parent even though it's always been you. To my other dad, Marc, for always being the sturdy, dependable rock of the family, and showing me real dedication through Buddhism even when I get antsy while meditating.

To my brother, Andrew, for showing me what it is to be a truly good person, and for putting up with being Mango's brother in high school (I'm sorry, forever!) and to Bruce.

To my best friend, my teacher, and the only person who gets to yell at me. This book wouldn't exist without you. You kept me on point and revived the project after I let grief take over. You inspire me Billy Bill, Jennifer Schultz.

To everyone else in my family: my dad's side, my mom's side, and the Joslyns. Thank you for always letting me be who I am.

To Will for being the beginning of everything. There are no words. I just love you. I wouldn't drop trou with anyone but you!

Jimmy! You're the light of all those NYC nights, the karaoke master, and my savior through dark times. Your friendship has meant more to me than I've ever been able to express.

To Seth, Ariel, Alexi. You're like family.

Carmen, John, Zooey, Michelle, Sunshine, China, Drew, Amy, Jennifer, and Elisa. Also to Jane for three of the best years while in New York and Italy.

To my babysitters, Lisa and Melanie. And my grade school teachers at Mt. Baldy: Ellen, Janice, and others. I know I was a handful, but you made it fun. My Bainbridge High School drama teacher, Mr. McAllister, for casting me in serious plays like The Crucible.

Harper Simon, Marci Klein, Mike Shoemaker, Fred Armisen, Horatio Sanz, Chris Parnell, Amy Poehler, Janeane Garofalo, Rachel Dratch, Tina Fey, Darrell Hammond, Jeff Richards, Ana Gasteyer, Molly Shannon, David Spade, Tim Meadows. Eva Mendez, Gary Shandling, Ted Demme, Amanda Demme.

Stacey Shear, Kari. Richard LaGravenese. Danny DeVito. Paul Thomas Anderson. Shauna Robertson for some of the happiest times. Maya, Parker, and Gracie.

Cameron for making me cooler than I was by being my friend, and also for teaching me how to handle fame.

Parker, the only woman who could be my man of honor—I love you more than words. You're both the good and the bad whisper in my ear. . .

To my friends, who appear then disappear, but remain unconditional and allow me to come and go in their lives without guilt. I adore you all. Call me!

To Mary Ellen Matthews for her brilliant photos.

To the Monday night guys.

To Paul Dinello and Amy Sedaris for jumpstarting my creativity.

To Travis Thrasher for organizing and polishing me up to sound like a real writer. Can I still call you and share stories?

To Alexa Stevenson for your brilliant editing, and everyone at BenBella for being patient and believing in me and this project.
To Steve Ross for guiding and pushing this project forward.

To Win Butler and the rest of Arcade Fire for personally allowing me to use a brilliant lyric and the most appropriate quote I could find for this book.

Adam Ginivisian

'Adam McKay

Adam Sandler

Alan Covert

Amy Heckerling

Andrew Steele

Andy Samberg

Anita Patrickson

Anthony Kiedis

Ben Stiller

Beyoncé

Bono

Brooke Shields

Charlize Theron

Cheri Oteri

Chris Henchy

Chris Redd

Christie Will

Colin Quinn

Conan O'Brien

Coolidge

Dana Carvey

Daryl Hannah

Dave Becky

Dave Chapelle

David Letterman

Denise Richards

Dianna Oliver

Ed Norton

Eddie Griffin

Ellen DeGeneres

Fax Bahr

Fiona Apple

Flea

Geoffrey Rush

Guy Oseary

Harrison Ford

Heath Ledger

Hugh Fink

Jake Gyllenhaal

James Brown, for teaching me to spin

James Franco

Jason Bateman

Jay Leno

Jennifer Allen

Jill Fritzo

Jim Wise

Joie Rice

Jon Hamm

Jon Lovitz

Josh Deu

Karen Maruyama

Kathy Griffin

Katie Feldman

Keanu Reeves

Kristen Bell

Kristen Purdy

Larry Mullen Jr.

Lisa Kudrow

Lyle Jackson

Madonna

Martin Short

Matt Piedmont

Melanie Graham

Michael Stipe

Mike Myers

Natasha Lyonne

Neal Brennan

Patricia Arquette

Patricia Heaton

Patty Stafford

Paul Reubens

Paula Pell

Phil Hartman

Renee Zellweger

Ron Burkle

Roy Jenkins

Scott Wainio

Steve Higgins

Steve Koren

Steven Soderbergh

Thomas Jane

Tom Cruise

Tom Hanks

Vince Vaughn

To Chaplin for The Rink and Modern Times

Buster Keaton for One Week and The General

W.C. Fields for It's a Gift and The Bank Dick

The Marx Bros. for Duck Soup and A Night at the Opera

Jack Benny

Bob Hope

Pinocchio

To anyone I may have forgotten, please forgive me.

ABOUT THE
AUTHOR

CHRIS KATTAN began his comedic career as a member of Los Angeles comedy troupe The Groundlings, of which his father was an original member. He joined the cast of *Saturday Night Live* in 1996, and over the next seven seasons, his recurring characters included Mr. Peepers, Mango, Azrael Abyss, Gay Hitler, Suel Forrester, and, most notably, one half of the head-bopping Butabi Brothers with fellow *SNL* (and Groundlings) cast member Will Ferrell. Kattan has appeared in numerous film and television roles. His credits include *A Night at the Roxbury*, *Undercover Brother*, the IFC series *Bollywood Hero*, *The Middle*, *How I Met Your Mother*, *The Tonight Show Starring Jimmy Fallon*, and *Late Night with Seth Meyers*. Kattan now travels the world doing stand-up, lives in Los Angeles, and enjoys making toast for house guests.

Bestselling author **TRAVIS THRASHER** has written more than 50 books and worked in the publishing industry for more than 20 years. He has penned fiction in a variety of genres, and his inspirational stories include collaborations with filmmakers, musicians, and athletes. Thrasher lives with his wife and three daughters in Grand Rapids, Michigan.